Leo Africanus

By

Joanna B McGarry

Chapter 1

The young man, a boy really, squatted beside the freshly dug grave of his mother and wondered why she had been taken so cruelly. Fourteen years he was, by his mother's reckoning, but he didn't feel like a man, although he had been supporting both of them when she died, and he had paid the funeral costs, and for a fine gravestone with the head of the goddess Ifri carved on it.

The boy was called Farinas. His mother had been cut off from her fiercely anti-Roman, Amazigh family, when she married a Roman auxiliary; not just any Roman auxiliary, but an Amazigh tribesman who'd joined the Roman army, by choice.

Farinas had never known his father. He'd left them when Farinas was still a babe. He'd probably been sent to some far-flung outpost of the Roman empire, to avoid him taking up with local insurgents. Despite this, his mother's family had left her to fend for herself and her child.

In the Roman garrison town of Theveste where he lived with his mother, Safiyya was considered slightly exotic with her glossy black skin, almond-shaped brown eyes, and long dark hair. She always smelled of perfumed oils and wore colourful robes and cheap, coloured jewellery.

Farinas had been aware of her visitors from an early age. One or two, he remembered being kind to him. A few had been cruel, when he was young and small, despite his mother's efforts to protect him, but most were oblivious to his presence as she entertained them behind a thin, brightly coloured curtain.

Farinas's reminiscences were interrupted by the arrival of three men who had left their horses at the foot of the hill and were labouring their way up towards him. He recognised his uncles, not Romanised Imazighen from the town of Theveste where he lived, but nomads from desert tribes that hadn't been subdued by the Romans, at least not yet. Farinas was young, but even he recognised it was only a matter of time.

Rome with its great aqueducts, straight roads, stone bridges, armour, superior weapons, and iron discipline, embodied in the mighty Third Augustan Legion would eventually subdue the whole of Tripolitania, north of the great desert. The boy had watched the legion drilling and training. He'd been impressed.

His uncles in their robes and turbans, with their thick black beards and piercing dark eyes, were coming closer and Farinas knew their arrival was not fortuitous. He had only ever seen them in the dead of night when they would arrive unexpectedly, crowding into the small room his mother rented. They'd ask about him, hand over money or food, then leave, cloaked, and hooded, keeping to the shadows.

He remembered his mother's hissed warnings not to mention these visits to anyone. Her brothers were fighting the Romans from their desert homes and were dangerous to know. There was another brother, the youngest, named Jilwa. Farinas knew little about him, except that he'd somehow, 'gone over to the Romans'.

The brothers had been raised on tales of their greatest hero Tikfarin who had led a rebellion against Rome. Farinas wasn't sure if his mother Safiya had been pressured into naming him after their hero, or if she'd thought to please her family by the gesture. If so, it hadn't worked.

His mother's tales that lulled him to sleep were gentler tales of secret hordes of gold and jewels, just waiting to be found by courageous and kind young boys, riding on flying carpets, assisted in their fight against the *jago-nini* and other monsters, by magic spells and sorcery.

Farinas sighed, got to his feet, and waited for his uncles. Khaled, the oldest led the way, his turban and cloak were black, and his beard was thick and unruly. His manner was always impatient, his hand never far from the angry-looking camel's head pommel on the single-edged sword, hanging from his broad leather belt. He called out, before reaching Farinas. "You're coming with us."

"I thought you had come to pay your respects to your sister," Farinas said quietly, knowing the brothers had little respect for a sister, forced to sell herself to provide for her son and herself.

Khaled spat on the ground near the stone. "Whores and traitors deserve no respect."

"She wasn't—" His denial was interrupted by a quick slap across his face, which brought him to the ground. Tareq, similarly dressed in black, but with light brown hair and a quick smile, placed his hand on his brother's arm. "Leave the boy. He's right to defend his mother, but he's one of us now." He turned to Farinas and explained how they'd found him. "The old leper told us you were here."

Farinas looked, but Idir the leper was no longer in his usual spot in the shade of the athel tree. His uncles' horses were now standing quietly under it. Unwelcome in the town, Idir sat on a mound beside the road, hoping mourners and travellers would seek to please their gods, by placing alms or food in the bowl he left at the bottom of the mound.

Idir had expressed sorrow at his mother's death and had spoken kindly to Farinas, although he knew the boy had no alms to give. Among the poor, the lepers were the poorest, and Farinas truly hoped Idir had been paid well for his information, however, he feared he might have paid with his life.

"Did you –"

Ramzi who had always seemed to treat his young nephew with deliberate cruelty laughed. "What? You think we would go near his diseased carcass? He ran off."

"Hobbled off," Khaled smirked.

Idir may have been shunned by everyone, but he was still part of the beggar network, a valuable part. Sitting on top of his mound, he was in a position to notice everyone entering and leaving the town. "The Romans will pay well for word of any brigands. He'll pass the word on," Farinas warned, hoping his uncles would leave.

The smirks turned to frowns and they glanced uneasily in the direction of the town. "You're coming with us," Khaled repeated, and it was clearly not a request.

"Now!" Ramzi added, kicking him in the ribs, as he remained kneeling by the headstone. He rolled to avoid another blow from a heavy riding boot.

"What for?"

"Your people need you." Khaled insisted. "Your mother kept you too long as a child. It's time to be the man the blood of your ancestors demands."

"You need to wipe out the memory of her treachery," Ramzi growled. "At least she gave you her Amazigh blood, and your father was a full-blooded Amazigh, even though he sold out this birthright by fighting for the oppressor."

Farinas stood and faced his uncles. "I'm happy here." This wasn't strictly true. Life had always been a struggle for his mother, and even when he was able to help with money and food, they'd remained outcasts.

"You're a full-blood Amazigh. Your father may have been a bastarding traitor to his people, but he was still one of us."

Farinas supposed that was true, but he had nothing in common with his uncles. Theveste was a Roman garrison town and he had always lived among Romans, and people of every race, creed, and colour, including 'Romanised' Imazighen. He'd mixed with foreign traders, merchants, soldiers, and officials who had passed through on the wonderfully straight Roman roads, bringing excitement and novelty to the young boy's life.

He never knew which came first, the old town with its small white buildings and narrow alleyways, or the Roman town with its wide paved streets, fora, baths, and temples. Whatever way it grew, Theveste was now most definitely a Roman town and, Farinas realised, he was probably as much a Roman as he was an Amazigh, despite his accident of birth.

If his uncles were trying to gain recruits for a rebellion against Rome, Farinas wanted no part of it, but he had seen the weapons they carried, and even without them, and their willingness to use them, he was no match for three grown men. He turned for a last look at the headstone.

"*Layàwn.*" He whispered a last goodbye to the only person he'd ever loved, and who had ever loved him and turned to follow his uncles.

Khaled, impatient at the delay, seized his arms, and slapped him, hard. "Are you slow-witted, or just don't understand the language of your own people?" he asked, "We have…to…leave…now!" he bellowed in his face.

Sensing another blow coming, Farinas stepped back, and the blow glanced off his cheek. "I understand and I'm not slow-witted." He stated then added, with emphasis, although trembling inside. "I…am…staying."

"You'll fight for your people, your blood kin," Khaled snarled. "You'll spill Roman blood until our people are free…or until your lifeblood seeps into the sand to mix with the blood of your ancestors."

"You can't win." Farinas knew he should keep his mouth shut but hoped they would leave without him if they saw he wasn't enthusiastic. "Your hero, Tikfarin couldn't do it —"

This time, it was Ramzi's fist that drew blood. "Don't soil his glorious name!" he shouted, and his hand went to his dagger. Farinas had been wrong; the only way they were leaving him there, was as a corpse.

He thought the bones on one side of his face had been smashed, and he tasted blood from a cut above his eye, probably from a heavy silver ring. He was trembling, amazed at his foolishness, but he also felt humiliated. He was a man. He should return the blow…with interest but knew he could not.

"Bring him along before we're discovered," Khaled growled, already walking away from them. "Knock him out if you have to."

Farinas found himself seized, and his hands were tied in front of him. Stumbling, and with his vision blurred by blood, he followed Khaled to the paved Roman road. It allowed them to take more grain and produce to Rome, instead of leaving it for the people to buy at reasonable prices. The Roman roads also allowed the legionaries to move quickly from one place to another, making it more difficult for the Imazighen to gather, to conspire against Rome.

Farinas looked at the huge horses waiting patiently and wasn't surprised Idir had left. He'd never been this close to even one horse before, and these didn't look any friendlier than their owners.

Khaled mounted a big black horse, and the other two stared at Farinas, "Get a move on," Khaled growled. "All we need is a funeral procession heading this way, or a Roman patrol."

Tareq mounted a grey horse. "Throw him up."

"I can't ride a horse," Farinas objected, backing further from the animals, and wiping blood from his eyes.

"You think we'd trust you with a valuable animal," Khaled growled. "Hurry up, Ramzi!"

Ramzi threw him across the horse's neck in front of Tareq, deliberately slamming his face against the animal and knocking the breath from him. When he did manage a deep breath, he smelled rank, sweaty horse. To be fair to the animal, it didn't smell much worse than its rider.

Ramzi then crouched and tied a rope around the one binding Farinas's hands, slid the other end under the horse and tied it around his ankles. When he started to slide, Tareq sitting above him, grabbed the back of his tunic and held him steady. "Just lie still," Tareq advised him. "I'll see you don't fall."

Ramzi mounted his own horse and, as Farinas tried not to bring up his last meal, the brothers dug their heels into the horses' flanks and broke into a gallop. Even with his hands tied, Farinas managed to grip the edge of the saddle and he hung on.

Soon they left the paved road and were racing across the scrubland bordering the desert where there would be nothing but sand and a few oases. The dust blowing into his face was bad enough, but Farinas wondered what the hot, gritty sand would feel like. The hood of his Roman-style cloak had fallen over his head and he was grateful for its protection from the sun.

Bushes and trees flashed past, and the hooves pounded on the short grass and low-growing plants. As well as feeling sick, he was becoming light-headed and dizzy and his vision blurred as the heat of the sun, a hazy circle of light, scorched him. His face throbbed from the punch but at least, in this position, the blood was running into his hair, not over his eyes and into his mouth.

Just when he thought things couldn't get any worse and he was begging the gods to save him, he became conscious of an increased sense of urgency. Tareq's hand tightened on his tunic, and he realised his uncles were urging the horses on to even greater speeds.

Worst of all, he could hear the pounding of horses' hooves behind them and he knew they were being pursued by Roman soldiers, probably an eight-man patrol, a *contubernium* of the Roman legion. He half hoped they would be captured, then he could be freed to return home, but he was sure, with his luck being what it was, he'd be taken for an insurgent and treated like his uncles.

He prayed to Mastinam for protection, but so as not to offend Roman deities, he included the Roman, Magna Mater in his panicked pleas for help. Maybe his own mother could be watching over him and she would help too. His thoughts were whirling around in his head and his last recollection was hearing Khaled let out a mighty roar, followed by a shouted curse from Ramzi.

Chapter 2

When consciousness returned, Farinas realised he was lying on a patch of grass beside a pool of water. His hands and legs were free, and he moaned as the blood flowed into them. The horses were standing beside him, eating grass, and showing no interest in him. Moonlight shone on the water, fresh and cold. He crawled and sucked it into his mouth before plunging his head in, then he gulped more water.

"Enough!" Tareq pulled him from the pool and rolled him onto his back. Farinas shivered and his uncle threw a rough saddle blanket over him. "Too much water is bad for you…all at once."

Farinas nodded and sat up, wincing as his neck, and back protested at the treatment they had received on the horse. He recalled the race across the desert. "The Romans?" His voice emerged as a croak and his throat stung.

Tareq handed him a waterskin. "Sip…slowly." He smiled. "Those jackals turned back as soon as we reached the sands."

"They fear our desert *jinns*," Ramzi called over and Khaled aimed a kick at his brother. "Fool! They fear moving too far from their base."

A few hours ago, Farinas had been wondering how he would get enough food to fill his belly for another day. Now he was wondering if he would see another day. "Do you think they will come back, with reinforcements?"

Tareq shrugged. "For three men and a captive? I doubt it. Don't worry, we know the desert better than them."

Farinas relaxed slightly. He wasn't ready to trust his uncles' judgement on anything, but they seemed confident the soldiers wouldn't return. They sat by a fire and ate pancakes with dried fruit and cheese. The food was sparse, especially for a growing boy, and he could hear his mother's voice telling him when he was little, he must have a worm in his gut, eating his food. He had cried until she hugged him and popped a sweetmeat in his mouth.

His uncle's angry voices, telling him to hurry, brought him back to reality and he ate quickly, with little pleasure. As they were getting ready to leave, Khaled pulled a brown woollen *djellaba* from his saddle pack and threw it at Farinas. "Take off that traitor's rag and wear your *djellaba* with pride."

Reluctantly, Farinas took off his cloak. His mother had sewn it for him, and her perfume still clung to it. He watched as Ramzi threw it on the fire, grinning at him. The cloak had been torn and dirty, but he knew no one rich enough to waste even such a garment. The *djellaba* would be cooler, but he missed the connection to his mother.

The sun was low in the sky when they left the camp, travelling more slowly now that they knew the auxiliaries wouldn't follow so far into the desert. Farinas was sitting behind Tareq on the horse. Maybe life in the desert wouldn't be so bad, he thought, but remembering the frenzied race to escape the Roman patrol, he didn't really believe it.

"Where are we going?" he asked Tareq who looked to his brothers for permission to give him any information.

"You'll see when we get there," Khaled growled. They rode in silence after that, until Khaled decided it was too dark to continue and ordered them to make camp for the night.

The temperature had dropped, and Farinas missed the many lamps and fires of the city. He wrapped himself in the *djellaba*, lay under the horse blanket, and fell asleep, listening to the horses snuffling nearby and the snores of his uncles. They took turns on watch but didn't trust Farinas to take a turn, for which he was grateful.

As dawn broke and the sun appeared over the horizon, warming the desert, they ate a quick meal and continued their journey, stopping only to water the horses and replenish the water skins. Acacia, palm trees and thyme provided shade when they stopped, and small birds fluttered through their branches breaking the silence. In the distance animals that Farinas had never seen before, prowled, and made strange noises. Ramzi took great pleasure in warning him about poisonous snakes, and ants that burrowed in the sand.

He hadn't realised there was so much life in the desert, but his uncles, for whom conversation appeared to be an unfamiliar activity, were reluctant to name them for him.

He ate the food and savoured the water, taken in rationed mouthfuls while crossing rough terrain in the baking heat, and he appreciated the thick white walls and latticework of the buildings in Theveste, designed to temper the heat of the sun. Here everything shimmered in a haze and the heat was relentless, even though they rested in the shade when the sun was at its hottest.

Late on the fifth night, Farinas was wakened from a troubled sleep by a kick from Ramzi. "Get up," he hissed.

"What's happening?" Farinas rubbed his eyes and saw Tareq already mounted and waiting.

"You ride with Tareq," Ramzi explained as Tareq motioned for him to get up behind him.

"Where are we going?" Farinas asked as they rode away from the camp.

"Tidamensi…to see your grandmother. Your mother might have called it, Cydamus…like the Romans." Away from Khaled, Tareq seemed more inclined to explain things to his nephew.

"Mum spoke of Tidamensi," Farinas said.

"Your mother was always sweet and kind. She was easily taken advantage of," Tareq said. It was the first kind thing he'd heard any of his uncles say about their sister.

They rode in silence after that. The cool silver sand was illuminated by the stars and Farinas saw movement, as small creatures came out to hunt and eat. Soon, he thought he saw buildings ahead, but it wasn't until Tareq spoke that he realised they had reached the end of their journey. "Tidamensi."

"Is this where you live?"

Tareq spat on the ground before answering. "In a Roman city? Our youngest brother lives here, like a Roman, with our mother. We are Imazighen. We live in the desert, as you will."

The town reminded Farinas of his hometown of Theveste. A solid white wall surrounded it, and palm trees swayed in the soft breeze. The gates were opened quietly and closed after them. The buildings were in darkness, and even the stars disappeared when they rode into a covered alleyway between buildings.

They dismounted and Tareq knocked on a door that was quickly opened by a servant, who slipped out and took charge of the horse. Tareq pushed Farinas into the building, then took a lantern from a hook in the wall and led the way to the second floor.

In a big open space, with brightly coloured carpets and wall hangings, low tables were set out with bowls of fruit and jugs of mint tea. Sumptuous cushions lay beside the tables. It wasn't Theveste, but Farinas thought he would enjoy living in a place like this.

Standing in the middle of the room, amidst the expensive wall hangings and rich cushions, was an old lady, who commanded respect by her age and dignity. She was dressed in a long, black woollen robe, which also covered her hair and the lower half of her face, and her very presence seemed to be a denunciation of the wealth and luxury surrounding her.

He bowed. "*As-salamu àlaykum.*"

"Is this the son?" she asked, coming forward to peer into his face while ignoring his greeting.

Farinas bristled at the disrespect to his mother, and he answered quickly. "I am the son of Safiyya of Theveste." Facing his grandmother, he realised he wanted nothing to do with these people and their futile war against Rome. He was determined to escape, although he had no idea how he would cross the desert alone and find his way back to Theveste.

The old woman grunted. "At least he looks like an Amazigh." Farinas realised that his black skin and thick curls had gained some favour with his grandmother. Still ignoring him, she turned and spoke to a servant. "Take the boy. Bathe him and give him clean garments. He has the stink of Rome about him." As he was led away he heard her say. "We can at least make him look like a man."

Washed and dressed in the loose clothing of the Imazighen, Farinas felt better. The desert dust and the dried blood were gone, and his skin and hair no longer itched. The clothes were cotton and wool, cool and soft against his skin. As he appreciated their comfort and quality, he felt disloyal to his mother, who could never have afforded such costly garments.

Back in the family room, his grandmother, seated on a Roman-style chair with a high back, was speaking to Tareq who was seated cross-legged on the floor, eating from a bowl of couscous. Farinas's mouth watered as he smelled the spicy sauce.

"Sit!" His grandmother scarcely interrupted the conversation. He sat and ate, ignored by his grandmother and uncle.

"You're a fool to have come here," she was saying. "It's too dangerous. The garrison is on high alert following a raid a few nights ago."

"They're not bothered by a few raids," Tareq answered. "They think most of us are happy, living under Roman Rule."

"Most of us are, including you, Mother," said a new voice, and Farinas realised his mother's youngest brother, his Uncle Jilwa, had entered quietly and had spoken.

Of his uncles, Jilwa looked most like Farinas's mother. He was clean-shaven, and his eyes looked gentle and kind. "I was sorry to hear of my sister's death," he said to Farinas. "You are welcome to stay here."

Farinas scrambled to his feet and made a clumsy bow. "I thank you, Uncle. I—"

"He is my grandson. He will go with my sons."

Jilwa shrugged. "I am sorry," he said to Farinas, who was disappointed beyond words that his fate now lay irretrievably in the hands of his renegade uncles.

"He'll be raised properly, as a real man," his grandmother answered. "He will not live in comfort, while the usurper lives off our land and steals our gold and salt, our crops and animals."

"And yet you are happy to live in such comfort, Mother." Jilwa's tone was quiet and respectful, but the words were barbed.

Tareq got to his feet. "That is disrespectful, Jilwa. At her age, our grandmother has earned the right to some comfort."

Jilwa nodded. "Maybe." His tone became resigned, and Farinas realised his uncles despised Jilwa while using him to further their cause. "What do you want this time?"

"We were near Theveste when we heard of our sister's death. We brought the boy to see his grandmother."

"And—"

It was his grandmother who answered. "They need a horse for him…a quiet one, a weapon, and supplies."

Jilwa nodded to a servant who left. Farinas's heart sank. If he could have lived in such luxury, in a town so like Theveste, he believed he could have been happy. Although looking at his grandmother's discontented expression, he thought perhaps not.

Jilwa was speaking again. "Finish eating and go. It will not benefit anyone if you are caught here. Feel free to go with your sons, Mother…the real men," he added bitterly. "I will happily provide another horse or a camel if you prefer, if this life is not to your taste." He left before his mother could answer, but Farinas thought his uncle would pay for those words, in many small ways.

"Drink your tea!" Farinas's grandmother barked, "And leave quickly. It will do you no good if we come to the attention of Rome."

The green minty tea reminded Farinas of home…not this home, his real home. He was unsure of what had been decided about his future, but he was sure it would not please him.

"Does he have to come with us," Tareq protested. "He can't even ride. With a weapon he'd be more of a danger to us than to the Romans," he added.

"*Amenzug*! Teach him! You need men to fight. He's young. He'll learn," Farinas's grandmother snapped. If his uncle had been named idiot by anyone else, the insult would have been answered by the sword, instead, he just hung his head and swallowed the slur.

They were no sooner finished the tea when a slave arrived to lead them out. In the stables, they found two horses, ready to ride. Both saddles had bundles attached. Farinas had expected no farewell from his grandmother, and he received none, but the servant handed him a thick warm burnoose, a gift from his uncle. "The horse is called Musad," the servant explained, "a quiet animal."

They left the town as secretly as they had arrived. This time Farinas rode his own horse. It was slightly smaller than Tareq's, but the saddle was larger. It held him more securely on the animal's back, and he hoped it would stop him from falling off.

As they rode away from the town, the sound of the gate closing behind them, seemed to indicate to Farinas the end of any family life he might have had. His grandmother had failed to meet his image of a kindly old lady, happy to meet her grandson, although Farinas realised, he should have expected no more from a woman who had denied her own daughter.

He struggled with the horse, although it seemed docile enough and followed Tareq's, with no encouragement or direction from its rider. Farinas's concentration was focused on staying on the horse, clinging to its neck, while his thighs burned with his attempts to clamp them around the animal's body.

Two men riding into the city, laughed as they passed. "My infant daughter rides better than this city-bred son of the desert."

The insult was designed to be heard. Tareq rode on without replying, but a short time later he snapped. "Use the reins, Farinas and sit up straight!"

Farinas breathed a prayer to Tannit that she would weave his home back into the pattern of his life. He wasn't hopeful. The gods hadn't seen fit to weave much happiness into his life recently, but he tried. He gave them respect and faith and hoped they didn't favour his uncles above himself.

"So, why are you taking me with you?" he eventually asked. "You could just let me return to Theveste."

"Because we need men, and you might have your uses. You know the ways of a Roman city and you can speak like a Roman. We'll keep you to provide information and when…if you are killed, our family will have one more hero to celebrate."

With that thought in mind, the remainder of the journey passed in a brooding silence, and Farinas was even more determined to escape from his uncles and their vision of him as a dead hero.

Chapter 3

When Tariq and Farinas rode back into the camp, Khaled and Ramzi were ready to ride, and they hurriedly unpacked the provisions provided by Jilwa. He may not have agreed with his brothers' way of life, but Jilwa had been generous with the provisions. As they were being parcelled out between them, Tareq threw a scabbarded knife to Farinas. He caught it and struggled to attach it to his belt.

"*Ahmaq*! Did your mother teach you nothing of our traditions?" Ramzi called over. "I was eight years of age when I was given my first *telek*. I killed a viper four days later."

Tareq laughed and came over and fixed the scabbard to Farinas's wrist, then slid the short-bladed dagger into the sheath. "It's a *telek*," he explained. Jilwa chose well. It will be easier for you to manage while riding, than a longer weapon."

Even without a sword, Farinas struggled with the horse, and after a few miles, Tareq held back to ride alongside him. "Trust your horse. If you are nervous, he feels it and becomes nervous too." Farinas listened and tried to release the tension from his hands.

"That does feel better... safer," he said, and soon he found he was enjoying riding and the closeness to an animal. He felt responsible for Musad, looking to the horse's needs, before his own, whenever they stopped.

Throughout the journey, Tareq rode with Farinas and coached him. By the time they could see Theveste shimmering in the heat, but still many miles ahead, he felt happier in the saddle, until Ramzi brought him back to reality.

"Musad is a good horse for beginners. He's making this easy for you. Wait until you're in a battle, though. The first charge will see you off your mount, to be dragged and trampled."

Farinas paid more attention to Tareq after that and worked hard on his riding skills, but he was never going to match his uncles, who had sat in saddles before they could walk. A few miles south of Theveste, with the sun low in the sky, they approached a stand of palm and acacia trees with low-growing shrubs among them. "We wait there," Khaled said.

As they approached, the normally well-trained horses showed signs of unease, tossing their heads, and trotting sideways. The men stopped and watched as a line of camels appeared from the trees, making its way towards Theveste.

"Horses don't like the smell of camel," Tareq explained softly.

"It's not the smell of camel that offends me," Khaled hissed. "It's the stink of the *dromedarii*."

Local tribesmen fighting with Rome, against their own people," Tareq explained.

"Traitors!" Ramzi snarled. "Like your father!"

They waited until the camels disappeared behind a sand dune, then walked the horses towards the oasis. With the scent of water attracting them, they were easier to manage.

The horses were watered, and the men were sitting in the shade, when two riders approached from the south, stopping within shouting distance. Khaled stood and called out a greeting. "*As-salamu àlaykum.*"

Greetings exchanged, the men approached, hands visible on the reins. When the horses were watered, the men sat and food was shared and eaten, although it was clear, even to Farinas, that there was serious business to be discussed.

Eventually, the older man sat back. He looked to Farinas to be old enough to be a grandfather, but he was still healthy and strong. Named Baragsen by his uncles, Farinas recognised a man of authority who commanded respect from them. A man with information that would have a massive impact on their lives.

Baragsen stood to address them. "My friends," he began, indicating his companion, who, although he looked younger, was clearly a seasoned warrior. "This is Harscheft of the Garamantes." Farinas gasped and drew his burnous close about himself. The Garamantes were fierce warriors; used by mothers to frighten naughty children. Farinas met Harscheft's glance and knew the tales had been true. This man was dangerous, in ways that even his uncles couldn't fathom.

The Garamantes were fierce desert tribesmen, known for their savagery in battle, often against the Romans, but just as often against any tribe living close to them in the desert. They were not known for showing mercy to their enemies.

Harscheft fitted the description perfectly. His eyes under heavy brows seemed to be assessing everyone as a possible enemy. The rest of his face and his head were covered by an indigo-coloured *tagelmust* which matched his *burnous*. He threw this back over his shoulder when he saw Farinas watching him, displaying a wool baldric holding a *janbīyah* in a curved, highly decorated silver scabbard. Farinas was sure the blade of the *janbīyah* was sharp and well-used to slicing through human flesh, like the sword in a leather scabbard hanging by the man's side.

To complete the intimidating display of weaponry, Harscheft leaned over and helped himself to a handful of dates, letting his sleeve fall back showing a straight-bladed *telek* in a sheath, strapped to his forearm.

When he had uncovered his face, Farinas had seen that his beard was short and neatly shaped, unlike his uncles'. It made his mouth appear thin and cruel.

Farinas looked from his examination to see Harscheft watching him closely.

"The boy?"

"Our sister's son," Khaled said. "He has much to learn."

"He speaks our language?" Harscheft asked.

"He does…and the language of the accursed invader." Tareq added this piece of information to excuse his presence here with warriors, but Farinas was sure it failed to impress anyone.

"It is safe to speak in front of him?" Harscheft asked, and Farinas thought his voice, a low growl, perfectly suited the man.

"I swear it, on his life." Khaled glowered at Farinas.

"I not kill." Next to his eyes, Harscheft's smile was the scariest thing Farinas had ever seen. "I let you live, boy but put out eyes, pull out tongue and cut off hands. By the horns of Gurzil, I swear this." The smile that accompanied this promise had the hairs standing up on the back of Farinas's neck.

There was silence after this announcement which no one thought an idle threat, and Baragsen seemed suddenly to have realised the nature of his ally. The silence stretched until Baragsen continued. "Our brothers in Theveste have sent word of a gold shipment going from the garrison at Theveste to the port at Hippo Regius.… We plan to seize it, with the help of a group of Garamantes led by Harscheft —"

"It will be well guarded," Ramzi spoke for the first time.

"If you are afraid—" Harscheft spoke softly but Ramzi was on his feet in an instant, hand on his sword. Tareq was as quick to his feet and caught his brother's arm.

"Ramzi is young and foolish, Baragsen, but you know he has proved his courage against Rome."

Harscheft had remained seated, indicating an insulting lack of concern at Ramzi's outburst. It was Baragsen who calmed the situation. "Sit, Ramzi. Your courage is not in doubt."

Harscheft's grunt suggested otherwise, but the younger man wisely chose to ignore it, and Baragsen passed round a wineskin.

"Stick to water, Farinas." Ramzi took the wineskin from him and passed it to Tareq. "You're having trouble enough with Musad, the gentlest horse in our stables." Farinas knew this to be true, and could do nothing but scowl at his uncle, as the men continued to ignore him.

"We have small groups of brothers, already gathering in the woods outside Theveste, ready to attack the wagons on the road to Hippo," Baragsen told them,

"Who are these brothers?" Khaled asked.

"Best you do not know, and few will know about you until we meet." The men nodded and Baragsen continued. "Once the gold is ours, we will load it onto camels and make our way south to our camp in the desert. We will take half, the Garamantes the other half.

"Those that survive," Tareq growled. "I have a young wife and child waiting for me."

"It is in the gods' hands. The names of the dead will be remembered long after the Romans have gone," Khaled told his brother. "Did you think to live forever?"

"I'd like to see a few more sons." Tareq smiled and added, "to pass on my illustrious name."

"Illustrious name first needs to be won," Harscheft murmured.

Tareq glared at Harscheft, then addressed Baragsen. "Can we trust the Garamantes?" he asked, and this time Harscheft was on his feet, hand on his sword hilt, as Baragsen once more tried to calm the situation.

"Relax, Harscheft, the Garamantes are known for many things. They are fierce and brave, great warriors, loyal to their own but ..." he hesitated, holding everyone's attention including Harscheft's, "as dangerous as a nest of horned vipers."

Farinas drew in his breath. Then a low rumble of laughter from Harscheft broke the tension and he slapped Baragsen on the back. "That is truth," he agreed, glaring at them. "Best not turn back on me."

In the silence that followed this advice, Farinas considered his unreadiness and his unwillingness to take part in such a venture, with such dangerous men. He'd seen horned vipers on his journey with his uncle. They didn't seem so dangerous, so long as you didn't upset them. He wasn't so sure about Harscheft.

"The boy? He will be more of a hindrance than anything else." Ramzi, young and hoping to impress the older men had picked on the only one less of a warrior than himself.

"We will train him on the way," Khaled stated with conviction, and Farinas contemplated his imminent death at the hands of the Romans, or perhaps at the hands of Harscheft.

Tareq smiled at Farinas. "He'll be fine. He's learning."

Baragsen and Harscheft got ready to leave. "I will join you at dawn, in five days, at the *stabulum* of Assellina Pertaca. You'll find it on the road between Thamugadi and Cirta, outside Ayn Malīlah," Baragsen told them.

"We aren't going to Theveste then?" Farinas had been convinced they were heading back to Theveste, where he'd thought to escape; to hide in the warren of familiar streets. His disappointment was obvious.

"You are not," Baragsen said. "You don't want to be seen anywhere near Theveste when the gold is being loaded onto carts and taken out of the city."

Before they left, Baragsen took the men's long swords and rolled them in a blanket before tying them to his saddle. Each man now carried a *janbīyah* hanging from a baldric, and a *telek* on his forearm; both weapons could be easily concealed while they were in cities.

Baragsen and Harscheft rode back into the desert.

"Don't even contemplate escape," Khaled warned, reading Farinas's thoughts. "Even if we had gone to Theveste as you hoped, you would not have evaded our brothers who live there like Romans, while secretly passing on information to us."

"You didn't think we only came to Theveste to visit you and your mother, did you?" Ramzi asked, and Farinas burned with shame, thinking that his uncles had come out of concern for him. "We came to meet our brothers living there, gathering information for the cause," Ramzi added spitefully.

"Enough!" Khaled spat the word at Ramzi. "Keep your information to yourself, brother and get ready to leave. We go through Thamugadi."

On the journey north, Farinas was young enough to be excited by new places they rode through and the many different *cauponae* and *tabernae* offering food and resting places for travellers. His uncles preferred sleeping outside, although they occasionally stopped to eat at roadside *thermopolia* where the food was cheap and not the best quality, but it was freshly cooked and hot. They reminded Farinas of street vendors in Theveste.

It took three days for them to reach Thamugadi. The layout was familiar to Farinas who was beginning to realise, that the Romans simply built the same city around the old cities they conquered. In Thamugadi, they passed the forum and continued east into the city where they spent the night in the home of a well-to-do ivory merchant. The horses were taken care of, and their host led them to a room, separate from the main household. Slaves provided facilities for them to bathe, before bringing food and green tea.

"Quintus is like our brother Jilwa," Tareq said when their host left to return to his family. He's Roman in all things but helps the Brotherhood to ensure favourable treatment if we are ever in power."

"And to avoid having his head cut off when that glorious day arrives." Ramzi sounded more convinced of the success of their cause than Tareq, Farinas thought.

"Men like them are useful to us," Khaled added, "but we know who the true freedom fighters are."

That night, Farinas was lulled to sleep by the familiar noises of the city, and he slept until wakened by Ramzi. By the light of a small lamp, they ate the food a slave brought. He also told them, with some urgency, that they were to leave before dawn.

The horses were saddled and ready and they made their way through the early morning bustle of traders preparing for the day. Penned animals and poultry added to the noise, as slaves called out greetings to each other while shopping for their masters' households.

Farinas eagerly tried to take in the sights, especially the narrow streets and old buildings that had been there before the Romans came. "I may never see these cities again," he whispered to Tareq.

"You will become part of the people who live in the desert," Tareq told him. "There is nothing so wondrous as lying under the stars listening to the wild animals, galloping on a fast horse across the sand or sleeping in a tent when the rain finally falls on the parched ground."

Farinas grunted but could imagine nothing worse.

Chapter 4

On the way out of the city, they joined prosperous merchants in lumbering ox-drawn carts or riding in fine carriages heading for the straight, paved Roman Roads leading to rich markets where they would trade their goods and become even wealthier.

"I'll be glad to be out of the filth and stink of the city," Khaled growled, and Farinas realised his uncles were uneasy in the crowded city, preferring the open spaces of the desert.

"I like the city," he said. "There's always something happening, people arriving from strange places, bringing wondrous goods—"

"We have our own wondrous goods, that the Romans steal from us." Khaled snapped. "Gold, silver, fine oils, and precious stones, and of course our grain. The Romans need our goods more than we need their pottery and cheap beads. Speak when you know what you're talking about."

Ramzi glanced over, grinning as he always did when Farinas was rebuked, and they continued the journey in silence.

By the time they reached, Ayn Malīlah, Farinas was saddle sore and exhausted and looking forward to spending a second night indoors at the *stabulum,* even if only in a loft above the stables.

Assellina, the tavern keeper, had been born in Hippo Regius to an Amazigh mother who embraced everything Roman. Her father too had been an Amazigh, but he had been a nomad from the desert regions and soon returned to the nomadic life to continue the war against Rome. Assellina, raised on her mother's tales of handsome young freedom fighters, was delighted to do her bit to further the cause.

Farinas later discovered that 'doing her bit', involved entertaining men like Khaled, in her private apartments. "He's trying to sire as many sons as possible before he dies a glorious death." Tareq laughed as he explained where Khaled was, and what he was doing with the young woman. For Farinas, it meant sharing a room in the main building with Ramzi and Tareq, eating delicious lamb and vegetable dishes, and sleeping on a soft bed with wool covers.

With the moonlight streaming through the latticed shutters, Tareq and Farinas spoke quietly as Ramzi cleaned and checked his weapons. Tareq had been trying to teach Farinas how to throw the knife he wore on his left forearm. It no longer felt awkward or uncomfortable, but they both knew it would be a long time before he would be able to use it effectively.

Tareq's last piece of advice to Farinas, about the raid on the gold wagons, had been. "Make sure your waterskin is full, watch what's happening, and ride south into the desert the first chance you get!" Farinas had taken this as a sign that Tareq did not expect the planned raid to go well.

Baragsen arrived early the following morning, tense and anxious to leave. "We need to be in place well before the gold arrives," he told them, hurrying them to the stables.

"When do we meet the others?" Tareq asked.

"When we get there. They'll be arriving in small groups, like us. The gold is being transported in two specially designed carts. They're ordinary *plaustra,* but roofs and sides have been added. They'll have an escort of auxiliaries."

"What about *dromedarii?*" Farinas asked, remembering the effect camels had on horses. He had no wish to meet armed and dangerous men mounted on camels, which would unsettle the horses.

"No camels…oxen and horses." Baragsen assured him. "Harscheft and his spearmen will lead the attack, on the signal."

"What signal?" Khaled asked.

"A horn blower will sound the *nafir* to signal the attack," Baragsen explained. "The first signal will be for Harscheft's spearmen. They are only ten in number, so the signal for our attack will come quickly. Be ready but wait for the second signal," he warned. "You don't want to be killed by a friendly spear."

Farinas had the feeling that he was being involved in more than just an isolated raid; it was beginning to sound like a minor war, but ten spearmen didn't seem much against Roman auxiliaries.

Baragsen was continuing. "Be ready to attack, before the convoy of soldiers and carts comes into sight. Attack on the second signal, break off on the third."

He stopped and waited, inviting questions. Farinas wanted to ask what the signal was to retreat but was afraid to ask, also he rather doubted there would be a retreat with Harscheft leading the attack.

"We will take the gold to an arranged meeting place in the desert. Harscheft and his men will take half. We will take the other half."

"We might have to fight the Garamantes for our half." Tareq's comment was ignored, but Farinas thought he was probably right.

"What about the auxiliaries?" Ramzi asked.

Baragsen shrugged. "To escort two carts? There won't be many. They have become complacent. We will easily outnumber them."

"We have to get the gold away fast, though," Khaled warned them, "before reinforcements are sent out from Thamugadi or Theveste."

Remembering Tareq's advice, Farinas made sure his waterskin was full and firmly attached to the saddle. Baragsen led the way, but rather than following the Roman Road, they took an old track that mostly ran parallel with it, though it often changed direction to take account of features in the landscape. They met few people along this route and soon arrived at the meeting place, which was dominated by a hillock, close beside the Roman Road.

Farinas felt his heartbeat thundering in his ears and his mouth dried up, as he realised he would soon be in a real battle, fighting armed Roman soldiers. He looked at his uncles, wishing he could be brave but knowing he wasn't. He was terrified.

Farinas's terror grew when Baragsen led them behind the hillock and into a clearing, sheltered and hidden by shrubs and trees. Waiting there, was a band of fifteen armed and mounted Imazighen. The uncles' swords were returned to them, and one was thrust into Farinas's hand. He held it clumsily and struggled to dismount with it in his hand. It was humiliating since three of the sword-wielding riders appeared to be the same age as he was and had the confidence of experienced riders and swordsmen.

"Stay in the rear," Tareq advised quietly. "Try to keep out of the fighting. There will be other battles."

Farinas nodded but wondered how Khaled would feel about that. Then a cloud of dust heralded the arrival of the Garamantes, led by Harscheft. Watching the fierce warriors, Farinas was even more convinced that they were in as much danger from the Garamantes, as they were from the Romans.

Unlike the robed Imazighen led by Baragsen, the Garamantes wore leather tunics to mid-thigh, covered by chain mail with studs that glinted in the sunlight. Their long boots were leather, and they wore bronze helmets. Each rider carried a throwing spear, and a sword hung in a scabbard at his side. Their silver rings and armbands were studded with brightly coloured gemstones.

The two groups remained separate. It seemed Farinas wasn't the only one who distrusted their allies, and the Garamantes made no attempt to disguise their contempt for the Imazighen.

As they waited, Farinas fought his rising panic. Terrified to the point that he could neither think nor move with any purpose, he wanted to turn Musad and ride away from the coming engagement, but he was sure the horse would never obey him, and what little control he had would disappear, once they became caught up in the charge.

Slowly as he sensed the tension growing and watched the determination on the men's faces, he felt the faint stirrings of belonging and a growing sense of pride. Maybe the blood of Tikfarin did run in his veins. He hoped it would stay there.

The heat was intense, and men and horses soon became restless. Standing beside Musad, Farinas grasped the reins in a hand that was slick with sweat. He covered his mouth from the gritty dust and the rank smell of horses and men. In the silence, he realised everyone was listening for the sound of heavy iron wheels, creaking leather, and jingling harnesses, signalling the arrival of the carts bringing the gold.

Tareq standing beside him whispered, "Remember, keep back and avoid the fighting if you can. There will be time to fight when you are older and more prepared."

Farinas nodded, but he knew he wasn't capable of making any decisions. His whole body was shaking, and he saw Harscheft watching him. How could he ride away with those eyes on him, and what would his uncles, Khaled and Ramzi think of him, if he did?

His thoughts were whirling around in his head when a rider approached Baragsen. Tension among the men rose and they mounted their horses. In silence, as Baragsen raised his arm, Harscheft led his spearmen out of the clearing, round the dune and onto the side of the Roman Road, followed by the Imazighen, Farinas with them, mounted and armed.

The Garamantes lined up facing the road but were still hidden by scrub and bushes. Behind them, the Imazighen formed two rows. Tareq manoeuvred Farinas to the end of the second row and they waited. Here, by the roadside, and out of the shade of the trees, the heat was brutal, and the dust scratched and scorched, but Farinas was only conscious of his own fear, as he clung to his horse while trying to hold the sword in a firm grasp.

The waiting stretched to breaking point, and then there was a slight movement from the end of the line, and they heard the sounds they had been waiting for. Looking to his right, Farinas saw four oxen emerging from the shimmering landscape. He wondered why the waiting force had not been seen by the leading auxiliaries, but it seemed that the vegetation, and the dust being thrown up by the carts, was enough to screen them from the road.

The leading soldiers had reached a point directly opposite Farinas when the horn blower sounded the call which rose above the noises of the convoy. Wild blood-curdling shrieks rose from the Garamantes, and the attack was on. The Garamantes launched their spears with deadly accuracy, speeding them towards the Roman auxiliaries who were marching in front of, and alongside the two carts. The Garamantes' aim was devastatingly true, and the spears should have taken out ten men. They didn't. With a swiftness that was completely unexpected, the auxiliaries raised and linked their shields, forming two shield walls, even as the signal for an attack was given. The spears hit and penetrated the shields, but not with enough force to reach the men.

Then, despite the failure of the spearmen, the second call sounded and, as the Imazighen rode out onto the road, the auxiliaries moved ahead of the carts and the two groups engaged. Farinas saw the Garamantes and the Imazighen racing towards the outnumbered auxiliaries, and he found himself waving his sword and yelling with the others, as Musad charged forward into the midst of a screaming press of men and horses.

Suddenly, the wooden sides of the carts crashed onto the road and swarms of auxiliaries jumped out and engaged the horsemen. In a heartbeat, the situation had changed. Trained auxiliaries swung their swords with deadly accuracy, bringing men and horses down in a welter of blood and gore. Farinas saw Harscheft's men following their leader - away from the conflict towards the desert. The Imazighen were on their own, and now massively outnumbered.

Suddenly Tareq, fighting beside Farinas, was pulled from his horse by a grim-faced auxiliary who slashed his throat, before letting him fall in a pool of blood. Stunned by the speed of the brutal attack, Farinas lost sight of his uncle, as Musad reared up, front hooves flying, trying to evade a Roman in full armour, holding the reins and stabbing with his sword. The animal eventually tore free and backed away, but the sudden change of direction was enough to unseat Farinas who crashed to the ground beneath hooves and feet.

Lying dazed in the bloodied dust, he heard the cry go up all around. "It's a trap! Disengage!" This was repeated, and the horn blew as horses struggled to back away from the fighting. Unseated riders tried to escape into the trees and undergrowth. Knowing they had won, the auxiliaries cheered as they charged and harried the panicked men who were putting up little resistance.

Farinas was struggling to get to his feet when he saw Ramzi lying in the dust, his bloodied, anguished face turned towards him. His uncle seemed very young, and Farinas forgot his enmity as he gazed into his uncle's eyes. Ramzi smiled slightly, in response to whatever he saw in Farinas's expression, just as an auxiliary plunged his sword into his back. Farinas watched in horror as blood poured from his uncle's mouth, and his eyes glazed over, lifeless.

Overcome by hopelessness, Farinas collapsed. His uncles' plans were lying shattered in the dust, and it seemed unfair that he was still alive. He looked for Khaled, their strong leader, but all he saw was confusion and terror. He buried his head in his arms, trying to avoid horses' hooves and bodies falling around him as he pressed his body into the bloody mud, overcome by fear, and the sounds of dying men.

He had decided he needed to get to his feet and at least try to flee the horrors surrounding him, when he felt a sudden agonising pain in his head, and he sank into a merciful blackness. His first battle was over, and he hadn't struck a blow. He felt nothing but gratitude to the gods for snatching him away from the horrors surrounding him.

Chapter 5

When Farinas opened his eyes, his body was rocking from side to side and his head throbbed, making him feel sick. He put his hand to his head and realised his hair was sticky with blood. His sword and *telek* were gone. He was lying in one of the Roman carts and as his head cleared, he remembered. There had been no gold. The Romans knew their plans and had set a trap. The carts had carried only Roman auxiliaries.

The cart Farinas was in, was now full of bodies. A few were obviously dead, others, like himself were conscious but injured. Over the top of the backboard, he could see auxiliaries leading captured horses away and he hoped Musad was one of them. Roman cavalrymen looked after their horses, and Musad deserved a good owner.

Farinas looked over the bodies trying to find Khaled, but none of his uncles, dead or alive, were in the cart. A stirring among the bodies drew his attention, and he watched as Baragsen drew himself up to rest his back against the side of the cart. Farinas half expected to see it crashing down like before, as Baragsen raised his head and looked around.

"We were betrayed, Brothers," he spoke quietly and there were murmurs of agreement as his men stirred. Those who could, sat up.

"What's going to happen to us?" The question came from one of the young warriors Farinas had seen before the attack. He looked just as scared now, as Farinas felt.

"We're alive," an older man growled. "Let's just thank the gods for that."

Farinas thought of the many ways the Romans executed their enemies and wondered if being alive was truly something to be thankful for.

"We survive to carry on the fight whenever and wherever we can," Baragsen said, but even to Farinas's ears, he didn't sound convincing. He certainly hadn't inspired anyone, and his words were followed by a gloomy silence. The journey continued and a few more men regained consciousness and sat up, but there was little conversation. Everyone just wanted to know where they were being taken and what would happen to them when they got there.

Farinas was beginning to feel dizzy from the heat and lack of water when the cart stopped, and the back was lowered. The cart was in a walled courtyard and soldiers dragged the men who were conscious, out of the cart. Those who were unconscious, or dead, remained in the cart as it turned and was driven back through the gate.

"Where are they going?" One of the men tried to follow the cart, but he was knocked to the ground where he lay, motionless.

"Pick him up, or he goes with them," a soldier commanded and two of the prisoners helped the man to his feet and held him upright, as a man who looked like a merchant, came out of the building, and approached the soldiers. There was a hurried conversation and he handed one of the soldiers a pouch full of coins.

The soldiers indicated to the prisoners that they should go into the building where they were directed to make their way to an underground cell. They were pushed inside, and the door was bolted.

Farinas recoiled from the foetid smell of sweat and human waste, mixed with damp mouldy straw. There were dark stains on the floor and walls, and small creatures squeaked and darted across the cell. In the gloom, he could see a foul-smelling waste bucket and a water bucket with a ladle. Besides Baragsen and the young man who had spoken earlier, there were four older men in the cell with him.

What do you reckon will happen now?" The man's question was met with shrugs and silence. Farinas realised none of the men understood what had just happened. They were from nomadic tribes and had little to do with city people, who lived with the Romans, dealing with them on a day-to-day basis.

"It seems the soldiers have an arrangement with the merchant. They sell some of their captives to him, to be sold on privately, no questions asked."

"How do you know that?" the young lad asked, and the others looked to Farinas.

"I speak the language," Farinas said. "I lived in a Roman town."

"What's going to happen to us?" an older man asked.

Farinas shrugged. "We'll be sold on as slaves."

No one spoke after that. There seemed nothing more to say, and they waited to see what would happen.

As the day progressed, the water bucket was soon emptied, and the waste bucket was filled. Everyone seemed to have sunk into a stupor by the time the door opened, and a bowl of tasteless-looking couscous and a bucket of water were pushed inside.

"Eat!" Baragsen growled, as no one moved. "Eat to keep your strength up. Maybe the others are dead. We are the only ones left to carry on the fight."

"As slaves, old man."

"Any way we can," Baragsen answered with contempt. "Have you given up the fight already, Sisangh?"

"You're right, Baragsen." Sisangh got to his feet and carried the food into the middle of the floor. "Come, eat this food prepared for us. Enjoy."

There were reluctant smiles, as the men moved to sit in a circle. They ate the bland food then moved back to try to sleep, to blot out the misery of their captivity, if only for a few hours.

The misery returned when the door was slammed back against the wall and men, armed with heavy cudgels, kicked them awake and forced them back up the steps. They stumbled into the courtyard as dawn broke and were marched to the far wall where slaves were waiting with chains. They manacled the prisoners and chained them to rings in the wall. The process had been carried out so efficiently, that no one had thought to resist.

"What's happening?" The young boy was terrified, and all evidence of the confident young warrior had disappeared. Farinas felt slightly better, knowing someone else felt as frightened as he did.

"We're to be sold as slaves," Farinas told him.

"Death might be preferable," another murmured, and Farinas's trembling legs almost gave way, as he thought about the many terrible things that could happen to a slave.

One of the slaves cracked a whip, and the dealer who had been standing in the background, shouted at them. *"Prohibere loquentes!"*

"Wh-what did he say?" the young boy asked.

"We've not to talk," Farinas told them, and the slave turned to use the whip on him. He dropped the whip and moved back, however, as the courtyard gate opened and two richly dressed men rode in on horseback.

They dismounted, and the dealer approached them, bowing so low, Farinas thought to see his beard trailing in the dust. He led the merchants to the men chained to the wall.

Only Baragsen objected to the examinations that followed. He pulled back when one reached out to move his *djellaba* aside. One of the guards struck him with the cudgel, leaving him bleeding and hanging unconscious from the chains.

The merchants, making no attempt to hide their disgust at the condition of the prisoners, pulled aside garments and probed their bodies, had them open their mouths so they could check their teeth, and ordered them to turn as they discussed the merits and otherwise of the men. The young boy was being examined more closely by one, and Farinas saw his lips quivering.

"They're supposed to have been captured after an attack on a gold shipment," the man examining him said. "This one looks more like a stableboy or a street urchin."

"He'd be no use to my client," the other noted. "Too timid."

"I can let you have him for a low price," the dealer said, anxious to get the slaves off his hands before the authorities found out about his shady dealings.

"I'll take him," the first decided. "My client's gardener needs a helper. This one will do."

The boy was released from the ring in the wall, although his hands remained manacled. He seemed petrified, and Farinas called out to him. "It will be fine. You won't be ill-treated." The slave was about to raise his whip to Farinas when the other merchant came over to examine him.

"You were told not to speak," he said, examining Farinas more closely.

Farinas shrugged. "I hope I made the boy feel better."

The merchant moved to open Farinas's mouth. The disrespect reminded him of the way men had treated his mother, and he pulled his head back and glared at the man.

"I'll take him," he said, smiling.

The slave bowed and released Farinas from the ring in the wall.

"Just the one, this time, *Domine*?" The trader asked. "I can give you a good deal."

I'm sure you can, Erdal." The merchant smiled. "You wouldn't want the authorities finding out about your little deal with the soldiers." The trader bowed and smiled but with little humour. The merchant continued, "My client needs just one. Deliver him to the *Ardeola* berthed at Hippo Regius... before it sails at midday."

"Midday, *Domine*, the trader murmured. "That doesn't give us much time,"

"You'll manage, Erdal. Payment on delivery. If the ship has sailed…no payment." The merchant mounted his horse, calling a farewell to the man he had ridden in with, then rode out leaving Farinas wondering where he was to sail to. He'd never been on a ship, never even seen one. He'd seen images of them on Roman walls and on mosaic floors, but he couldn't imagine one, and he was sure he didn't want to go on one. On the other hand, he didn't want to think about what would happen if he was returned to Erdal.

One of the cudgel-wielding thugs dragged him from the others. A small, fast cart was driven up and Farinas was thrown in and chained to the side of it, then the thug climbed up beside the driver and they drove out of the courtyard.

It happened so quickly, Farinas had no time to think or to say anything to the others left behind. He sat against the side of the cart in a daze. He had no idea where they were, but there was a welcome breeze, and the air was cooler than he was used to. He knew they were heading to the coast and looking out of the back of the cart, he could see they were in a Roman city. The road was steep, and the city seemed to have been built on a rocky hillside. It wasn't a city he knew.

Very soon the roads became busier with carts and horses laden with goods going to and from the port, and even inside the cart the air was fresh and cool. Then they were driving alongside the sea. To Farinas, it looked like an enormous blue desert, only it moved and made a roaring sound as the water crashed against the sides of the boats bobbing on the waves. The air was full of the cries of birds, lots of screaming birds, not the quiet solitary ones that flew high above the desert sands, and there were people everywhere; carrying loads, pulling or pushing carts, rushing and shouting, navigating narrow gangplanks and weaving in between carts and carriages He was so amazed by the sights, he didn't realise they had stopped until he was released and dragged out of the cart.

"Wait here," the man ordered the driver, then led Farinas by his chains along the harbour to one of the ships.

"What keeps it up?" Farinas asked, gazing at the massive wooden structure, creaking, and swaying on the waves.

"It's in the hands of the gods," the guard answered, laughing at his ignorance. "Now get a move on. I'm not taking you back to Erdal." He prodded him, and Farinas stumbled up the gangplank. After his first glance at the waves crashing so far below, he stared straight ahead and tried not to think of what lay beneath him, or in his future. One looked as bleak as the other.

"Hurry up." The guard dragged him to his feet when he fell. "You'll get used to it." He laughed, not unkindly. "It's like being rocked in a cradle."

Farinas couldn't remember being rocked in a cradle, but he doubted it would have felt like this.

Chapter 6

Farinas managed to clamber up the gangplank and he stepped onto the deck where the guard removed the chain. A seaman fastened a shackle and chain to his ankle before leading him down a flight of narrow wooden steps to a small door with an iron bolt. The man pushed him through the door into a low-ceilinged cell and attached the chain to a beam in the wall.

When the seaman left, and the door was shut and bolted, Farinas looked around. He saw a straw-covered floor, a bucket of water with a ladle, and a waste bucket beside the door. He groaned at the sight of yet another waste bucket and was startled when a voice called out to him.

"It's not so bad. They change the buckets regularly."

Peering further in, where it was cooler in the shadows, he saw two straw palettes on the floor. A man was sitting on one of the palettes, watching him with interest. "I wondered if anyone else would get here before we sailed." He sounded rough and spoke Latin with a strange accent, but he didn't sound unfriendly. "Who are you?"

"Farinas, from Theveste." It seemed important to say where he was from. That was where he belonged, not here on a ship that was rolling alarmingly from side to side. Even more alarming was the creaking and groaning coming from the ships' timbers. It sounded as though the ship was starting to come apart at its seams.

"Well, Farinas from Theveste, sit before you fall." He waited until Farinas sat down on the pallet. "I'm Videric from the land the Romans call Magna Germania. I fought the Roman legions, and now I'm here on the *Ardeola* at a place named Hippo Regius."

He stood and scooped water from the bucket with the ladle and handed it to Farinas. "Drink, you need to drink as much as you can. You'll probably be sick later."

"Why will I be sick?" Farinas asked, drinking the water like an obedient child.

"Ships make people sick at first. You get used to it, then you stop vomiting."

Farinas looked at the man. He was big and very pale-skinned, apart from where he was bronzed by the sun. Farinas thought him to be quite old, possibly thirty or slightly more. His eyes were very pale blue, and his hair and beard were fair, or they would have been if they'd not been matted and filthy. Although he was obviously a foreigner, Videric was dressed like Farinas in loose trousers. His *alasho* was keeping the heat from his head and neck, but his *djellaba,* tunic and sash were folded beside his boots.

"It's so hot." Already, Farinas could feel sweat pouring down his face and body.

Videric threw a ladle of water over his head and handed him the refilled ladle. "Drink! Stop complaining."

Farinas tried not to stare at the battle scars, livid against the pale skin of his chest, but Videric had seen his glances. He seemed fine about it, even proud of them. He grinned. "I gave as good back…and I'm still alive!"

Farinas nodded and wiped the sweat from his face. Despite a slight breeze blowing between the closely fitted wooden slats, the cell was hot. Farinas's fine *burnous*, the gift from his uncle, had disappeared along with his weapons.

The door opened and a bowl was placed on the floor, then the door slammed shut. Videric used a wooden ladle to spoon the broth. He pointed to a similar ladle on the floor beside Farinas's palette. "Eat while you can," he said. "Although you'll probably bring it back up again." He seemed quite amused by the thought of Farinas's coming sickness.

Farinas did as Videric said, and discovered he was hungry enough to eat the flavourless mess of *seksu,* although he missed the spices and pieces of meat his mother always added to her broth. When the broth was finished, there was nothing else to do but lie back and endure the oppressive heat.

"It'll be cooler when the ship's moving," Videric promised.

They were drifting off to sleep when there was a sudden roar and a sound like thunder beneath them. Farinas sat up, rattling the chains with his sudden movement. "Wh…what's happening!"

"Relax," Videric groaned. "It's only the oars being run out."

"Oars! What are oars?"

"The oars move the boat when there's not enough wind for the sails," Videric explained, "or when the boat is being guided out of the harbour. At least we don't have to row the boat," he murmured. "It should get cooler now," he added.

Farinas lay back on the palette, fearful of the new things that were happening to him. He longed for Theveste. Mostly, he longed for his mother, bathing his forehead, and telling him everything was going to be all right. He fell asleep eventually but woke feeling ill, not just ill. He was convinced he was dying. His skin was slick with sweat, he was shivering despite the heat, and he just managed to reach the bucket before vomiting.

"You're seasick," Videric muttered, and Farinas moaned as he emptied his stomach into the foul-smelling bucket. He remembered little after that. Videric must have helped him to the bucket when necessary, and forced him to drink, although he could remember most of it coming back up.

Coming out of his period of violent sickness, he realised that the ship was moving over a sea that was relatively calm, but for a long time, he found even that motion unbearable. When he wasn't kneeling by the bucket, he lay shivering under a blanket, 'moaning pitifully', was Videric's description later, although he did help Farinas to keep hydrated by forcing him to take small sips of water, often.

It could only have been a few days before he recovered, but the days and nights shivering on his sweat-soaked palette or being violently sick seemed endless. Gradually though things did get better, and he was eventually able to sit without his head spinning and his stomach emptying. He struggled unaided to the water bucket and drank.

"How do you feel?" Videric asked.

"Better," he moaned, then he considered. "Well better than I was." Lying on the sweat-soaked palette, its sour smell hit him, and he almost lost the water he had drunk.

"Just as well," Videric said. "I didn't fancy having to carry you off the ship."

"When?" He had never longed for anything so much as the feeling of firm ground under his feet, the sun on his back, and a fresh breeze on his face.

"Not sure," Videric told him. "According to the lad who's been bringing our food, the actual time depends on the weather, the tides, and the gods; all of which are unpredictable".

"Praise to the gods," Farinas sighed, feeling at last that he might live. "I'll be so happy to get off this ship."

The next morning, Farinas was awake when the lad brought their food. "You look better," he said. "I have good news. The ship should berth soon."

"Then what?" Farinas asked, struggling to eat some food and keep it down.

"You're to travel north, then take another ship to Britannia." He backed out hurriedly, afraid he'd said too much. "That's just what I heard," he added.

"No, no," Farinas moaned, holding his head in his hands, and rocking from side to side in his misery. "No, I can't, not another ship. I'd rather die. I probably will die."

"Best finish your food," Videric said, ignoring his self-pitying moans. "We might not get the chance again for a while."

Farinas forced himself to eat. He was learning how unpredictable life could be, and that he needed to be prepared. "Do you think we're going together?" he asked, fearful of losing his new friend…his only friend.

"Looks like it," Videric said, as the thunder of oars being rolled out, warned them they were heading into the harbour. "At least we'll be out of this stinking hole, and able to feel fresh air and sunlight."

"I think I've forgotten how to walk," Farinas stumbled over to the water bucket, bent over to avoid his head touching the ceiling, and realised it would be even more awkward for Videric who was much taller.

"Maybe you'll learn on the way to the next ship." Videric smiled, but Farinas could see he was worried too.

Their evening meal had been brought to them, by the time the ship was safely berthed, and the unloading begun. They ate quickly, then dressed, despite the heat, expecting to be taken out, but it was full dark when the door was finally thrown open.

"On your feet!" The armed seaman unfastened them from the rings in the wall and pushed them out of the cell. "On deck!"

Farinas struggled to walk upright on legs that trembled. He heard Videric moan and knew the bigger man was suffering as he tried to straighten up. Eventually, they managed onto the dock without falling, and breathed in the cool salt air, thankful the sun had disappeared below the waves.

"Into the cart!"

With the chains clanking and dragging on their feet, they eventually managed to climb into a cart waiting on the dock. Inside, they were chained to iron rings fastened to its sides. There were some rough woollen blankets and a water bucket lashed to the side with a ladle.

"What now?" Farinas asked, and Videric shrugged.

"Wait and see. I think someone's coming."

They heard sounds of a scuffle from outside, then a loud angry voice blasted through the silence. "I've told you. Cináedus was my bastardin' Roman name. I'm called Cináed…Cin…á…ed!" The sound of laughter was followed by the angry voice again. "Aye, go on laugh, but this is a proud name back home."

"Well, wherever back home is, he speaks a type of Latin," Videric noted. He seemed amused by the exchange, but Farinas was fearful of the violent-sounding person who appeared to be joining them.

"But you're not at home, Cináedus." It was clear the man speaking was fast losing patience. "Just get in the cart or we'll throw you in."

There was the sound of chains clanking, and the angry voice again. "I can get in myself. Take your hands off me."

A group of armed men appeared and manhandled a man into the cart where his manacles were chained to the side of the cart. "Enjoy the journey, Cináedus. They're not so patient where you're going." The men laughed and tramped back along the dock, as the new man sat up and looked around.

Farinas drew back into the shadows and examined the man now slumped against the side of the cart. He was almost as tall as Videric and well-muscled. His skin was as pale as milk, except where the sun had browned it, and his red hair stuck out all over his head blending with a bushy beard and a long moustache. He was the first person Farinas had seen with hair, moustache and beard the colour of the desert sands, burnished by the setting sun.

The three sat considering their situation, then Videric broke the silence. "You'll be Cináed, then?"

The newcomer hesitated then laughed. "Aye, that's me, Cináed from Caledonia."

"Videric, from Magna Germania, and our young friend here is Farinas from Theveste."

"Have you seen any guards?" Cináed asked, pulling on the chain, where it was attached to his manacles. "This could be our best chance to escape."

As Farinas and Videric considered the ridiculous proposition, they heard hooves on the paved surface and a horse and rider appeared at the back of the wagon. The rider wore a heavy indigo cloak, pinned on one shoulder by a large gold *fibula*. Under the cloak, his tunic was pale yellow and looked like silk. Black trousers were tucked into high leather boots. His hair was short and very fair, and he was clean-shaven. The fading light shone on gemstones set in silver rings on his fingers and he wore a long sword in a decorated scabbard on his left hip. He was loosely holding the reins of a magnificent black horse and his bearing proclaimed wealth and confidence.

"Those chains are very strong, and the connections are solid. I wouldn't give another moment of valuable time to the consideration of escape," the rider advised, in a confident voice that carried easily. He spoke the version of Latin employed by soldiers and officials throughout the empire and, so long as he spoke slowly, the others could understand him. "I really wouldn't like Madray or Guyar to have to destroy any of my property… filthy and miserable looking as it is."

On hearing their names, two of the biggest dogs Farinas had ever seen, appeared and looked over the backboard of the wagon. They were big, but lean, with fine grey-black hair. They growled, which was scary enough, but then their lips curled back, and they snarled.

A click of their master's fingers sent the dogs back to sit quietly behind the horse, which showed no fear of the animals. "Don't worry," the rider explained, "they only attack on my command, or if I order them to give chase." He considered the men, as they watched the beasts. "I very much doubt you would get far with those chains…or without them."

"I had a beast like those, once," Cináed said, the anger had left his voice, and Farinas heard longing in it. "Back home…Aye back home."

"They are bred and trained in Caledonia," the rider explained.

"Aye, well I wouldn't want to get in a fight with one of them," Cináed said. "Bonny hounds they are, and great hunters."

"Well, there you are," the rider said. "As Socrates advises. 'The secret of change is to focus your energy, not on fighting the old, but on building the new.' So, you should stop fighting and try to sleep before you start building on the new... Unless you'd rather walk."

Heads were shaken and the three prisoners settled back, as the rider rode off with Madray and Guyar loping easily behind him.

"That settles it, then," Videric announced. "Let's just enjoy being out of that stinking cell, and not having to walk."

"Oh aye, let's enjoy being slaves, and being chained to a stinking cart," Cináed growled, and Farinas wondered if he was going to start shouting again.

"Well, there's nothing we can do about it, so let's just try to sleep," Videric said.

"If you keep being so reasonable, I might just have to knock your head off." Cináed threatened, but he did settle, and soon his snores were drowning out the sounds of the cartwheels trundling along the streets, taking them away from the harbour and from everything Farinas had ever known and loved.

Chapter 7

It was dark when Farinas woke and realised the cart had stopped. Videric and Cináed were already awake and looking over the backboard.

"Looks like a *mansio,*" Videric said, examining the fine white buildings surrounding the courtyard.

"*Mansiones* are too good for the likes of us," Cináed muttered. "They're for officials and travellers with lots of gold."

Soon after, a figure peered into the back of the cart. His delicate features curled in distaste, and he drew back slightly. "This is so disgusting," he complained, waving a wood and ivory-handled, ostrich feather fan in front of his face. Moonlight gleamed on gold and gemstone rings…a lot of them. "I really don't know why slaves can't be cleaned before they're sold."

"Maybe you'd like to do it," Cináed growled, glaring at the man who was dressed in wide loose-fitting trousers and tunic, with a soft woollen cloak thrown casually over his shoulders. He was big, but it was mostly fat, and the walk from the door to the cart had left him breathless. His velvet indoor slippers looked comfortable but impractical.

"Oh, dear me, no. That is not what I am employed to do." His voice rose an octave, at the horror of the suggestion.

"You're here to guard us, then?" Cináed was becoming increasingly aggressive.

"Guard you? I mean…Do I look like a brute?" In no way intimidated, the man smiled and clicked his fingers. The massive jowls of Madray and Guyar appeared over the backboard, calming Cináed immediately. The man stroked the massive heads, while crooning to the animals. "There, my lovelies, you can relax. Pelias is perfectly safe." With another click of his fingers the dogs visibly relaxed.

"So why are you here, Pelias?" Videric asked.

"I am to look after you on the journey. See to your every need, as it were."

"So, you're our servant?" Cináed laughed but kept his distance from the backboard…and the dogs.

"Of course not. You could say I'm your trainer. I have been tasked with improving your fitness." He examined them carefully and gave a great sigh. "There is so little to work with. It will take all my considerable skill."

"You?"

"Well not just me, of course." He gave a delicate laugh and fluttered the fan. "I will oversee your training, supervise any medical needs you may have, and see to your food."

"Medical needs?" Farinas didn't like the sound of that.

"Training will be…difficult," Pelias breathed out the last word and smiled. "Yes…arduous." There was silence as they considered this, and then Pelias snapped the fan shut. "Now, you will be taken to the bathhouse to use the facilities, then food will be brought, but don't take too long. It is late, and your training will start early in the morning." He gave a little wave and made his way back to the *mansio*, stepping delicately in his velvet slippers, followed by Madray and Guyar.

Two guards stepped out of the shadows and pulled the backboard down. A young lad clambered in and released their chains from the side of the cart.

"Out!" The guards, openly displaying large, curved swords, stepped to the side and waited, as they climbed out trailing their chains. In a small bath house at the back of the courtyard, they were directed to the latrines then their manacles, shackles and chains were removed, and they were ordered to strip.

They removed their clothes and went through to a sunken bath. The water was hot, and Farinas smiled as he felt it soak away the caked blood, sweat and grime. He plunged his head under the water and scrubbed his scalp and body with oil from *amphorae* on the side of the bath. The guards pointed to *strigils*.

"Scrape that muck off. If you're too slow, the dogs will get your supper."

Clean and dry, they were handed breech clouts, loose-fitting cotton trousers and tunics, and woollen cloaks. Instead of boots, they were given leather hob-nailed sandals, similar to the ones Farinas had seen Roman soldiers wearing.

A slave came and fastened a chain around their waists. It hung loosely between them, allowing them to move more easily.

Outside they were told to sit on a bench, and bread and bowls of thick vegetable broth were brought from the *mansio*. When they returned to the cart, they found fresh blankets and cushions, and clean water in the bucket. The ends of the chain were attached to the rings on the side of the cart. Despite the chains, Videric smiled. "Things are looking better."

"There's a reason for it." Cináed was not impressed. "Slaves don't get treated this well. This means trouble."

"You always so cheerful?" Videric asked.

"No. I can be a right miserable bugger at times." Even Farinas managed a smile, thinking maybe Cináed wasn't so bad after all. In clean clothes and with soft bedding, they fell asleep quickly.

They were wakened while still dark, by the guards hammering on the sides of the cart. They were hurried to the latrines then given food, and before long they were chained up in the cart again.

Pelias came from the *mansio* wearing more substantial footwear, and a warmer cloak. "Well gentlemen, I do hope you are rested. Training starts today." He spun around, cloak flying in a circle and clapped his hands.

A young man, wearing a tunic to mid-thigh, a band of crimson silk confining his thick black curls, and leather thick-soled sandals laced to his knees, ran from the *mansio* to the gates of the compound. He was a big man, and as he went through a series of stretches, they could see firm muscles rippling under his bronzed skin.

A guard entered the wagon and unfastened the chain.

"Out!" Pelias snapped his fingers, and as they climbed out, Madray and Guyar, lying beside Pelias, raised their huge heads and watched. "You will not need your cloaks," Pelias told them. "We will be following in the cart, but these lovely hounds do like to run ahead and keep an eye on things. Don't you, my lovelies?" He stroked the animals' heads and they drooled happily, showing long sharp fangs. "Now, in a single file. Run! Follow Teo." When no one moved, he flapped his hands. "Go on then! Go! Don't keep Teo waiting. He can get quite cross."

"Teo?" Videric asked.

"That superb bronze god you see before you." Pelias waved his hand towards the young athlete waiting by the gates.

"How far?" Cináed growled.

"Just until he stops," Pelias answered, smiling. "Then you can walk." When no one moved he placed a hand on each of the hound's heads. Both growled and Pelias smiled. "I really would start running," he advised. "Teo has been tasked by our master, to ensure you keep up. These two lovelies," he smiled, "will be on hand to assist him."

They looked at each other, then at the dogs and finally, they watched the broad, muscled back of Teo, as he raced out onto the road, and they ran. Cináed was in front with Farinas in the middle and Videric at the back. "How will we keep up," Farinas gasped. "These chains are heavy."

"Depends on how fast that big brute runs," Videric answered, already gasping for breath.

"Save your breath for running," Cináed snapped. "I'm not being slowed by you two."

The sun was not nearly as hot as it had been when they left Hippo Regius. In fact, everything seemed very different to Farinas, but it was warm, and as they ran, they soon became sticky with sweat and covered in dust from the road.

Although running along a straight paved road, the countryside was different to the one Farinas was used to. It was greener, and there were lots of strange plants and trees. They passed few people, but those they saw were pale-skinned and dressed differently, especially the women, who wore drab colours and left their heads and faces bare.

Teo remained a speck in the distance, but they managed to keep him in sight, even when it rained. At first, the rain cooled them but soon it became cold, adding to their misery. Farinas's breath was coming in gasps, and his legs were burning, when he saw Teo running back to them. He turned then walked ahead of them.

"Walk!" he commanded, and they walked.

"I didn't think I could run that far," Videric gasped.

"You look like a soldier. I thought they could run for miles," Cináed taunted him, although he was finding it hard to draw breath too.

"That was many years ago when I was fit," Videric explained. "Like young Farinas here." The two men looked at Farinas, red-faced and gasping, then at each other, and they broke into laughter.

Farinas decided he would show them. He would keep up with them. He had no idea how far they walked, but he found he was managing it quite well. He was breathing easier and, as his breathing slowed, he felt quite comfortable, but he was pleased when Teo led them into the courtyard of another fine white *mansio*, just off the road.

They used the latrines then Teo chained them to rings in the wall at the back of the courtyard. Trees kept the worst of the rain off. "So, you kept up, "Teo said, "but the pace was ridiculously slow. You will do better." He looked them over and checked their feet. "Pelias will give you paste for your feet. Next time, we run faster."

"You ready for that, Farinas?" Cináed asked.

"As ready as you," Farinas answered. "I just hope the paste works on these blisters."

"It is a good ointment," Teo said. "Now I will send out food. Eat it, and drink lots of water." He ran over to the main building and soon a young boy came over carrying a big bowl of barley porridge and vegetables. Farinas didn't know if the food was as good as it tasted, or if he was just very hungry.

They were examining their feet in gloomy silence when the cart pulled into the courtyard with the dogs trotting alongside. Pelias climbed from his seat beside the driver and went into the *mansio*. The dogs remained with the driver as he tended to the oxen.

"I hope we don't have to run again," Farinas said.

"Not on full stomachs," Videric decided. "I think we'll have a rest first."

"I want to know what's going on." Cináed was still miserable. "I never heard of slaves being this well-treated. I'd put money on us riding in the cart now…with its fancy cushions and blankets."

Cináed was right, and when Pelias returned, it was to lead them back to the cart. He gave them the promised paste then attached the ends of the chain to the cart and left.

"This does feel good," Farinas murmured, gently massaging the paste into his feet, but the other two had finished and fallen asleep. It was not long before Farinas was sleeping too.

As the light faded, Teo returned with the guards. There was no sign of Pelias or the dogs.

"Why is it still raining?" Farinas asked and the others looked at him. "In Theveste, the rain only lasted a little while, then the hot sun dried everything."

You're not in Theveste now," Videric pointed out, as the guards undid the chains from the cart. "You're in Gaul. Sometimes it rains for days, and you don't see the sun at all."

"I like that it's not too hot here, but I hate the rain, and the clouds that always hide the sun," Farinas decided.

They ran and walked until darkness fell. This time they were sure the distances were longer, but they managed to keep Teo in sight until they reached the stopping place, where they ate a hurried meal then slept.

Teo ran faster each day, and they covered more distances. They did notice that the food ration increased in quantity, though the quality remained the same. To Farinas, used to spicy dishes, it was bland but filling. However, on the second day, a drink was added to their diet, with some important information.

They had stopped for the night and were looking forward to a long cold drink of water, but there was none waiting for them. Instead, it was Teo who brought the waterskin and a jug to them.

"I'm parched." Cináed reached for the waterskin, but Teo handed him the jug. Cináed shrugged and took a long drink before pulling the jug away and spitting the contents of his mouth onto the ground. "I'm not drinking this," he roared. "It tastes like…like camel piss."

"How do you know what camel piss tastes like?" Videric asked, taking the jug and sipping from it. Farinas watched, desperate for a drink, but Videric spat his mouthful out too. "I think you're right." He nodded at Cináed and handed the jug to Farinas who sniffed it and tried to hand it back to Teo.

Teo stepped back and shook his head. "Good for you. Specially brewed for gladiators."

There was a sudden stillness as they considered this, then Cináed spoke up. "What's gladiators got to do with us?"

Teo shrugged. "I know gladiators drink this. You must drink it."

"We drink water," Videric insisted.

"And wine, and beer…" Cináed added.

"You drink water…after you drink this." Teo was adamant, and Farinas decided it was worth drinking anything, just to eventually feel the cold water soothing his parched throat.

"I'll drink it," he declared. He looked at the others, now watching him with interest. Teo handed him the jug and Farinas quickly swallowed a mouthful…then he threw up. "Water," he begged. "I drank it." Teo reluctantly agreed and gave him the waterskin.

While this was going on, Pelias had come over from the *mansio*.

"What's this about gladiators?" Cináed demanded.

Pelias looked surprised. "You don't know?"

"No, we don't know," Videric answered softly.

"Your master…and mine, the esteemed Caelus Gallio Flavius, owns gladiator schools. You are training to be gladiators." Pelias answered. "Your training will continue…If I think you are good enough," he added.

"I don't want to be a gladiator." Farinas knew about gladiators from the arena at Theveste. His mother had taken him once, and he'd been thrilled by the spectacle, but eventually, there was so much blood and noise, they'd left early.

"Don't be such a babe," Pelias said sharply. "You really do not understand how lucky you are. You could be on the way to a salt mine, or a galley to be a galley slave. You could be —"

"We know what we could be," Cináed snarled. "So why aren't you a gladiator, if it's so wonderful?"

"I have other talents," Pelias sniffed. "I was educated in the great city of Alexandria. I am far too refined for the arena." He looked them over and added. "Unlike you people."

Cináed looked ready to attack someone, but he seemed to think better of it and sank back onto the bench. "We need water."

"Drink the drink of the gladiators…then water." When Teo turned to walk away with the brew and the water, they gave in. Videric and Cináed drank the brew. Both managed to keep it down, unwilling to show weakness. Then they drank the waterskin dry.

"You see," Pelias smiled. "That really wasn't so bad." He turned and walked away.

"It tastes so bad going down, your body fights to stop having to taste it coming back up." Cináed decided.

Farinas shuddered. "Just thinking about that, is enough to make me sick."

"You'll get used to it," Teo assured them. "Makes bones strong…for when you fight." He gave them a warning look as he followed Pelias. "You drink it, or I break your bones."

They drank it every day after that.

Chapter 8

The next day, Teo woke them early and showed them exercises that they had to do first thing in the morning...every morning, then he made sure they were repeating the movements correctly. While they exercised, Farinas saw a figure standing by the entrance to the *mansio*, watching. As the sky lightened, he recognised the horseman from the first night off the boat. Caelus Gallio Flavius was keeping an eye on his property.

These exercises were added to their day, and the number of times they repeated each, increased steadily over time.

"Do you think the people that watch us on the road, think we're gladiators and the chains are just to make us stronger," Farinas wondered one night as they lay in the wagon.

"You're thinking of those pretty ladies that we passed today," Cináed mocked. "You believe that if you like. I could see they were only interested in me, chains or not."

Farinas laughed. "It's your funny milky skin and wild hair, the colour of the desert sands at sunset."

"It's not. It's my tight muscles." Cináed said. They laughed but they knew they looked fitter since they'd begun training with Teo. People along the way often stopped to watch them. Many called out insults or laughed at them, but others shouted encouragement. They knew the ladies' admiring looks were generally for Teo, although Farinas's dark skin caused quite a few compliments.

They didn't mention the gladiator school and Farinas tried not to think about it. Maybe Pelias had got it wrong...but if he had...what was the alternative?

The day after the 'special drink' was added to their diet, they followed Teo into their first stopping place just before midday and saw Pelias waiting for them with a bundle of wooden practice swords.

"Now, this I can do," Cináed growled. Teo was already thrusting and parrying with an imaginary opponent, adding flourishes for effect.

"He looks good," Farinas said, and Cináed snorted.

"Pretty moves don't win fights."

"I think he heard you," Videric grinned, as Teo glanced in their direction. Pelias handed each of them a sword.

"I've fought with real swords," Cináed announced.

"That was before you got old and slow," Teo responded, then made a few quick, confident movements. He stopped with his sword point resting against Cináed's throat.

Cináed wasn't happy, but he nodded. "Aye, you could be right."

"Right, Farinas," Videric was handling his sword quite expertly, "looks like it's you and me."

"Maybe not." Farinas was watching two other men, every bit as strong and fit-looking as Teo, walking towards them, carrying practice swords.

"Pay attention, Cináed!" Teo's shout was followed by a cry of pain from Cináed, as Teo slammed his sword down on his wrist, sending Cináed's sword spinning onto the ground. You won't be able to beat everyone into submission," he added. For once, Cináed didn't respond with blind anger. He picked up his sword and paid more attention to Teo's instructions.

Farinas and Videric took up their swords and faced the newcomers. Farinas hoped they would show consideration for his youth and general lack of skill, although he doubted it. As they stood waiting, the two men exploded into action, and Farinas fell under a barrage of blows. He glanced across and saw Cináed and Videric on their knees. Three wooden swords lay in the dust.

Teo and his companions stepped back casually and waited until the three men got back on their feet, holding the swords. They attacked, only to find themselves back on the ground almost immediately.

At one point, a very bruised and battered Farinas was holding the sword in both hands and swinging wildly, as his opponent's sword darted in and out stabbing and slashing. The man eventually stepped back and dropped the point of his sword. "Stop!" he roared.

Farinas stopped and watched as the man went through a few moves with him and then engaged in a lesson rather than a contest. Despite this, there came a time when Farinas was lying in the dust, his body in agony, and he knew he was finished.

Maybe the beatings would stop if he just lay there. Breathing was painful and he was wondering how many ribs had been cracked when Cináed called over.

"You havin' a rest, boy?" Despite the mocking words, Cináed was panting, as he struggled onto his feet, but he was still fighting back. Videric was on one knee, but also struggling to get up.

"Just…catching…my breath!" Farinas gasped, as he leaned on the sword and got back on his feet.

"Good lad!" Videric managed to get up, then crashed back down, struck by a sword blow on the back of his knees. Cináed followed and then Farinas found himself on his back, having had his feet kicked away. As they lay in the dust, exhausted, battered and bruised, they heard laughter and realised their three adversaries were enjoying themselves. Not only that, merchants, and travellers, coming in to spend the night at the *mansio,* had come to watch. They formed quite an audience.

Ridiculous odds were being offered on them being able to; land a blow, stay on their feet for the count of ten, or force their adversaries to retreat by a couple of steps. There were no takers that Farinas could see.

At one point, Cináed caused considerable confusion and loud laughter, when he staggered as far as the chain allowed, trying to hit out at a particularly vocal spectator. Everything stopped, as attention turned to the unplanned entertainment.

"What's happening?" Farinas asked. He hadn't understood anything the locals had said since he'd got off the ship, but he was more than happy to take a break.

"That fancy-dressed merchant's been insulting 'the barbarian with the orange hair' and Cináed got annoyed." Videric wiped the sweat from his face and watched as Teo dragged Cináed back into line, encouraged by the jeers and laughter of the crowd.

The uneven fight lasted until past the time they would usually have eaten. By then, the spectators had lost interest and wandered off to resume their journeys or settle in for a relaxing evening in the *mansio*.

Finally, Teo nodded and the other two threw their swords on the ground and jogged back to the *mansio*. They had barely exerted themselves. Farinas, Cináed and Videric had been knocked down numerous times and they lay there panting, greasy sweat coating their faces and bodies.

"You're piss-poor at fighting," Teo informed them. "Those of you who could fight, have forgotten most of what you learned. Bits of you would be scattered over the arena if these had been real fights." He looked much as he had done at the start. His breathing was normal, and his body glistened with a healthy glow.

Farinas knew Teo was being overly critical. Videric and Cináed had been good...just not good enough for the experts they had been fighting, but he knew he had to work hard. He was piss-poor.

"We wouldn't be chained together if we were in the arena. These chains are heavy." Videric complained.

"You'd be wearing armour." Teo squashed that excuse, adding. "Armour's heavy."

Farinas looked at Cináed and Videric, gasping, caked in sweat and grime, red-rimmed eyes staring from bruised and swollen faces, and knew he looked even worse.

"You have to work harder." Teo picked up the bundle of wooden swords and walked away.

"Right, which one of you is ready to take me on," Cináed gasped.

"Well, I would, but Teo has taken our swords," Videric pointed out.

"Aye, so he has," Cináed agreed. "That's too bad."

Farinas looked at them, and his shock must have registered because Videric attempted a laugh through a split lip and swollen jaw. "Don't look so worried, Farinas, I can't even get off the ground, and I don't think Cináed can either."

"I'm just going to lie here," Cináed said, panting and gasping. "If Pelias wants me in the wagon, he'll need to carry me."

Farinas breathed a sigh of relief. "It's not just me, then?"

They lay there gasping for breath, trying to find out if any bones were broken or if their bodies were just badly bruised. "I think help is on the way," Videric said, as Pelias approached, followed by three young boys. Farinas wasn't so sure. He could see the boys were carrying large leather buckets.

Pelias removed the chains and stood aside. "Right, lads." The boys approached and threw the buckets of cold water over them. It was refreshing at first, but the sun had gone below the horizon, and soon they were shivering, and their teeth were chattering. Pelias threw towels and clean clothes down.

"Take those wet clothes off and get dried and dressed," he ordered. "Food's coming."

"Right, let's get moving," Cináed ordered, struggling to his feet, and grabbing one of the towels.

Dried and dressed, the chains were attached adding to their discomfort, and Pelias fastened them to rings in the courtyard. They ate the flavourless food and drank the disgusting brew, then, meal over and released from the rings, they rattled back to the cart to be fastened in for the night.

"Life would be so much easier without these chains," Videric complained, as they lay on the blankets, being careful of their new lumps and bruises. For once Cináed had no response, and Farinas kept his mouth shut, although he was wondering if they would ever be free of the chains.

The next day, Teo wakened them as usual for their exercises, before the food arrived, and the day continued as before with sword practice added to the daily regime. Surprisingly, their aches and pains seemed to ease with the exercises, and Pelias provided them with a liniment to put on their bruises.

"This is good stuff." Videric smelled the liniment. "It has myrrh and laurel oil in it. They must really want us in good condition."

"Well now we know why they want us in good condition," Cináed grumbled. "It's not for our benefit. We've been bought to die in the arena, as gladiators, making more gold for wealthy bastards."

Chapter 9

During the whole journey from the ship, they had stayed on the straight, paved Roman Roads, only leaving them to avoid busy towns and villages. At night they made camp in open spaces, or in the courtyards of *mansiones*. Then one day, not long after their humiliating fight with Teo and his comrades, they found themselves confined to the cart after the midday meal when they should have been running.

"I reckon we're coming into a port," Videric announced. "The lad on the last ship said we'd be going to sea again."

"You could be right." Cináed nodded thoughtfully. "I've noticed a change in the air, and I've seen sea birds, lots of them."

"And there's lots more buildings," Farinas said, gazing in wonder at buildings that weren't blindingly white, but a muddy brown or grey in colour. The streets were narrow and filthy and even the people seemed grey. Farinas shivered in his cloak, missing the bright colours and sunshine of his home.

"We're in Gaul," Cináed said, "so I reckon we're heading into Gesoriacum."

"How do you know?" Farinas asked.

"When the Romans brought me here from Caledonia, they sold me in the slave market at Gesoriacum."

"We won't be sold in the market, will we?" Farinas asked, wondering if that would be worse than becoming a gladiator.

Cináed shook his head. "No. Merchants like Flavius sail from here, with an escort of Roman naval ships for protection. These waters are full of pirates. We must be going on board soon, or we'd be running behind Teo but I'm not complaining." He sighed contentedly and lay back on the cushions.

"I hate ships," Farinas said. "I don't ever want to go on another one."

"It won't be so bad," Videric explained. "You've got over your sea sickness. You'll be fine now."

"Are you sure?"

"Of course, I am."

"Although the sea between Gaul and Britannia can get rough." Cináed was delighted to share this information. "Waves like mountains sometimes."

"Stop worrying the lad," Videric laughed. "It's not the time of year for rough seas."

"That's true." Cináed seemed disappointed but soon cheered up. "Of course, there's always the sea serpents and the *cirein-cròin*."

"What are they?" Farinas asked. He had a notion of what a sea serpent might be, but he had no idea about the other. He just knew he didn't want to meet one; especially when he was on a ship, out at sea.

"Giant sea creatures that –"

"Legends and stories to frighten children." Videric interrupted Cináed's account, and Cináed laughed.

"Aye, and it's working. Just look at the lad."

"I'm not frightened," Farinas muttered. Even as he protested, he knew he lied. He was afraid. He had heard tales of such beasts from travellers back home. Beasts like the *jago-nini* that lived in water but came out to eat people. He wondered if one of them could climb onto a ship.

"Toughen up, lad, some gladiator you'll make." Cináed grinned. "The sooner we go on board, the sooner we'll be in Britannia, and that's close to the most beautiful country I've ever seen - Caledonia."

The cart pulled into docks that looked just like the one they'd landed at before. "Right, everyone! Out you come." Pelias appeared at the backboard, and Teo climbed in to undo the chains. Drawing their cloaks around themselves and lifting the chains, they struggled out and stood among the busy throng of merchants, traders, and dock workers.

Farinas gazed at the ship towering over them and saw a line of slaves, chained together, walking unsteadily down the gangplank and onto the dockside. Farinas noticed a few dark faces and wondered where they had come from. As the slaves left the gangplank and trudged along the harbour, Pelias called out over the constant noise. "Now we can go up."

He led them up the gangplank with Teo following. As usual, Farinas was between Videric and Cináed and he struggled with the constantly swaying board beneath his feet. He clung to the ropes on either side, and it didn't help when Cináed growled. "You fall; we fall; so, don't."

They made it safely to the top, but instead of going below like before, Pelias led them up onto the deck where they were able to see the harbour and the city of Gesoriacum spread out in front of them. Pelias led them to the mast and attached them to it by the chain. "You stay here until your cell gets cleaned out from the last lot."

"Good luck," Teo called. "Remember everything I've taught you."

"And work hard at the school," Pelias added. "It can be a good life… a gladiator's."

Pelias and Teo left, but armed seamen stood close by guarding them. Farinas huddled into his cloak and shivered. "Do you think we'll ever see them again?"

"Probably not," Videric said, watching the two men leave. "They were all right," he added, "for slave masters."

Cináed nodded. "I've known worse." He said no more, and no one asked about his previous life. They all had things in their past they wanted to forget.

"It's so cold," Farinas complained, getting up and walking up and down as far as the chains allowed, rubbing his arms inside the cloak.

"You'll have to get used to the cold in Britannia," Cináed told him. "This is as hot as it gets over there." Farinas wasn't sure he believed him but was afraid he was telling the truth.

"Lots of ships," Videric remarked, as they looked out on a sea of swaying masts and creaking timbers. Ships were being loaded and unloaded, carts laden with goods were being driven to and from the ships, and merchants in rich clothes mingled with sailors and dock workers. The buildings looked like huge warehouses and granaries, and the narrow streets were jammed with carts and wagons.

"The harbour's close enough to the Roman garrison town to benefit from its protection." Cináed pointed out the fort in the distance, beyond the harbour and warehouses.

"The city over there reminds me of Theveste," Farinas said. looking across at the white buildings in the Roman section of the city where the fora and temples, the arches and monuments, stood out from the drab local buildings.

"The Romans always build bigger and more elaborate buildings than any in the old towns they occupy," Videric said. "They like to make sure everyone knows who the conquerors are."

"There weren't any Roman towns where I lived," Cináed pointed out proudly, "only a few Roman forts and they were mostly made of wood and turf."

"That's because no one wants to live in Caledonia…except the Caledonii," Videric answered. Any reply Cináed was about to make, was prevented by the appearance of three young lads carrying buckets of hot water, tubs of paste, little amphorae of oil, and scrapers.

One of the armed guards removed the chains. "Strip!" he ordered. "This is the last chance to bathe before you reach Britannia."

"I'm getting used to this oiling and scraping," Cináed grinned.

"I'd heard the Caledonii don't wash," Videric said, keeping a safe distance from Cináed.

"Lies!" Cináed roared but he seemed happier now they were close to Caledonia, and he didn't take Videric's comments too seriously.

Farinas was happy to feel short hairs starting to grow on his face. He thought his beard would probably look very impressive when it grew in properly; thick and black, like his uncles'.

"Stop admiring yourself, Farinas! There's no women on this ship." He looked over to see Videric and Cináed grinning at him. When they were finished, they poured the contents of the buckets over each other. Dried and dressed in clean breech clouts and new sandals, they were chained together and led across the deck by the guards.

As they reached the top of the stairs, Cináed appeared to lose his balance and he fell heavily. The chain tightened, and Videric and Farinas both fell beside him in a tangle of arms and legs and clanking chains. As they struggled to their feet, the guards looked on with stony faces and folded arms. Eventually, they reached the cell, where clean clothes and heavy woollen cloaks waited for them, on clean straw palettes. They were fastened to the wall and the door was bolted.

"It was nice to be outside, without having to run or exercise," Farinas said, remembering the feel of the fresh air.

"That's not something you'll be saying very often, once we reach Britannia," Cináed laughed.

"Never mind that," Videric said. His tone had changed, and Farinas realised he was very serious. "What was that about?"

"What do you mean?" Cináed tried and failed to look as though he had no idea what Videric was talking about, but Videric was determined.

"Well?"

Cináed shrugged and pulled a pointed iron spike out of his breach clout. "You could have done yourself a serious injury with that." Videric pointed out, and Cináed grinned. They stared at the spike which had four sharp edges along the shank, leading to a narrow point.

"What are you going to do with it?" Farinas asked.

"Pick my teeth." It had been a stupid question, so Farinas kept quiet, and let Videric ask sensible ones.

"When you get out of the chains, what will you do?"

"I hadn't thought that far ahead." Cináed looked slightly taken aback. "I just saw it lying there, waiting to be picked up."

Videric nodded as if it made complete sense.

Farinas grabbed his cloak and wrapped himself in it, suddenly realising how much he missed his home, the narrow alleyways and white houses, the bright sunshine, and the heat. He understood Cináed's desire to be free of his chains now that he was so close to home.

"I'd do anything to get back home," he said.

Videric and Cináed examined the chain where it looped and fastened. "That's the weak point," Videric said, pointing to a link on the chain. "Try putting the spike through there and twisting." Cináed went to work with the spike, as Videric held the chain taut. Working on the chain was keeping their minds busy, but Farinas knew how much trouble they would be in if the spike was discovered.

As they worked and cursed whenever the spike slipped, Farinas heard the bolt sliding back and he threw his sandal at

Videric. "Someone's coming," he hissed, and Cináed slid the spike under his pallet. Farinas felt his heart hammering in his chest, and his palms were slick with sweat. If Cináed was found with the spike, a potentially lethal weapon, it would not go well for any of them.

Chapter 10

The door was opened by the armed guard, and a boy about ten years old, with dark curly hair and a cheerful grin slipped in. The door closed behind him. The boy was wearing a woollen tunic trimmed with blue braid and Roman-style leather sandals. He put down a bowl of food and a jug of their special drink and said something that appeared to be a greeting.

"That sounds like the language they speak here in Gaul," Cináed said. "I wasn't here long enough to learn much of it. Never wanted to talk to any of them anyway," he growled, clearly remembering his days as a slave in Gaul.

The boy backed away from Cináed and looked at the others. Farinas smiled, feeling sorry for him, meeting Cináed for the first time.

"Aigulf," the boy said, slowly, in a form of Latin they could understand enough to carry on a basic conversation.

"Farinas." Farinas pointed to himself then to Videric and Cináed. "That is Videric. The angry one is Cináed. Sometimes he's not so angry."

The boy smiled but kept away from Cináed. "Gladiators?" he asked.

"In chains? Do we look like gladiators?" Cináed growled.

"We're training," Farinas said. "What's this?" he asked, examining the food in the bowl.

"*Hordearii*," Aigulf told him. "Made from barely. Better with fruit or honey, but not too bad.

"You'd better get used to it," Cináed added, dipping a ladle into the bowl. "It's like the porridge we eat in Caledonia. We make it from oats."

"I could do with some meat, though," Videric said. "*Sauerbraten*," he murmured. "That's the best meat dish you'll ever taste, fresh meat soaked in wine…then cooked…delicious."

"*Seksu* is delicious, with a spicy broth, vegetables and lamb," Farinas offered, remembering the very few occasions he and his mother had been able to enjoy such an expensive dish.

"There's nothing like a nice hot greasy piece of deer or hare …or… boar roasted over a fire of pine chips," Cináed said.

Aigulf had been trying to follow the conversation and he smiled. "Gladiators not eat meat," he told them.

"I don't think I want to be a gladiator," Cináed growled.

"Not much choice." Aigulf glanced at the chains, then skipped smartly out, slamming the door behind him, and they heard the bolts being pushed into place.

"No choice! We'll see!" Cináed ate quickly, then pulled out the spike and attacked the chain links again. Videric pulled the chain tight, and Farinas sat by the door listening. He thought of the land they were going to; a land that seemed so different from his own home. He'd heard nothing good about the place, but surely, he thought, it can't be so bad if Cináed wants to go back so much.

When Cináed threw the spike across the cell in disgust and sat back against the wall, Farinas tried to find out. "What's this Caledonia really like?" he asked. "Is it a wonderful place?"

"Only if you were born there!" It was Videric who answered.

"Aye, that's maybe true," Cináed agreed, with something like pride in his voice. "It's a rough, wild place, cold and *dreich* sometimes, but it's always bonny... Aye really beautiful."

"Herodian wrote that most of Caledonia is marshland," Videric told them. "He also said the barbarians swim in these swamps or run in them practically naked because they don't want to hide the pictures they have painted on their bodies. They're fierce and dangerous fighters, and the atmosphere is always depressing because of the thick mists that cover the land…constantly." He laughed at their surprised looks. "I've listened to learned men…and even read the writings of some of them. I wasn't always fighting."

Cináed grunted. "Aye well, we're not barbarians but your man Herodian got the bit about the fighters right. The rest... that's just lies."

Lying against the wall, taking a break from working on the chain, Cináed offered the spike to Videric and Farinas. "I reckon we could escape once we reach Britannia. Then it's not far to Caledonia. My people there, the Vacomagi, will welcome anyone escaping the Romans," he added. "We need good fighters, but I could convince them to take you in although you're both still piss poor at the fighting."

"I'll take you on any time," Videric smiled. "But what would me and the boy do? he asked. "Trying to avoid Roman patrols in Britannia, then freezing our *testes* off, struggling through the swamps in Caledonia."

"I told you…that's lies!" Cináed roared but relaxed when he saw Videric smiling.

"It's different for you," Videric explained. "You'll be in a country you know. Me and the lad are better as we are for now, besides, we'd only hold you up."

"If everyone is as white as you, I'm not going to blend in," Farinas pointed out.

"That's true. Except for some of the Roman soldiers and officials, most look like me," Cináed agreed. "Just not so handsome."

"Ugly as well as savage," Videric noted, but Cináed just laughed.

"If you do ever escape, head for Vacomagi land. My father's the headman of a village there, so I'm what you might call a prince in your country. If you mention me, you'll be safe…and we're not the barbarians Rome calls us," he added proudly. "They spread lies about us because they've never beaten us…well only once, at Mons Graupius…and we don't talk about that," he growled.

"What happened?" Farinas asked, then ducked as Cináed lashed out at him.

"I told you!" he roared. "We don't talk about it!"

"You've frightened the boy." Videric laughed.

"No, he hasn't! And I'm not a boy!" Farinas recovered quickly and joined in their laughter.

That was the most they had heard Cináed say, and for the first time Farinas wondered if he might be right about his people. It was Videric who broke the silence. "Let's get that link open, so you're ready when the chance comes."

Thinking about his homeland made Cináed even more determined, but the chain links were well-made and solid. It took a lot of work and cursing, for them to finally prise one open and separate it enough for the chain around Cináed's waist to be taken off. Cináed stepped out of it and took a few steps, swinging his arms, and bending his body from the waist. "That's me ready to go," he laughed.

"There's no point in escaping while we're in Gaul," Videric reminded him. "Not when we're going to Britannia anyway." He handed him a piece of leather thong from his sandal. "Fasten the link with this and be careful. If it breaks or comes undone…you'll be lucky to stay alive."

Cináed fastened the chain around his waist again, but he couldn't stop grinning. Farinas wasn't the only one unsettled by this. "Stop grinning, Cináed," Videric told him. "It's not natural."

"It really isn't," Farinas added, and Cináed growled at them.

"That's better," Videric laughed as they lay down and slept, lulled by the gentle movement of the ship.

The next morning when Aigulf brought their food, Farinas woke with no sign of sickness. He ate everything, and drank the brew without complaint, as Aigulf told them what he knew about their voyage.

"Sail soon, Roman navy ships, protect us to Portus Ritupis in Britannia. After that, sail on our own, no protection, just crew and oarsmen."

When Aigulf left, Videric decided they should do the exercises Teo had taught them, while confined to the cabin. These were done from a lying or sitting position. The low roof of the cell made anything else impossible. "If you escape," he explained to Cináed when he grumbled, "you'll need to be fit, or you'll be captured and be even worse off than you are now."

Thoughts of escape kept Cináed eager to train, so he agreed. Videric and Farinas just liked to be moving. Teo had trained them well, and their bodies demanded exercise, even when they really wanted to sleep.

Soon after, as they lay recovering from the exercises, they heard the oars being run out then felt the ship moving. They were on their way to Britannia.

Chapter 11

When Aigulf brought their food, he told them they'd reached the south coast of Britannia. They'd left the naval ships berthed at Portus Ritupis and they were sailing north, unescorted. Farinas added pirates to his list of things to worry about. He'd also lost his appetite, but Cináed, as usual, finished what was left. Aigulf was leaving with the empty bowl when a horn sounded. This was immediately followed by the thunder of oars being shipped, and footsteps pounding on the stairs, racing to the top deck.

"What's happening?" Farinas asked, happy he'd left most of the meal. The way his stomach was churning, he knew he wouldn't have kept any food down.

"Sounds like we're under attack," Cináed guessed. This was confirmed by the shout, "Repel boarders!" followed by the clash of weapons and shouts, then the screams of men in agony.

"Stay here!" Videric shouted as Aigulf turned to leave. "Safer... out of the fighting."

They sat in the almost dark cell, listening to the sounds of the fighting raging above them. "All oarsmen and seamen will be fighting," Aigulf said. "They're well-armed. They'll drive them off."

"They can't row and fight," Videric pointed out. "We can't outrun them, so we won't be going far until the battle's over, one way or another."

They had no idea how the battle was going, and Farinas thought that having a sword and fighting would be better than sitting helpless, not knowing what was happening.

"If the ship goes down, we're done for," Cináed muttered.

"Our men will fight them off," Aigulf repeated with less conviction. Farinas recognised fear when he heard it, and he wasn't convinced. "Ba'al Ḥammon preserve us," he pleaded, although he wasn't sure his god would help, so far from home.

"The gods help the deserving," Videric growled as they listened to the screams of injured and dying men. "We need to do something to show we're deserving of their help."

Cináed nodded. "Or we die like rats." He pulled and broke the thong holding the chain together and stepped away from it, before pulling the spike from under his palette and handing it to Videric.

"No!" Aigulf cried out, his eyes widening in fear. As he turned to run, Cináed caught him and pushed him onto a palette.

"Just stay quiet, lad. We're not going to be trapped and dragged under by these chains."

Aigulf lay still, wide-eyed as Videric went to work on the chain. "This won't …open…" Videric was panting, as he tried to force one of the links apart.

"It wasn't easy," Cináed conceded, leaving Aigulf and going to help Videric.

"What are you waiting for?" Videric asked, working frantically on the chain. "This is the best chance you'll get." He had a sudden thought. "You can swim, can't you?"

Cináed nodded. "I can't just leave you and the boy." Together they went to work on one of the links while trying to work out who had the upper hand in the battle going on above them.

Suddenly, the ship shuddered, and the sounds of clashing steel and the noises of the battle were drowned out by the deafening shriek of ripping timbers. The ship heeled over sending them tumbling along the tilting floor. When the ship settled, there was silence.

"Sounds like we've rammed the pirates," Videric said.

"Or they've rammed us," Cináed suggested.

"The ship's sinking!" Farinas felt sheer terror take hold of him. What would it be like to be under the water, with no air? "We're trapped!"

"It's not sinking yet," Videric said, sitting up and carrying on working on the chain. "If it sinks though, we don't stand a chance."

"Get away, Cináed. What else can you do?" Videric gasped. "Stay and hold our hands as we drown?"

"Go, Cináed!" Farinas managed to speak, despite his fear. "You're nearly home." Despite his brave words, his voice trembled, as a body came crashing down the stairs and thudded against the door. Blood thick and dark seeped under the door.

"We can do this together!" Cináed joined forces with Videric and, straining desperately, they managed to pry open the link. freeing Videric.

"Go now!" he insisted as he began working on Farinas's chain, but Cináed grabbed the spike. "We know how to do it now," he panted, as they worked together. "It will be quicker."

Aigulf lay on the floor where he'd rolled, watching the men struggling with the chain. He could have got out, but he didn't. He was imagining what it would be like to be chained to a sinking ship. "Guards don't bolt the door," he told them. "Only when I leave."

Cináed laughed. "I hadn't even thought of the door."

The ship was now steady, although lying at a steep angle. Agonising screams, mixed with shouts and curses, filled the cabin, but finally, Farinas's chain fell away, and they were free. Videric handed Cináed the spike. "You might find this useful." Cináed nodded and hid the spike in his clothing.

Then, over the noise of battle, a horn sounded, and a voice roared in the hush that followed. "To the oars!" They heard running feet on the deck then footsteps thundered down the stairs. The desperate cry, "To the oars!" was repeated over and over.

"The master must be trying to free the ship and outrun the pirates." Videric was pushing Cináed ahead of him. "This is your chance to get away, Cináed."

"What will you do?"

"Some oarsmen will have been killed; others will still be fighting. They'll need men. We'll help man the oars."

"I've never even seen an oar," Farinas panted, wild-eyed at the thought of going out into the fighting.

"It only takes brute strength," Videric told him. "You've been training and at least we'll be doing something, not sitting waiting to drown or be killed."

"Me too!" Aigulf scrambled to his feet, and they made their way out of the cabin and joined the men storming down the stairs.

When they reached the lower deck, Aigulf approached a tall man who was directing men to the benches. Like the others, he was bloodied and sweat-stained. Everyone looked exhausted, but they were moving quickly; three men on each bench, spaced apart enough to allow them to move their arms freely.

"Adalhard!" Aigulf called above the noise. "We've come to help!"

When the man saw them, he hesitated. "Have you rowed before?" he barked.

They shook their heads, but Videric insisted. "You need every man you can get."

"Aye, well…We've lost a few right enough, just go with the rhythm. Don't fight the oars." As he was speaking, Adalhard was directing each of them to a bench, placing them with an experienced rower on either side. He looked at Aigulf and smiled. "I doubt you'll be strong enough to man an oar, but you can maybe help with the balance."

He put Aigulf between two huge men, each of them looked as though he could man an oar by himself, but they grinned and made way for the lad. "Just go with our rhythm," one of them told him. "Rest when you need to," Aigulf nodded and grasped the oar.

Farinas sat and watched as the benches filled up. There was less noise now, as most of the fighting men were manning the oars. He imagined the pirates must have withdrawn to try to save their own ship.

Looking around, he saw Cináed, sitting in the middle of a bench across from him. He hadn't tried to escape. He was going to help too. Cináed looked grim but he nodded encouragement, then, at a signal Farinas was unaware of, the oars moved, and he understood the sound he had heard before, as they were pushed through grommets, held in place by rings, then they stopped and hovered above the waves.

As Farinas was desperately trying to understand what he should be doing, the oars dipped into the water and began a sweeping movement. He remembered not to fight the oar but that was all.

"Go with the rhythm," the man on his right grunted. Farinas tried to relax into the movement and soon felt confident enough to put his weight into it. "Good!" the man nodded, and they moved the great ship together, rows of men, bloodied and battered, grunting with the effort, but moving smoothly to a common rhythm.

Farinas wondered where the drum was. The one that was supposed to mark time on galleys, but this great sweeping movement seemed too smooth to be governed by a drumbeat, anyway, he doubted it would be heard over the roar of battle, and the thundering of waves.

Were they chasing or being chased, hunter or hunted? His muscles were straining, sweat was pouring off him, and his legs burned with the effort of pressing on the deck, as his arms and upper body helped to work the massive oar.

Then there was a tearing and screeching noise. "Easy," the man beside him grunted, "work with us. We've broken free of the pirate ship. We'll be changing direction soon."

Farinas eased back until he felt the rhythm pick up again. He saw Cináed working on his oar and wondered if he had surrendered his chance to escape, to help save the ship.

"Stop!" his companion urged. "Just place your hands on the oar and rest." Farinas did as he was told, panting, and gasping as he tried to pull air into his lungs, then he felt the ship slowly changing direction.

"Right, we'll be going forward now," his companion said. "When you feel the rhythm, put your weight behind it."

Farinas nodded and he was soon moving smoothly in time with his two companions. The ship surged forward, and it felt amazing to be part of the ship's company, moving in perfect time, speeding the ship across the waves to safety. If he could have found the breath, he would have cheered!

His exhilaration didn't last long though. His arms were soon burning, and each breath was painful. Every part of his body ached and strained and there were spots dancing in front of his eyes. By the time darkness fell, he knew he would not be able to carry on much longer. He thought of Aigulf, younger and less fit, and of how he must have been struggling. Then, as suddenly as they started, they stopped. The men collapsed over the oars, now hovering motionless above the water.

"*Colligere arma!*" Adalhard roared, and they pulled the oars in, and leaned on them, waiting, surrounded by silence. There were no sounds of battle, only the sounds of waves gently lapping against the hull, and the laboured breathing of the oarsmen.

In the silence, an exhausted Adalhard stood and addressed the men in a voice that carried the length of the ship. "Well done, men. We've left the pirate ship holed. It's probably at the bottom of the sea by now." There were a few tired cheers then he continued. "The master tells me the wind is favourable, so rest now. Bonuses when we land."

Adalhard walked back, making sure the oars were secure, before allowing the men to leave. When the oarsmen, including Aigulf had left, Adalhard spoke to Videric and Farinas. They didn't know if he realised one man was missing, if so, he didn't mention it.

"Come with me." As they followed him to their cell, he nodded his approval. "You did well, but I have to lock you in."

They staggered into the cell on legs that trembled and collapsed onto their palettes. The door slammed shut, the bolt slid into place, and a guard positioned himself by the door. The chains lay in a heap where they had dropped them.

Chapter 12

Farinas and Videric sank down on their palettes and lay breathing hard. Farinas was shivering as the sweat cooled on his body and Videric threw a blanket over him. "You don't want to get chilled," he said, wrapping himself in a blanket.

"Do you think Cináed got away?"

Videric grunted. "If his gods were with him, he might have escaped the sea and the pirates. At least he seems to have got off the ship. I hope—"

The door opened and the man they'd first met on the docks in Gaul, Caelus Gallio Flavius, owner of the gladiator school, came in. Gallio's arm had been wrapped in linen strips and was still seeping blood. It seemed as though every able-bodied man had been involved in the fighting.

He lifted the chain and examined the links. "I don't suppose I can blame you, in the circumstances, and you did help on the oars." They waited. "The other one?" Gallio asked. "The Caledonii?"

"The last time I saw him, he was on the oars," Farinas answered truthfully, and Videric nodded his agreement.

"Well, he's not on the ship." Gallio sounded surprisingly calm. They waited to find out what their punishment would be. "Don't get any ideas." He warned them. "Your friend might survive the sea and the pirates. He might even get past the Roman patrols, but we're still a way from Caledonia. He won't get any help this side of the Great Wall." He looked again at the chains. "Adalhard said you did well." He nodded and left, and they heard the bolt sliding into place.

"Maybe he really did get away," Farinas whispered.

Videric nodded, but neither really believed their friend could have escaped. Exhausted, aching and trembling from the effort he put in on the oar, how could he have survived the cold water?

"Anyway," Videric said, "it's time we did our exercises."

Farinas was shocked. Today he'd done man's work. He thought what Cináed would have said, and grinned. "Go ahead. I'll just lie here and watch."

Videric laughed. He'd never intended exercising. He could barely stand, but he was pleased that Farinas hadn't just agreed with him. "Maybe you're right. We've exercised enough today."

Soon after, as they lay on the palettes, Aigulf came in carrying a bowl of *hordearii*. They were too exhausted to talk and Aigulf left them to eat. Soon after, however, he returned, smiling. He was carrying a wineskin and three bowls. "Adalhard gave wine to men. Gave me ...to share."

"Like the ambrosia of the gods," Videric declared, and Farinas didn't know if that was because it was good wine, because of their recent restricted diet, or because they'd earned it, but they enjoyed every drop.

"Any news about Cináed?" Videric asked, and Aigulf shook his head.

"That's good, isn't it?" Farinas asked.

"He probably made it into the water, but …" Videric stopped and shrugged. "No matter, his gods be with him; he deserves his freedom."

They nodded and drank to Cináed, then Aigulf coiled the chains and picked them up. "To be fixed," he said, struggling to carry them. They listened, as he clanked his way below.

"Take your time," Farinas shouted after him, but not even the thought of being chained, could spoil their pleasure and the sense of achievement they felt.

"Maybe the blacksmith will have so many weapons to repair, he won't have time to work on the chains," Farinas suggested, before falling into an exhausted sleep.

They were wakened by the door banging back against the wall and a voice bellowing. "Get up! Your jewellery's here."

"Funny!" Videric groaned, still half-asleep, as the ship's blacksmith walked in carrying chains.

"I think so… every time I say it." The blacksmith laughed and fastened them back in the chains. These had been shortened and held only two loops which he fastened round their waists. "Right! I've made a proper job of this." He pulled the chain tight and fastened one end to the ring in the side of the ship. "You won't open these links…but you can try." He grinned and turned to leave as Aigulf came in. "Young Aigulf here wanted me to bring leg irons, as well, but I don't have any small enough for your dainty ankles." They could hear him laughing all the way along the passageway, as Aigulf protested.

"No! Did not!"

"We know you didn't," Videric smiled. "It's just him, trying to be funny."

They sat with the bowl of food, and the jug of special brew, no wine this time. Life was back to normal it seemed, but without their companion.

"No news?" Videric asked, and Aigulf shook his head.

"Nothing."

"That means he may have reached shore," Farinas said, and the other two nodded, although they knew it probably meant he'd drowned.

"Do they think the pirate ship sank?" Videric asked.

Aigulf shrugged. "Maybe - if hole low. Not, if above water."

"Why?" Farinas asked. He had heard something in Videric's voice that made him think there was more to the question than there appeared.

"I don't think Cináed would have been able to survive in the cold water for long...but...he might have reached the pirate ship."

"Do you think they would have taken him on board?" Farinas asked.

Videric nodded slowly. "They'd have seen he's not a friend of Rome, and he's from the island, even if he's from further north, so they might have helped him."

"He said he was a kind of prince." Farinas was trying to convince himself that Cináed would be safe in the strange land they were going to.

"Everyone I've ever met was a prince or a king in their own land, but I hope he escaped." Videric turned to Aigulf. "So, what's happening now?"

"Call in at Arbeia, near fort on Great Wall. Unload some cargo and mend ship."

"Will we get off the ship, while it's being repaired?" Farinas asked, but Aigulf shook his head.

"Go on other ship, leaving soon," Aigulf said, as he left.

Farinas sat with his head in his hands, thinking of more days at sea, possibly even another attack.

"Right, Farinas," Videric interrupted his gloomy thoughts. "Now it *is* time for our exercises." That was the last thing Farinas wanted to do but he knew he would feel better after, so he nodded.

Teo's training had been the only reason they had been able to keep time with the men on the oars, so keeping fit could only be good for them. They worked their muscles, they sweated, and they exercised until long after Farinas felt he had to stop. Eventually, Videric collapsed, and they lay still.

"If the roof was higher, we could at least practise sword fighting moves," Videric sighed. "I don't know how we'll do, next time we have to fight."

Farinas nodded. "Even wooden swords sting when they land." He remembered the bruises he'd received previously and knew he would be no match for Teo, or even Videric, who had been recovering his old skills with a sword.

When Aigulf came in a few days later with their food and the news that they would be berthing later that afternoon, they were delighted. Any change to the routine was welcome.

They had become used to the sounds of the oars and of the men working the sails, but in the harbour the sounds were different. They knew they had berthed by the shouted commands and tramping of many feet. Heavy items were thumped on deck and, when Aigulf brought their evening meal he told them they had berthed in Arbeia.

"You leave soon, join the *Halisa*. You sail north in convoy, taking supplies to forts in north. Good luck," he said. "Maybe hear tales, when you become famous gladiators."

"You be careful," Videric said. "Find work on land. It's safer."

They said their goodbyes and Aigulf left them to their meal.

"The food might be better on the next ship," Videric said, as they ate the monotonous and largely tasteless *hordearii*. The farther they sailed, the fewer ingredients there were to add to the basic meal.

"Can't think the native food is very good," Farinas moaned. "Not if the land's covered in marshes."

"Remember what Cináed told us," Videric warned. "Especially if it's about people Rome hasn't been able to conquer, like the Caledonii."

The noises continued late into the night, as the ship was unloaded ready for the carpenters and blacksmiths to begin work, then as they were settling down to sleep, the door was thrown open and they were unfastened from the ring in the side of the ship.

"Get dressed!" The man standing over them was only a huge shape in the dim light, but they could see the coiled whip he carried. He cracked it once and they got to their feet, scrambling to dress in tunic, trousers, and sandals. They threw their cloaks over their shoulders and followed their guard off the ship and down onto the harbour, with no idea of where they were going or what they would meet when they got there.

Chapter 13

Their chains rattled, as they hurried past the shadowy shapes of ships, rocking on the moonlit water. Despite the late hour, men were still working in the dim light of torches, and they had to make their way through stacks of cargo, and carts laden with supplies. They were jostled by impatient labourers, and the threat of the whip kept them hurrying along the side of the harbour with the waves crashing below.

Eventually, the guard led them up a gangplank to a ship much like the last one and into a cell; small, low-ceilinged, and dark. He fastened the chain to the wall and left without a word. They found two pallets at the far end of the cell and sat down.

"At least this ship doesn't have a hole in it," Videric said.

"Is that the best you can come up with?" Farinas replied, and Videric looked at him, surprised by his answer.

Farinas laughed. "I was just thinking what Cináed would have said."

"Aye, that's just what he would have said."

Very soon they heard the oars being run out, and they felt the ship moving. "We're on our way," Videric said. "Won't be long now."

"I suppose anything will be better than this."

Videric nodded, but they fell asleep with little hope for their future in the strange, cold land.

The next morning, they awoke to a surly young lad who banged their bowl of food down and left without saying a word. The food itself was a disappointment.

"What is it?" Farinas asked, peering into the bowl. "It looks like lumpy *uji*."

"It's a bit like the *hordearii*," Videric said when he tried it, "but stickier. We'd best eat it while it's hot, whatever it is. I expect we'll feel the cold more, the farther north we go."

When they weren't exercising, they huddled under their cloaks and hoped it wouldn't get any colder. It did. As they sailed farther north, the seas became rougher, and the cold seemed to penetrate their very bones. They could hear the wind howling and tearing at the rigging, and when Farinas wasn't panicking about the ship sinking, he was wondering if the howling was from a *cirein-cròin* that Cináed had talked about or a *jago-nini*. "There are no monsters." Videric tried to reassure him, but even he looked uneasy during the worst of the weather.

A few days later, just after midday, they heard unusual activity, and they guessed the ship had arrived at its destination. When the boy brought their food, Videric asked what was happening.

"We're docking at Trimontium in the province of Valentia, in Caledonia." He shuddered. "I hope we leave soon. It's a miserable place full of barbarians." He hurried away, leaving them feeling even gloomier than before.

Guards soon came to take them ashore, still chained together. When they climbed the stairs and emerged on deck, Farinas hadn't expected to see a blazing sun and blue skies, but he was shocked by the scene before him. Everything from the grey sea to the sky and the surrounding countryside looked dull and colourless, and he had to assume the pale circle moving towards the horizon, was Caledonia's version of his golden, hot sun. "There's no colour!"

"It reminds me of home, wild and savage. It's not easy to make a living in this kind of land," Videric said, but he didn't look too displeased by the prospect.

"I don't think it would be easy to do anything in this land," Farinas moaned, looking over the barren landscape as they were taken off the ship and led along the harbour to a man waiting beside a large horse. Both man and horse looked sturdy and well used to the harsh conditions.

"These for the gladiator school?" the man asked, handing over a parchment to one of the guards. "Caelus Gallio Flavius passed me on the way here. He gave me this."

The guard studied the parchment, then slid it into a pouch on his belt. "That's them, Petronas. Don't look like gladiators to me."

Petronas nodded. "We'll sort them out...or kill them trying." The guards laughed and returned to the ship.

The man they'd called Petronas stepped forward, unlocked and removed the chains. "Welcome to Caledonia. The bad things you've heard about this barbaric, cold, bleak land are true," he said. "But it's not a bad life…if you work hard."

"No chains…?" Farinas asked, enjoying the feeling of lightness that came with their removal.

Petronas looked back at them and shrugged. "Where would you go?"

His two prisoners gazed at the bleak landscape, the massive fort walls ahead of them and the cold grey waters of the river. "He's right," Farinas agreed. "The only place I want to be right now is inside, out of this wind."

Petronas nodded and rode ahead along the road, expertly guiding his horse between the carts and wagons heading to and from the harbour. His two charges followed, side by side, in step, as if still connected by chains. The wind tore at them and, not for the first time, Farinas shivered and thought he'd never felt so cold in his life.

They stopped to draw breath after the climb from the river, and they gazed at the walls of the fort, looming ahead of them. Rome's power was once more on display to intimidate the native population.

The fortifications were made of the muddy wet turf Farinas could see everywhere. The main military buildings were made of harsh grey stone that looked well able to withstand the elements as well as an attack from the natives. There were other buildings attached to the fort and they too blended in with the landscape.

The settlement outside the walls of the fort had clearly been built to provide services, local goods and produce for the officials and soldiers. The houses and trading establishments lined narrow alleyways and were as colourless as everything else Farinas could see.

The ground was brown, wet, and soft, and it was cold. His feet sank into it and the mud seeped into his sandals and squelched in between his toes as Petronas led them past the settlement and through the gates.

"Trimontium," he said, then pointed to a separate walled compound on the left. "The Gladiator School of Caelus Gallio Flavius."

Once the formalities had been seen to, with the Roman authorities, Petronas led them to the school. He took them through the entrance to an underground cell in the main building. There, by the light of a small flickering lamp, they saw a small, dark room. Farinas moaned when he saw the familiar waste bucket and smelled the stench seeping from the damp walls. When Petronas left, taking the lamp with him, they wrapped themselves in rough blankets and sat on a stone bench built into the wall, listening to the sounds of men going about their business.

"Maybe we should have run when we had the chance," Videric said, but Farinas thought of the wind howling across the colourless landscape and shuddered.

"Maybe they won't keep us here long," Farinas said, trying to see what was causing the scratching noises in the walls. "Do they have rats in Caledonia?"

"I expect so," Videric answered, sounding less cheerful than usual. "I've never seen a place that doesn't."

Fortunately, Petronas soon returned with slaves carrying palettes, a bowl of food, a barrel of water and heavy woollen clothes.

"Eat while it's hot," Petronas advised. "It will get colder in the night."

"How can it get colder?" Farinas moaned.

"How long will we stay here?" Videric asked.

"Not long."

Petronas left, and they heard the key turning in the lock. Farinas took a handful of the food. In the gloom of the small lamp, it looked like *hordearii* but tasted different. He knew he had to eat it but found it difficult to swallow.

"How do you like the food?" Videric asked.

"I don't know," Farinas answered. "It's different and it's hard to swallow…It's thick…and sticky."

Videric chewed the food carefully. "It's not too bad and it *is* hot. It should help keep us warm."

Farinas hoped so. As soon as they'd eaten, they used the water to wipe off the worst of the mud, then they put on the clothes that had been left for them. After the trek through the mud, they appreciated the woollen foot coverings, sturdy sandals, and the thick woollen material of the new garments.

"These clothes feel so heavy," Farinas said remembering the light, flowing material of his homeland.

"Don't worry," Videric tried to cheer him up. "You'll get used to them and they're warm."

"I've had to get used to a lot," Farinas replied, thinking of his past life, and wondering how many more things were going to change.

"But you're alive," Videric pointed out. Farinas tried to feel happy about that. He had to try very hard.

They wrapped themselves in the blankets and lay on the stone benches, hoping to sleep, as the wind battered the building and nasty creatures scratched inside the walls.

Chapter 14

The new day brought stiffness to their joints and more aches in their bones. Farinas almost cried out when he stood up. There was no sunlight to chase the bone-chilling cold of the night, and he and Videric shivered together on the bench until a slave came bringing food. He lit the lamp that had gone out in the night. and they saw the bowl was full of a hot grey porridge that was welcome, if only because it warmed them. "Gods!" Farinas moaned. "Is everything in this place grey!"

"It's not so bad in summer," the slave answered, not very convincingly.

"How long do we have to stay here?" Videric asked.

"Not long. The *lanista* will come for you soon, to see how fit you are, and decide if he wants to train you."

"What happens to those he chooses not to train?" Videric asked.

The slave shrugged. "We don't see them again." He left and they had barely finished the porridge when Petronas arrived and led them to the main building.

Farinas and Videric were wearing every item of clothing they had been given, yet they still shivered as they followed Petronas to a small amphitheatre where rows of seats surrounded a circular patch of grass. Two men were practising with wooden swords. They were pale-skinned and wore woollen tunics and trousers.

The practice bout ended when one fell beneath the blows of the other. One of the reasons for the fall may have been the slippery mud underfoot, but the call was made, and the one standing was declared the winner. They left together, passing two men on their way into the arena. These two immediately began running on the track that circled the arena.

"Take the cloaks off!" Petronas waited until Farinas and Videric had taken off their cloaks, then nodded at the two men. "Follow them," he ordered.

"You want us to run?" Farinas asked. His joints were so stiff, he'd barely been able to walk.

"You do not question orders." This was said quietly, but the message was clear, and Videric walked into the arena, followed by Farinas. As the runners passed them, they fell in behind them and ran.

"This isn't too bad," Videric encouraged Farinas. "It's like training with Teo."

"No talking!" Petronas's voice, amplified by the design of the stadium, carried easily, and they ran in silence. As the runners increased their speed, Farinas was soon gasping for breath. He didn't think collapsing in the mud would help his chances of becoming a gladiator, so he forced himself to speed up.

Then, just as Teo had done, the runners changed the tempo, reducing their speed until they were walking, and Farinas and Videric were able to catch their breath.

"Exercises!" The voice from the seats carried to the walkers and the four men were soon carrying out the exercises Farinas and Videric had been taught by Teo. Like everything else, these were made more difficult by the wet grass and mud, but Farinas and Videric managed to keep going until the next command. "Swords!"

"Nooo!" Farinas moaned as he rose, exhausted, from the last exercise. Videric slapped him on his back and laughed.

"At least we've no chains. It'll be easy."

Wooden swords were brought and Farinas and Videric faced the two men. Nothing was said, and they went through moves they had learned from Teo. Farinas realised Videric was being pushed harder than he was, but he thought they were doing quite well until the fight moved up a notch and Farinas and Videric found themselves watching their swords flying through the air, as their opponents calmly walked back into the building.

"You have much to learn if you wish to stay alive!" Petronas's voice echoed throughout the arena, as he came from the seats and walked towards them.

"At least we're warm," Videric said.

"For how long?" Farinas questioned, looking at the muddy amphitheatre and the leaden grey sky. "Where's the sun?"

"That disc that looks like the moon," Petronas explained. "That's the sun."

He turned and led them through one of the arches into the building. They followed him through corridors until they came to one lined with doors…lots of doors. Petronas opened one door into a room barely big enough to hold the wooden bed frame with a palette, and a wooden chest.

"Yours." Petronas indicated that Videric should enter the tiny room.

Petronas opened the door to the next room. "Yours," he said, and Farinas entered.

"At least there's no bucket," he noted. The room was tiny but clean and lacked the foul stench of their previous cells.

"We are not barbarians, although we live among them. We have latrine blocks and bathhouses," Petronas informed him. "Remain here, until someone comes for you."

Petronas left, and Farinas was pleased to see his cloak lying on the palette. When Videric came in, he was wrapped in his cloak. "We've to stay here until someone comes," Farinas told him. "I wonder where everyone is?"

Videric shrugged. "I expect we'll find out soon enough."

Almost immediately, a young lad entered. "I am Tòmachan," he said. "You are to come with me." He led them back along the corridor and pointed out the bathhouse and latrine block, before continuing out through the arches and into a separate block.

Here the floors were paved, and they could feel glorious heat beneath their feet. The walls were painted with pictures of gladiators, and niches in the walls contained the images of various gods; some they recognised, others were unfamiliar. Farinas was surprised to see an image he recognised of the god Gurzil, carved in black wood. He stopped and gently stroked the god's head, asking for his blessing.

Tòmachan named rooms as they passed, including the *armamentarium*. "Lots of weapons, very secure," he advised, and the *valetudinarium*. "Where the *medicii* will treat you when you get injured."

"If," Farinas countered, slightly annoyed by the lad's superior attitude. He looked even younger than himself.

Tòmachan looked him over and smirked. "Oh, you'll get injured."

Videric laughed. "We'll both be grateful for the services of a *medicus,* I'm sure."

"If they agree to you being trained."

"What do you mean?" Farinas could feel himself beginning to panic, remembering the earlier comment from Petronas. Videric was sure to be taken on. He'd been a soldier. He was stronger and fitter, and he could fight.

"Not everyone is accepted into our *familia gladiatoria.*"

"What will happen if they don't take us into the family?" Farinas asked.

Tòmachan shrugged. "You'll be sold at the market." He paused. "Maybe sent to the salt mines." He looked Farinas over and smirked again. "Maybe an old man will be pleased by you."

Farinas could only imagine what a salt mine was, but he had no wish to be sent to one and he certainly had no wish to be an old man's plaything. He shuddered, wishing he'd put more effort in when the *lanista* had been watching them in the arena, but it was too late now. Tòmachan knocked on a carved wooden door, then entered and led them into a warm, comfortable room. He remained standing by the closed door.

Farinas and Videric regarded the men sitting behind a long wooden table. These were the men who would decide their fate. They recognised Caelus Gallio Flavius who was dressed in a richly dyed linen tunic and woollen trousers with a fine leather belt and boots.

Videric bowed to him and greeted him with respect. "*Domine.*" Farinas followed his example, and Gallio nodded. Farinas hoped he would look favourably on them. He wasn't sure he wanted to be a gladiator, especially in that particular outpost of Rome, a grey shithole of a place with no sun, but he had a feeling the alternatives would be even more unpleasant. Petronas sat on Gallio's right, and on his left was the man who had fought Videric earlier in the arena with the practice sword.

"You have met my manager, my *lanista*, Petronas," Gallio said, then indicated the man on his left, "and this is Kyrios, my *magister hoplomachōrum.*

"*Hoplomachi?*" Videric asked, and Farinas heard the interest in his voice.

It was Kyrios who answered. "I train the gladiators named *hoplomachi*. They fight with a spear and short sword."

"Kyrios fought in the arena for many years and was awarded the *rudis*, so won his freedom. Fortunately for the school, he chose to remain with us," Gallio told them.

Videric bowed respectfully to Kyrios. "I have used spears and swords in battle."

The men nodded, and Petronas continued. "We are aware of your fighting experience. In the arena, *hoplomachi* train and fight with *murmillones* who fight with a sword and shield."

Farinas and I train well together," Videric pointed out.

Farinas nodded eagerly. "I can fight with a sword," he added. If he could only stay with Videric, he would be happy, even in this grey wilderness.

Kyrios turned to Gallio and Petronas. "I doubt he has ever fought anyone, with anything, and his skill with the sword is …well…" he spread his hands. "Any of our youngsters could easily best him."

"He can learn," Gallio intervened. "His dark skin will be an attraction in the arena. Ladies here favour those from Africa Proconsularis for their exotic looks."

"That's certainly true." Kyrios nodded in agreement. "And he is quite pleasant to look on. If Alkestis agrees to train him as a *murmillo*, the helmet would protect his face from ugly scars" He considered Farinas then added. "Still, pleasant looks are no use if he can't fight."

Gallio nodded. "True, but he has stamina and he's stronger than he looks; he worked the oar well when the pirates attacked. I rather think the other one will help with his training."

"Yes, *Domine*. That I can do." Videric promised.

"We will give it our consideration," Gallio answered. He looked over at Tòmachan and nodded. "Find them something to eat."

Videric and Farinas followed Tòmachan to a large room with wooden tables and benches.

"Wait here," Tòmachan ordered and left them to worry over their future.

"They'll take us on." Videric tried to reassure Farinas. "We'd be a good match; *hoplomachus* against *murmillo;* white against black.

"You can fight," Farinas moaned. "They know I've never been in a real fight." He remembered the raid on the gold and added. "Well, not really."

"But you have such a pretty face…and…exotic looks." Videric laughed. "Cheer up, you don't want to frown and spoil those looks." Farinas had to laugh, but he wasn't sure Videric was right.

They cheered up when Tòmachan returned with slaves carrying bowls of thick vegetable broth and flatbread that tasted like the *khoubz* Farinas's mother had baked. They found they had developed an appetite and ate the food, as Tòmachan poured them generous measures of the special brew they were becoming used to.

"No wine?" Videric asked, with little hope, and Tòmachan laughed.

"You'll find it hard enough to keep up with the others, even without a head befuddled by drink; no wine!"

"This drink is for gladiators, isn't it?" Farinas wanted to know if this meant they had been accepted, but Tòmachan just shrugged.

"Good for everyone," he said, leaving them to their meal.

Time passed, and groups of men came in to eat and chat, but no one spoke to them or even acknowledged their presence. They visited the latrine block and admired the marble baths with the blue tiles and fish mosaics, then waited until Tòmachan returned.

"Come with me," he said.

Chapter 15

Tòmachan led them back to the amphitheatre where they found two lines of men positioned opposite each other in the middle of the arena. They held batons and Tòmachan led them to the head of the columns.

"Don't hesitate," Videric muttered. "This looks like an initiation…a test. If you fall…do not stay down!" As they approached, the men raised their batons to form an archway.

"Run between them to the end," Tòmachan told them, before stepping back. "When you get knocked down…get back up! If you stay down… you leave!"

"You go first," Videric told Farinas. "I'll be behind you, but it's best if I don't help you. Whatever happens, don't stop. Keep going 'till the end."

Farinas shook his head. "You go first. If I fall, I don't want to hold you up. I'll follow you…so run fast!" He tried to smile, to show confidence he didn't feel, but the men were becoming impatient.

"Well! You running or not?" one shouted.

"We're running," Videric answered. They stepped up to the space between the first two men and looked along the path they had to run. Farinas thought it looked very long, very grey, and terrifying.

"When you get to the end, you'll be in gladiator school," Videric hissed the promise in his ear, and then he ran.

Farinas watched as he passed the first two couples who beat him with their batons, at the third couple he stumbled, and Farinas ran. He'd perhaps thought to help Videric, but he soon realised how futile that thought was. The blows rained down on him and he gritted his teeth to stop himself from crying out.

In front of him, Videric was on his feet, head down, arms across his chest, ploughing between the batons, and Farinas followed. His body jerked trying to avoid the blows, but it was not possible. Instead, he tried to ignore them, staring at Videric's back and running until he was stumbling, and then he was on his knees. The blows didn't let up and he struggled to get back on his feet, but he was beaten to the ground. The men's laughter spurred him on, and he staggered to his feet and ran. Ahead of him, he could see Videric stumbling forward and then collapsing. This time, he didn't get up. Farinas sobbed and forced his battered body on still hoping he could help Videric. When he fell again, he realised Videric was standing at the end, urging him on.

Back on his feet, he stumbled forward, blinded by the blood running down his face, but he kept going forward, and the batons raining down on him kept him in line, as he staggered from side to side. "Not far, not far…." he repeated until he collapsed and felt himself being lifted and carried from the field.

When he came to, he was lying on a clean, soft palette in a warm room. He rubbed the blood from his eyes and looked to his side where Videric lay on a similar palette. "Did we make it?" he gasped.

"We made it." Videric groaned. "I'm not sure I want to be a gladiator if this is what the training's like."

"It's not always this hard." Gallio was standing with Kyrios and Petronas, smiling.

"Not always, but don't think it will be easy," Kyrios warned them.

"What do you think, Petronas? Can we make something of them?"

Farinas held his breath, waiting to see if the run and the beating had been worth it.

"So long as no lasting damage has been done, I think they'll do," Petronas said. "Get the *medicus* in and we'll see."

The three men left and a *medicus* came in and introduced himself as Epeius, one of the school's *medici* who looked after the health of the gladiators. He bathed their cuts in a warm vinegar solution and rubbed an ointment of arnica and hypericum on the bruises. After a quick examination of the two men, he declared their injuries, 'superficial'.

"No lasting damage," Epeius told them. "You will have to come to the *valetudinarian* tomorrow for a full examination. We work like an army hospital and our gladiators need to pass a strict medical before joining." He saw the anxiety on their faces and smiled. "Don't worry, you look healthy enough and you did the trial in good time. You should be fine."

He took a bottle of clear liquid from a shelf and poured a small amount into two cups. "Drink this. It will help you sleep." Videric and Farinas drank the draughts without question. Sleep was what they wanted, oblivion and freedom from pain.

"Someone will take you to your rooms." Epeius left and Tòmachan came in.

"Epeius says you're well enough to go to your rooms." He looked at them and grinned. "You don't look that well to me. Do you need to be stretchered back?"

Farinas looked at Videric. "No!" Videric tried for a strong response, but his voice came out in a low moan. Farinas decided to make do with a shake of his head then wished he hadn't, as a sharp pain and flashing lights behind his eyes almost blinded him. Despite this, neither wanted to be seen being carried through the school.

"Right! Up you get. They'll be wanting these beds soon."

With no help from Tòmachan, who seemed to be enjoying their misery, Videric and Farinas got to their feet and clung to each other until they reached Videric's room. Tòmachan opened the door and Videric stumbled over to his cot as Tòmachan slammed the door shut before moving on and opening the next door.

Farinas stared at the open door. Willing his body to stay upright, he moved away from the wall and immediately collapsed with a groan on the floor. Tòmachan pulled him to his feet and dragged him into the room. "There you go!" he muttered, throwing him onto the cot before going out and closing the door.

Farinas knew nothing until the following morning when a young lad came in and wakened him. It took a few minutes for Farinas to understand where he was and to remember the events of the previous day, but the lad seemed used to dealing with injured men. Once Farinas was able to understand what was happening, the lad introduced himself.

"My name is Lachlann. I've to take you to the latrines and then to the bathhouse. After that you can eat, then go for your health check." Lachlann picked up a bundle of clothes he'd brought with him and stood waiting.

"You want me to get up…now?" Farinas peered through swollen and bruised eyes at the boy. He reminded him of Aigulf, with his cheerful manner and dark curly hair.

The boy nodded patiently and waited as Farinas tried to make his legs move, but it was a struggle. Eventually, he rolled off the palette then used it to pull himself to his knees, from there he held onto the wall and got to his feet. "Right, let's go," he said.

Lachlan opened the door and waited, as Farinas painfully made his way to the door, balancing himself against the wall.

In the corridor he saw Videric ahead of him, accompanied by Tòmachan who was carrying a similar bundle of clothes.

They shuffled along to the latrines where they managed to smile at each other, grateful at least, not to be balancing over filthy buckets, then on to the bathhouse. In a small entrance hall, the lads skilfully stripped them of their soiled garments before leading them into a room where they helped them to lie on raised platforms. They oiled their bodies then wiped them with soft linen cloths.

"What are you doing?" The angry voice disturbed the quiet peacefulness of the room and made Farinas's head hurt.

"The medic said, 'No strigils', Tasgall. They have cuts and bruises," Lachlann answered, as he continued to wipe the oil and dirt from Farinas's body.

"That's those Greeks for you." Tasgall watched what the lads were doing with a look of disgust on his face. "Bringing their soft ways over here."

He looked down on Videric and Farinas. "I'm Tasgall. I was born near here of the Selgovae, although we look and sound like Romans now. At least they're not as soft as the Greeks." He sighed and turned to the boys. "That's enough patting and wiping. Get them in the water and make sure you take them to the *frigidarium* before you leave."

"The medic said no cold —" Tòmachan spoke quietly and firmly, but Tasgall had clearly heard enough advice from the medic.

"I don't care what the Greek said, Tòmachan. Here we do things my way."

The boys helped Farinas and Videric into the warm water where they relaxed and eased some of the stiffness and pain from their battered and bruised bodies. Too soon, the lads helped them from the water, wrapped them in warm towels, and took them through to the frigidarium. Farinas shuddered and clutched his towel, as he looked at the still, cold water.

Lachlann left them shivering and ran to a door opposite the one they'd come in by. He looked out in the corridor then beckoned. "Right," he said, laughing, "we've been in the *frigidarium*. Let's get you to your rooms and dressed."

"I don't think that was what Tasgall meant," Tòmachan said, but he was smiling.

"That's exactly what he said," Videric agreed. "Thanks, lads."

Once Tòmachan and Lachlan had helped them to dress, they met in the corridor again.

"You've to get something to eat in the canteen but it's best if you get there on your own," Lachlann advised them.

"You need to look strong at all times," Tòmachan added.

Videric nodded. "Good advice, lads. Thanks." He turned to Farinas. "That's not a problem, is it? We're as strong as any of them, aren't we?"

"Keep telling yourself that," Farinas grimaced as a new pain shot up his leg, almost bringing him to the ground. "I'll just try not to look as weak as I feel."

They grinned at each other, straightened up and walked along the corridor to the canteen. Before going in they stopped, took deep breaths, and marched in – to an empty room.

"Where is everyone?" Videric looked around, as Farinas collapsed on the nearest bench and put his head down on the table.

"Can I stop looking strong, now?"

"You don't look very strong to me." A man had appeared behind a counter, and he was watching them with some amusement. "I'm Bretislav, retired auxiliary, now cook to the gladiator school. I've got some oatmeal ready for you. It'll build you up and make you strong." He watched them then shook his head. "Do you expect me to serve it as well as make it?"

Farinas was sorry he'd sat down, as he struggled back onto his feet and followed Videric to the counter. They took the bowls of hot oatmeal back to a table and spooned it quickly into their mouths. "It's good," Farinas said.

"Of course, it's good," Bretislav said. "You don't get legionary rations here." He brought a jug of watered, spiced wine and two cups. "And we don't give you *posca* to drink either. Well, not if you're gladiators. There's a special brew, especially for them."

"We know," Farinas shuddered, then enjoyed the spiced wine.

Bretislav eyed them critically. "You'd better finish up and get along to the medic. You both look like you need him." He laughed and walked back behind the counter.

Both passed the medical without any problems. "The school's lucky to have us," Videric decided, and Farinas agreed.

Chapter 16

Although the trial with the batons had made them anxious about the harshness of the school's training methods, the warmth and comfort of the bathhouse and the canteen had made them more complacent. This complacency was shattered the next morning when they were wakened by Tòmachan, hammering on their doors.

"Practice field .... NOW!"

When Farinas staggered out of his room, he found Videric waiting for him. Dressed in a hurry, they stumbled out to the training field where various groups of men were exercising. Kyrios marched over to them and pointed to the outer track. "Run...until I tell you to stop!"

They'd missed breakfast and Kyrios kept them on the field until after the midday meal. They ran. They shadow-boxed. They exercised. They used their practice swords on a stuffed wooden dummy, and if they stopped, Kyrios was there to make sure they didn't stop for long. When they eventually staggered into the canteen, the others were leaving, passing Farinas and Videric without so much as a glance.

"Probably haven't left us any food," Farinas muttered as they made their painful way to the counter.

"You're in luck lads. There's some porridge left but it's gone cold. You're late."

"No one woke us this morning," Farinas complained.

"And why would anyone do that? You're not infants." Bretislav leaned on the countertop and watched them walk to the table.

"You were an auxiliary. Soldiers keep each other right, don't they?" Videric said, annoyed that the other gladiators were being so unhelpful; not one had even spoken to them. "We didn't know about the training."

"Well, you should have known. It's up to you to find out what you need to know. You aren't soldiers. No one here's going to have your backs." Bretislav looked thoughtful then continued.

"You're a fighting man. You and your mates looked out for each other. Right?"

"Right," Videric spooned the sticky cold mess into his mouth, and he and Farinas listened.

"Did you have to do your damnedest the next day... or a few days later, to maim or seriously injure one of your mates, before he did the same to you?" Bretislav asked.

Videric shook his head, seeing the point he was about to make. "No. No, I didn't."

"Right! These men aren't your mates. Remember that. You can have mates from the settlement, once you're allowed outside, but no one has mates in here, not among the gladiators anyway." Videric and Farinas nodded their understanding and ate the porridge in gloomy silence.

"Cheer up, lads," Bretislav called out. "The ladies in the settlement love a gladiator, and you two have the looks to attract them...Just like me!" He grinned, showing off his few remaining teeth, then returned to his clearing up. "Ask Tòmachan or Lachlann to give your doors a bang on their way past in the mornings, until you get used to it. They help me get breakfast ready, so they're here early. You can make it up to them when you start getting gifts from your admirers." His laughter made it clear he didn't think that would happen any time soon.

Every morning after that, they were wakened for training by the boys until eventually, they found themselves waking before the boys hammered on their doors.

They settled into a routine that included regular training and exercises, but they also helped the swordsmiths and the shoemakers. They helped in the laundry and in the kitchen. They dragged fallen gladiators from the amphitheatre and spread dry sand over the blood and gore after each bout, and they helped the medics patch up the injured. They never left the compound, but they were learning about the life of a gladiator, the most common types of injuries they were likely to suffer in the arena, and hopefully, how to avoid them.

Farinas grew in height, and he bulked out with the gladiators' diet, putting on a layer of fat to give some protection from stabs and slashes, but he was impatient. He'd watched the various types of gladiators practising with real weapons; swords and spears of different shapes and lengths, tridents, even slings, darts, and nets and, what Farinas thought most strange, the scissors. The *scissores* were most often matched with the *retarii* who used their nets to foil them.

"When do you think we'll start proper training?" Farinas asked Videric, weeks after they had been accepted into the school. They were sitting in the canteen and Farinas had been watching the gladiators coming in from 'proper training'.

Videric shrugged. Not so young and impatient, he was content to take things easy. He'd experienced warfare and wasn't that keen to get back in the fray. "When they think we're ready."

"I think I'm ready."

Andosteni, an older man from Gaul, who usually fought with a short sword, was sitting nearby and he laughed. "What you think doesn't matter. You've got a long way to go before you're ready, boy."

"I'm not a boy and I'm ready to start training," Farinas ignored Videric's warning look. He could see Andosteni was just looking for a fight, having recently lost his third match in a row in the arena, but Farinas wasn't about to back down.

"You'd cut yourself just cleaning my sword." Andosteni stood up and Farinas did the same. As the two stood, facing each other, there was a definite stirring of interest in the room. Entertainment was in short supply in the school, and this looked like it would be interesting, although the obvious outcome meant no bets were being taken. There was a moment's silence broken by Bretislav. "Videric, you're wanted!"

Videric stood, torn between looking out for Farinas and obeying Bretislav, and Farinas realised what Bretislav was doing. He was making Farinas stand on his own two feet and stop depending on Videric, for both their sakes.

As Farinas's attention switched from Videric and Bretislav, he stepped into a meaty punch from a grinning Andosteni. Farinas was using the table to drag himself to his feet when a swift, sharp kick to his thigh, brought him back to the floor, bouncing off the table on the way down.

Through the fog of pain in his head, he heard the laughter of the other gladiators and he determined to fight back. Struggling to his feet, he swayed to the side and narrowly missed another punch, but it was a fluke and Andosteni landed a quick uppercut that finished him.

When he regained consciousness, he was in the *valetudinarium* having his bruises examined by a medic who gave him a small cup of bitter liquid to drink, then turned to shout at a young assistant. "Right, take him away! He'll live and I've enough to do, dealing with real injuries."

Farinas didn't see how he could walk but the painkiller was taking effect, and with the assistant's help, he managed back to his cell where he collapsed on his bed and slept until Videric looked in to check on him. Farinas sat up with a wide smile on his face, clearly the result of the painkiller.

"You look happy, considering the number of lumps and bruises I can see," Videric said, pleased Farinas hadn't been seriously injured.

"It's nothing. Wait 'till you see Andosteni."

"Somehow I don't think he's suffering very much," Videric said, "The medic gave you some painkillers, did he?"

"I think so. I'm not sure, but I don't hurt like I did before." Farinas said, still smiling.

"Kyrios said you won't get painkillers next time you get into a fight. You'll be flogged."

Farinas nodded. Even in his drugged state, he realised he had been foolish. "I know," he whispered. Another grin and he slid down, closed his eyes, and was soon snoring.

Early the next morning, Lachlann, knowing the state Farinas would be in, banged on his cell door then opened it. "Get up! You don't want to be in more trouble!" When Farinas only moaned and rolled over, Lachlan threw a jug of water over his head. "Now! Move!"

"Now?" Farinas sat up but Lachlan had already left. Dried and dressed, Farinas staggered along the corridor to the canteen and slumped down in the seat opposite Videric.

"Keep away from Andosteni. He's been confined to the school for ten days for fighting. You've got extra duties," he added.

Farinas nodded, knowing he deserved the punishment. He drank the warm *calda.* Bretislav had brought to the table. "Better drink up, this will settle your stomach."

The *calda* worked until Farinas began his punishment duty after the day's exercises were over. Even the hot drink couldn't stop him from emptying his stomach as he worked, cleaning out blocked latrines, surrounded by the stink of shit. He worked until after dark then washed the worst of the muck off before heading to the bath house.

When he finally staggered into the canteen he was met by a chorus of groans. "What's that smell?" someone called out.

"Smells like shit!" It was Andosteni who answered, but he was laughing, and Farinas decided wisely, to smile and walk on. Clearly, everyone knew about his punishment duty, but Farinas was too tired to care. He took his bowl of *puls* and a piece of cheese back to a table where Videric was sitting, and collapsed, almost too tired to eat.

"I don't really smell, do I?" he asked. Videric and the others at the table laughed but the general opinion was he smelled like one of Kennora's girls, from the amount of perfumed oil he'd used.

That night he lay in bed, determined to work hard, and be selected for training as soon as possible. He knew he had to stop depending on Videric.

Chapter 17

They didn't have to wait long for Videric's 'real' training as a *hoplomachus* to begin, and with it came closer contact with the other gladiators, and a decrease in the time spent with Farinas. Both men accepted this as a necessary part of the life of a gladiator.

Videric specialised in the armour and weapons of a *hoplomachus*. He used a heavy spear, a *doru*, with an iron, leaf-bladed tip, but as a counterbalance and additional means of attack, the *doru* had a bronze butt spike, heavy and lethal. For close-quarter fighting, the *hoplomachus* carried a leaf-shaped, short sword based on the design of the Greek, *Gladius Graecus*, and a *pugio*, a dagger with a shorter blade.

The *hoplomachus* wore a loincloth held up by a broad leather belt. His legs were wrapped in thick linen and covered by metal greaves and a metal arm guard on his right arm provided additional protection. He carried a distinctive round, bronze shield which could also be used as a weapon. Videric's shield was decorated in his colours of blue, yellow, and white. The typical *hoplomachi* iron helmet, the *falconum cassis*, had a wide rim and a visor. Videric's was decorated with feathers, also in his colours, allowing the spectators to differentiate him from other gladiators in the arena.

Videric needed intensive training over many months to become skilled in the use of so many weapons while wearing heavy armour before taking on a real opponent in the arena. The first time he practised in full armour with his weapons, Farinas watched from the banks of seats and wished he was doing the same. When Videric finished the exercises, Farinas went down and took his shield and spear, surprised by their weight.

"You looked good," Farinas told him. "You'll be in the arena soon."

Videric grunted and lifted the helmet off. His face was red and slick with sweat and the linen padding was soaking wet. "I'll need to get used to this armour," he muttered. "It's hot and heavy."

When he finally entered the arena, it was against untrained locals who had been found guilty of law-breaking in the settlement. For these 'warm-up' matches, full armour, and a variety of weapons were not required. His skill with them was further developed before he was ready to be matched against a fully armoured gladiator, and it was months after that, before he even managed to achieve a draw in the arena. This was greeted with loud roars of approval from those in the audience who had been following his progress and could see they might eventually win some money on him.

Shortly after Videric's minor success in the arena, the *magister murmillonum* sent for Farinas. He sat down and Alkestis pushed a mug of wine across the table to him.

"I've agreed to train you as a *murmillo,*" Alkestis told Farinas. "You need to fatten up. You've got the height for the long shield, but you don't have the strength yet to carry it and the helmet." He waited for an objection, but Farinas had learned his lesson. He nodded in agreement and Alkestis continued. "We'll start you off with a lighter helmet and a shorter sword. When you go into the arena, you won't be up against any real opposition for a while. In the meantime, I've heard you ride?"

Farinas nodded, remembering Musad. "Only horses," he admitted.

"What else would you ride?" Alkestis asked, genuinely interested.

"Camels," Farinas said. "I don't ride camels," he added firmly.

"I'll remember that, if any come our way," Alkestis said. "I want the crowds to see you. You'll ride around the arena before the contests and put on a bit of a display. The women will love you."

"I haven't been on a horse for a long time," Farinas confessed. He recognised how docile and easy to manage Musad had been. He could imagine being thrown from a horse in the middle of the arena; humiliated before the contest even began.

"Take this tablet to the gatehouse at the fort. They'll sort you out with an animal," Alkestis said. "The training with the horse is extra. You do the regular exercises as well."

Farinas had visited the settlement a few times where he'd sampled the local beers in the Aquila Alba, the White Eagle Tavern, and the more exotic ladies in Kennora's *lupinara*, attached to the settlement's bathhouse, but he'd never been to the fort. It was much like the school, with the same sense of discipline and routine, but bigger and noisier. There he was taken to the stables and given access to a big, black horse called Libertas.

"This old boy's seen a lot of fighting. He's earned his veteran status," the officer in charge of the stables told him. "He's getting on a bit is Libertas, but he still likes to be ridden and he's used to battle noises so he's not going to panic in the arena."

Farinas took Libertas out into the exercise grounds and found him to be almost as placid as Musad, but bigger and stronger. He was given a pass allowing him to ride Libertas in the training area at certain times. "You treat him right, or you'll have most of the cavalry to answer to," an officer warned him.

The gladiators never fought on horseback. The arena at Trimontium was too small. A few of the gladiators would ride into the arena and put on a show for the spectators, then dismount to fight on foot. The horses were mainly used to intimidate the local hotheads and persuade them against any form of uprising. The Romans lived in constant fear of uprisings, especially living so close to the northern savages and so far from Rome and reinforcements.

Farinas looked forward to riding the big cavalry horse and he knew Libertas would make him look good in the arena. His time with Libertas helped make his general training less onerous, although he took longer than Videric to build up his strength. Eventually, though, Alkestis decided he was ready to train as a *murmillo*.

Like Videric, Farinas fought bare-chested, with his legs and striking arm protected by linen padding and metal greaves. His main weapon was the Roman *gladius*, and he carried a *scutum*, a large heavy rectangular shield that could be used to charge an opponent, as well as for protection. Where Videric's *hoplomachi* weapons were based on those of the Greek soldiers, known as hoplites, Farinas's were typically Roman.

His helmet was bronze, with a metal grille that covered his entire face. Farinas never forgot the panic he felt when he first put the helmet on, the breathlessness and the sound of his breathing echoing in the helmet and quickening, as he struggled with his restricted vision. Of course, he became used to it. He had to. Times like that reminded him he was just a slave.

When he and Videric started winning against skilled gladiators, they built up a following of admirers and settled into the life of the school as fully-fledged members of the *familia gladiatoria* of Caelus Gallio Flavius. Farinas felt good belonging to the family, even if it wasn't the usual kind of family. When he went to the settlement and visited the taverns and brothels, he was recognised as a gladiator, one of Flavius's men.

As Farinas became popular, the spectators began calling him, Leo Africanus. A female admirer gave him a large, square, gilded-silver belt buckle decorated with the head of a lion and other small lion-themed gifts followed. Petronas the manager, encouraged this, and Farinas was quickly listed on posters as Leo Africanus. The regular fish decoration on his helmet was replaced by a lion's head complete with horsehair plumes, dyed the colour of a lion's mane. Black and gold became his colours.

Farinas happily adopted the role chosen for him. He received many expensive gifts from his followers who were mainly, but not exclusively female and he wore increasingly elaborate jewels and clothing when he visited the settlement. Videric was less flamboyant although he was also a favourite and had his own band of followers. Neither ever had to pay for their drinks and they were always welcome at the *lupinarae* scattered throughout the settlement, although Kennora's remained their favourite.

The downside of life as a gladiator was the injuries. Fighting skilled men with bladed weapons designed to slash and stab made wounds inevitable, added to that was the fact that bloodletting was an essential part of the games, demanded by audiences.

Owners of gladiators accepted this but took steps to mitigate the effects. Gladiators were costly to purchase and maintain. Their diet was designed to bulk them out, to provide a barrier of fat against deep, penetrating wounds. Well-trained and experienced medics were on-hand to provide the best treatment possible. The gladiators themselves quickly learned how far to penetrate, to provide enough blood to satisfy the paying customers, but not far enough to kill or do lasting damage.

The first time Videric was injured, Farinas couldn't believe the amount of blood he lost before his opponent Kosyo, was declared the winner, and Videric was dragged unconscious from the arena.

Kosyo fought as a *thraex*. *Thraeces* were slimmer than other types of gladiators and fought with smaller shields and *sicae*, short swords with curved blades. This allowed them to be exceptionally mobile and Kosyo made Videric look slow and clumsy in this, his first bout with a *thraex*.

Farinas remained at the arena helping to drag fallen gladiators out, but he went to see Videric as soon as he could. He was surprised to see him sitting on his cot, looking pale but much livelier than Farinas had expected. Many of his wounds had simply been cleaned and wrapped in linen strips, others had needed to be stitched by the medic's assistant.

"I thought Kosyo had killed you!" he said.

"Kosyo is very good at making his opponent look stupid, but he also knows how to spill a lot of blood, without much damage. We need to learn to move faster against gladiators like Kosyo."

"He uses a spear too sometimes." Farinas was beginning to see that how his opponents fought, was as important as working on his own skills.

"I'm lucky he didn't use one today," Videric confessed. "He could have slowed me down even more." He lay back, clearly exhausted. "Pass me the mug." He grimaced as he took the mug and drank deeply. "The medic says I need to drink more of the special brew, and I'll be fine tomorrow."

Not all injuries were so superficial and both Videric and Farinas required more radical medical attention, on many occasions throughout their careers with the school.

Deaths of gladiators were not common. The desire of the audiences to witness severe injury and death was generally satisfied by the killing of condemned criminals, known as *noxii*. They were unskilled prisoners given unfamiliar weapons and little protection, so they posed minimal threat to trained, armoured gladiators.

"You'll not be coming to the tavern tonight, then?" Farinas asked and wasn't surprised when Videric decided to stay in his room, drinking the special brew, and sleeping.

"I can't be late for training tomorrow after that performance today. I owe Kosyo a drink, though. He could have maimed or killed me easily."

"That wouldn't have pleased Gallio," Farinas pointed out.

"No, but it's probably what I deserved." Videric put the empty mug down and his eyes were closing as Farinas left.

After this humiliation, Videric made it his business to find ways of developing skills to deal with lighter, faster opponents like Kosyo, and his determination paid off. Five years after joining the school, Videric was awarded the *rudis* and his freedom, after a particularly difficult and bloody bout with a thraex. Since then, he had fought as a *rudiarius* and his popularity grew when it was known he had chosen to continue to fight as a free man and Videric carried the little wooden sword with him everywhere, as proof of his status.

"Wouldn't you like to live as a free man?" Farinas once asked him over a drink in the Aquilla Alba.

Videric shrugged. "I've no skills, no way to make a living and I'm too old to want a family. I like feeling part of something. As long as the crowds like me...I'm fine here."

Occasionally, a high-born lady, living in the officers' accommodation at the fort, would take a fancy to one of them, and the *lupinarae* would be without their custom for a few weeks, but this type of relationship often came with problems, such as angry husbands and vengeful fathers, but it was a part of the life of a gladiator that they enjoyed.

Chapter 18

One cold wintry night, when the gladiators were finishing their evening meal, the school's routine was disturbed by the announcement that Petronas wanted to speak to everyone. The canteen was warmed by the kitchen's ovens and a few braziers Bretislav had placed in the corners of the room. The staff of the school had joined the gladiators and the room was rapidly filling up.

"I wonder what he wants to tell us," Farinas murmured. "Announcements are usually posted on the general notice board." As they waited, Farinas noted some of the changes that had been made in personnel, since he'd arrived at the school. Lachlann and Tòmachan had completed their training as gladiators and were becoming successful in the arena, replacing older gladiators. Two young lads, Brude and Ruaraidh, had taken their places, and would soon begin training. They were about fourteen years old; the same age Farinas had been, when he came to the school, ten years before.

Videric, in his prime, according to his lady friends, but old for a gladiator, continued to fight successfully in the arena, but he also spent time training the new lads. It was generally accepted that he would soon begin to fight less and train more, possibly becoming one of the school's *magistri*.

Conversations stopped as Petronas walked in and made his way to the front of the room. "Right, lads, you've probably heard of the unrest north of the Antonine Wall. For a start, the wall's a joke, the Romans abandoned it years ago and it's nothing more than a long line of ruins across the country that the locals use to shelter their animals in.

"There's nothing now between Trimontium and the barbarians. The garrison soldiers are shitting themselves at the thought of hordes of painted savages pouring down from the hills and slaughtering them before reinforcements can get here from the south."

He waited as latecomers arrived. "What's that got to do with us?" Lachlann called out.

"What's it got to do with us? Have you seen our stores of weapons and armour? Those naked savages would do anything to get into our *armamentarium*." He hesitated then continued. "Besides, you lot wear more jewellery than Kennora's girls. There must be a fortune stored in the chests in your rooms." There was some laughter, and the tension in the room eased slightly.

Petronas continued. "Soldiers at the fort are jumpy at the best of times. Now they're on high alert, inclined to act, and ask questions later. So!" Petronas paused and made eye contact with as many men as he could. "From today, the school will be locked down from the start of the second watch." He waited for the murmurs to die down. "Be back before then. If there is trouble, we want you back here, not being picked up, or killed, by over-enthusiastic, shit-scared soldiers, patrolling the settlement looking for trouble. Is that clear?" The last was roared and everyone jumped and nodded, but no one was happy.

"What about my family, sir? Can I still visit them?"

There was silence as Petronas turned his icy glare on the young gladiator who'd spoken. "You're a slave, Borja. You don't have a family." Borja wasn't the only one with a woman and children in the settlement, but he was the only one stupid enough to mention it.

"If you did have a family, Borja...which you don't, you could visit, but you would have to be back at the same time as everyone else!" He glared at the hapless Borja before addressing them all. "Right, you've been warned. Back here before the start of the second watch...whether you have a family, which you don't...or not. Is that clear!"

There was a chorus of, "Yes, sir!" and men started to get up, until Petronas held his hand up.

"One more thing. Our glorious emperor, Marcus Aurelius has died and his son, Commodus, who ruled jointly with him, is now the emperor." He waited as if expecting a response, but there was none. No one knew the man who had died or his son. It mattered little to them who the emperor was in far-off Rome.

"What difference will that make to us?" Andosteni called out. Andosteni would be retiring from the arena, to become a full-time trainer, when Kyrios retired.

"Our esteemed local governor, Wilbeorht Stanier, funds the games. He wants the next games to be special, to show due respect to the dead emperor and to celebrate the new one. He also hopes to ease the tension between the fort and settlement, given the current unrest."

"I'll fight Wilbeorht!" A voice called out. "That would be special." There was laughter at the thought of the flabby, self-important local official taking up weapons to fight in the arena.

"What does the whoreson want us to do now?" Kosyo asked. He had reason to be bitter. On a previous occasion, Wilbeorht had put a trained gladiator into the games, among a group of condemned unskilled criminals. Kosyo had been drawn against Wilbeorht's fighter. Instead of an unskilled and terrified criminal, he found himself unexpectedly fighting desperately for his life, against an equally desperate, experienced professional.

Wilbeorht and his cronies had hoped to make a killing on the betting. Kosyo had finally won the bout, but his injuries had been so serious, he'd been unable to fight again. Petronas had allowed him time to recuperate and then appointed him bathhouse attendant when Tasgall died of a flux. Kosyo's only satisfaction had come from the knowledge that Wilbeorht had lost a fortune on the outcome of the contest. He'd lost most of his friends too.

"He wants what all the fat, stupid officials want," Lachlan answered. "They want blood!"

"So long as it's our blood." Andosteni called out, reflecting the views of the others, disgusted by repeated calls for 'more blood', from the spectators and officials, none of whom had ever shed blood.

"We make that fat bastard money," Andosteni called out. "Why does he hate us so much?"

"You're everything he's not," Elekos suggested. "He likes having power over you." Elekos had taken over as chief *medicus* when Epeius retired and returned to Greece, and he'd been surprised by the variety and severity of the wounds he'd had to deal with. He remembered each of the men he'd been unable to save, and he admired the gladiators.

There was silence as the men considered this, then Petronas, looking more uncomfortable than anyone had seen him look, raised his voice, and spoke. "The thing is, Wilbeorht Stanier funds the games, so sometimes we must do what he wants, and he wants something special for these games.

"What do you think Wilbeorht is planning?" Farinas asked Videric.

"No idea, but he's twisted. It won't be pleasant."

They listened as Petronas spoke into the silence. "Tomorrow, Wilbeorht will be posting notices proclaiming games in honour of the dead emperor and to celebrate the new one. The details will be posted then."

Everyone was tense. Petronas had long resisted attempts by officials to bring wild animals into the games. Was that what he was introducing, now?

"The games will include one match...to the death, *sine missione*...between gladiators," Petronas added.

There was an angry roar as the meaning of the announcement became clear. Gladiators did die in the arena, but it was usually by accident. They did not go into the arena determined to kill each other, unlike gladiators matched against criminals and 'enemies of the state', who were only there to be executed to provide entertainment for the crowd.

Elekos raised his voice above the protests. "Didn't Augustus, ban fights to the death between gladiators?" he asked, and Petronas shook his head.

"He discouraged them...not the same thing, especially this far from Rome," Petronas answered, and it was clear he would have welcomed such a ban.

"Do we draw lots?" a voice called out, quietening everyone. It was the fairest way, but it put everyone in danger of being selected.

Petronas waited for complete silence before speaking. "Wilbeorht has the final say. The names will be posted tomorrow."

Chapter 19

Ten days after Petronas's talk in the canteen, Farinas lay back in the warm water and felt the pain from a long day of training, easing from his muscles. Looking at the marble columns and mosaic tiles he might have been in Rome itself. A wealthy young nobleman perhaps, rather than a slave in one of Rome's far-flung outposts.

Soothed by the warm water, Farinas fell asleep dreaming of a warmer land where dark-skinned, brown-eyed women, dressed in flimsy garments, danced for him. When water splashed against his face, he opened his eyes to see Videric lowering himself into the water. They sat together, quietly content. Life had been good.

Videric grunted as the water eased his joints. "Quiet in here today," he murmured.

The warmest place in the compound, the bathhouse was usually crowded with gladiators, recovering from practice bouts or gladiatorial contests. That day, the atmosphere was different, more subdued.

"They're giving us time alone," Farinas answered, though he knew Videric understood. "You don't think you need extra practice before the games tomorrow?" he asked.

Videric grinned wolfishly. "Death's a gladiator's constant companion; best you make friends with him. The governor loading the dice, won't make any difference to me. I'll accept whatever the gods decide."

Farinas knew it to be true. but he couldn't be so accepting of the situation. Tomorrow, he or Videric would die.

As Petronas had told them, Wilbeorht Stanier had decided to give the locals what they wanted, and he had posted notices proclaiming that the games in honour of the emperors would include one bout, between gladiators, to the death, *sine missione.* The gladiator contest designated *sine missione* would be between the school's two best gladiators, Videric and Farinas.

When this was posted throughout the settlement and in the fort, interest in the games had ramped up to a frenzy and spectators were expected from settlements for miles around. Betting was fierce, with vast amounts being staked on each man.

Farinas and Videric were often matched against each other, and they always provided a skilful and realistic display. They didn't follow the patterns and set displays that lesser schools favoured, consequently there had been many occasions when one or both had been glad of the professional, life-saving services of the school's medics.

"We're evenly matched. We'll fight until there's a winner," Farinas insisted, although seriously doubting his own words.

Videric shook his head, realistic as always. "The locals don't appreciate skill and technique, the way the garrison troops do. If we don't give them blood, the governor's afraid they'll start fighting amongst themselves or worse, against corrupt officials like himself. A bloody day at the arena will keep them quiet…for a while."

"It's madness to kill off your best gladiators."

Videric shifted in the water, trying to ease his aches and pains. "The governor doesn't give a damn about the gladiators. He's only interested in saving his corrupt neck, so he can carry on stealing from the locals."

Farinas knew this was true, and he knew more killing of gladiators would follow once the locals got used to the bloodshed. Life at the school would change. He looked at the blue and green tiles shimmering under the water, wondering if he would ever see them again, then realised, with a sickening feeling, if he ever did, Videric would no longer be with him.

"Gallio did his best." Videric reminded Farinas. "He managed to limit it to one professional bout, but that was on condition it was between the two best gladiators. Most of the blood and guts will still come from convicted prisoners."

"It's just a pity the blood and guts of gladiators will come from us; you and me."

"That's because we're the best," Videric pointed out with pride. "Wilbeorht insisted on it."

"That doesn't seem like such an advantage, now." For the first time, Farinas truly appreciated the fact that he was just a slave, despite the honour and glory heaped on him in the settlement and the admiration of the townsfolk. "You should get out of it. You're a free man. You fight by choice."

Videric shrugged. "Where would my reputation be then? I'm getting old. It's time I went, while they still want to see me fight, and I have old friends waiting to welcome me to the gods' table." He paused for a moment then became serious. "I want a quick, clean death. I don't want to be kneeling in the sand, while Wilbeorht takes pleasure in playing to the crowd, considering how to have me killed."

Farinas nodded, knowing what Videric was asking. "It's more likely to be me." He was being honest. "I'm still not as good as you."

"You've bested me six out of our last sixteen bouts, we've drawn three times, so it's in the lap of the gods." Videric thought about it. "Wilbeorht is likely to demand both our deaths, regardless of who wins—"

"No, he couldn't," Farinas insisted but Videric continued.

"He could and he would, but we'll take that power from him. We give them the best, most realistic contest they've ever seen. It ends only when one of us is dead, and the other must be reprieved because he fought so well."

Farinas realised what Videric was saying. They had to try to kill each other, using every skill they had. Sadly he had to agree. "It's the only way."

"I'd not be sorry to go, while I'm still popular, and before they start sending me out against beasts. That'll be Wilbeorht's next idea. At least I'll be mourned by Doireann and Eyona —"

"Bedelia, Conwenia, and Kevia —"

Videric shrugged. "What can I say? The ladies love me."

It was true. Ladies loved the gladiators. They loved the aura of confidence and danger that surrounded them, and the acclaim they received in the arena.

Soon others came into the bathhouse to ease away their aches and pains and talk about the coming games. Not something they would discuss in front of Farinas and Videric, but there were sympathetic glances cast their way and shouts of 'Good Luck', and 'Gods be with you,' which the two acknowledged, equally casually. Well, there was no point in getting upset about it. Killing and dying were an accepted part of a gladiator's life, although the odds were usually considerably better than fifty-fifty in the gladiator's favour.

They said their own goodbyes as they left the bathhouse, punches to the biceps and, 'See you in the arena', but there was more to it this time, and they both felt it. The next day would be different to anything they'd experienced before.

Back in his cell, Farinas found a flagon of excellent wine – a small flagon. There was enough wine to ensure an untroubled sleep, but not enough to impair him in the arena the next day. Gallio had to go along with the man holding the purse strings, but the wine was his way of saying he wasn't happy with the decision.

Farinas drank to Videric, knowing he would be drinking to him, in his cell. Each knew he would be fighting for his life, against the best in the school.

Chapter 20

Early the next morning, Farinas ate little, knowing it could be his last meal, or Videric's. As he considered which outcome would be worse, Ruaraidh and Brude came in carrying his armour and equipment.

"Be careful with that!" he barked. Suitably subdued, they carefully placed the items on the cot. Brude made a hasty exit while Ruaraidh waited. Farinas handed him a vial of oil he'd had prepared for him by Old Eithni, a local wise woman. Everyone knew she was a druidess, but no one ever mentioned druids. The Romans worked hard to maintain the myth that they'd driven them out.

Ruaraidh oiled Farinas's body until his dark skin glistened then he handed Farinas the vial. He was pleased the lad had remembered this part of his pre-game's ritual. Farinas always applied the oil to his hair and worked it into his tight curls himself.

That done, Ruaraidh fastened the soft padding to the tops of his feet, his legs and his striking arm, and fixed a bronze greave around his right leg and arm. A wide metal studded, leather belt with his signature lion's head buckle, fastened the loincloth. He fixed the sandals securely and stood back as Farinas tested everything was secure, without restricting his movements.

"Come back when it's time for my first contest," Farinas told him.

"Yes, Sir!"

The lad bowed and left, and Farinas knelt on one knee before his altar. It was in the Roman style, but the figure on it was distinctly un-Roman. It was carved from black wood and the name the trader gave it, Uzivelele, had sounded familiar, so Farinas had bought it – at a vastly inflated price, since they both knew he would not find many black figures, in a land of pale-skinned people. Uzivelele became his special god.

As he burned incense, he could only ask Uzivelele to give him a good outcome in the games. The only contest he was concerned with was the final one against Videric. For that one, he would not ask for a win.

As the incense filled the cell, he stood and raised his bronze *cassis crista* with its grille and lion's mane plumes. For a moment he remembered, as he always did, the panic when it was first put on, then he placed it carefully on the cot and waited for his first encounter of the day.

When Ruaraidh returned, Farinas secured his weapons and picked up his shield. Ruaraidh walked in front of him carrying his distinctive helmet, into the tunnel leading to the arena. Two contests had already been fought with the expected outcomes. The gladiators had easily killed their inexperienced opponents, and the iron smell of blood tainted the air.

The sound coming from the arena reverberated through the tunnel; the roar of the crowd competing with the musical notes of the *citharae* and *timpani,* and the beat of a *scabellum* marking time.

Vendors were doing brisk business among the crowds. Only those taking bets were having a lean time. Who was going to bet on the outcome of a contest between Leo Africanus, and a pathetic native who had spoken out against the emperor, or stolen a few beasts or coins?

As the crowd roared its welcome to a favourite, Ruaraidh solemnly placed the helmet on Farinas's head and adjusted it, before assisting him to mount Libertas. The experienced cavalry horse showed no signs of unrest as it waited for its rider to mount. With the helmet and armour, this was no easy task, and Ruaraidh did a bit of shoving and steadying before Farinas felt secure enough to take his shield and parade before the crowd.

Riding with the helmet cutting off much of the sound, Farinas felt lonely, a little island in a sea of noise. The faces before him looked bestial, as they roared and screamed his name, and he realised, for the first time, only Videric really cared for him. What the spectators wanted, was for him to kill, or be killed, and put money in their pockets from their wagers. He shook his head, smiling. This wasn't like him. Probably it was the effect of the day. Since it was possibly his last on earth, it was bound to make him thoughtful.

Libertas tossed his head and rolled his eyes, responding eagerly to the acclaim. Farinas had him rearing a few times before returning to the centre of the arena where he dismounted, trying not to tumble into the sand; an inauspicious start to any contest. Ruaraidh was on hand to steady him, discreetly, and ensure everything remained securely in place.

As Libertas was led away, Farinas stood in the centre of the arena, waiting for his opponent. The first man he would have to kill or be killed by, but he felt no fear or concern. He was only eager to move on to the final contest. The most important of his life and one in which there would be no winners, although one man would survive.

Farinas was aware of the music building to a crescendo, but the crowd had become restless. There was a buzz of conversation, and the vendors were still busy among the spectators. They knew, as he did, that this contest, like previous ones against convicted criminals, would not test his fighting skills, and there was little interest in a contest where the outcome was a foregone conclusion.

He stilled his breathing and made sure his helmet was fixed in a position that allowed the best view of the arena, drew his sword, watched the tunnel, and waited. He reminded himself to be on his guard. In the arena, nothing could be taken for granted.

Suddenly, loud war cries echoed off the sides of the arena, and three Caledonii raced from the tunnel. They were naked, with thick beards and long straggling hair and, although small, they looked strong. Their loud cries and their dangerous-looking swords caught the attention of the jaded spectators, but Farinas knew these men would have been more familiar with shorter, leaf-bladed swords. The ones they were brandishing so impressively would have been handed to them as they left the tunnel, putting them at a further disadvantage as they faced the well-equipped gladiator. Wilbeorht Stanier was taking no chances. Leo Africanus would survive to take part in the main event of the day.

A roar from the crowd indicated a surge in interest, now the odds had changed, even if only slightly and spectators hastily left the queues at the vendors, to return to their seats. Bets were placed, and new odds calculated.

These were not the usual miserable wretches needing to be whipped into the arena by the *lorarii*. These were desperate men whose only chance of being reprieved, was to fight well enough to be judged deserving of life. There was very little chance of that happening, but it was enough, and they were proud men. They were determined to fight well or die well. Screaming their battle cries they charged, as Farinas calmly waited.

They could have attacked from three sides, and with the helmet restricting his vision, their chances would have been considerably greater, but they were undisciplined and too panicked by the noise and the crowds to think clearly.

As they charged, Farinas easily stepped aside and brought down the one on his left with a deep laceration below his ribs. A quick turn, as he dragged the sword through flesh and muscle, followed immediately by a stab through the thigh brought down the warrior facing him, The weight of the man falling helped to pull his sword clear.

Seeing the others brought down, the last man turned from his charge and faced Farinas, who led him away from his comrades. He'd seen men brought down by a sword slash from an injured opponent lying, apparently harmless, in the sand.

Farinas wasn't even breathing hard at this point. It had been too easy, and he felt no sense of victory. The man still standing was a decent enough swordsman but unused to the heavier weapon. He hacked, inflicting a few minor injuries and Farinas parried easily until the man was exhausted. Sensing the crowd becoming bored by the man's display of brute strength and his own constant dodging, Farinas moved in for the kill.

The Caledonii saw it in his eyes, and he shook his sweat-matted hair from his face and tried one more time, to get beneath his opponent's guard. Farinas used his shield to block then he brought it up hard, under his opponent's chin. As he fell, it was a simple matter to thrust the sword blade into his heart. He'd fought bravely. He at least deserved a quick clean death.

As Farinas followed the bloody trail left by the tribesmen's bodies as they were dragged out of the arena, he doubted anyone would pay for their burial and they would soon be forgotten in the contests that followed.

Farinas had no interest in those contests, remaining in his cell even when Videric fought, never doubting the outcome. No one disturbed him, sensing his desire to be left alone. Sounds from the arena carried to his cell, but he tried to concentrate on his memories, even back to his home in Theveste when his mother still lived. He wondered if she would be waiting for him if he died. He hoped so.

When Ruaraidh came to lead him to the arena for the final contest, he was calm and resigned to whatever the gods decreed. He would fight as well as he was able, as would Videric. They would make sure no one could deny the winner of this contest, his life.

This time, the roar of the crowd drowned out the sounds of the musical instruments. This was the contest they had been waiting for. More money had been bet on the outcome of this fight than on all the others that day.

No one stood by the vendors, waiting to be served food or drink. No one even sought out the *scorta;* the women waiting to service their customers in dark shadows under the tiers of seats. No more bets were being taken. Everyone's attention was on the arena and the atmosphere was tense with blood lust.

At the end of the tunnel, Ruaraidh placed the gleaming *cassis crista* on Farinas's head, making sure it fitted snuggly.

"Gum beannaicheadh Cailleach thu." The lad bowed and, recognising a local deity in the phrase, Farinas nodded his thanks for the blessing, while hoping others were offering blessings to their gods, for Videric.

There was no Libertas waiting in the arena. There would be no display of horsemanship on this occasion, to distract from the main business of the day. The contest between the school's two best gladiators, *to the death*, was what this crowd had been waiting for.

Marching alone into the arena, to the cheers of the crowd, he saw Videric striding across from the opposite side. Videric carried the double-ended spear and a small round shield. Over his shoulders and crossed over his chest were two baldrics supporting his sword and dagger.

Farinas was aware of the spectacle they made with their gleaming armour and weapons and the warlike plumes making gaudy distinguishing crests above their helmets. The crowd stood and roared as the two men met in the middle of the arena. This fight, no one wanted to miss.

Through the grilles, they gazed into each other's eyes, expressing forgiveness and acceptance for whatever was about to happen and promising to do their best for each other. Farinas shook tears from his eyes, as they each hoped for the same outcome, life, or an honourable death at the hands of a brother.

Chapter 21

The referee waited, building the tension, as a hush spread over the massed ranks of spectators, then gave the signal for combat to begin. They raised their weapons in salute and engaged in the fight of...and for... their lives.

Videric was fast, he threw the heavy spear, but they had practised the move many times. Thrown with his right foot forward, meant Farinas had to move to his left to avoid it. Overcome by the thought of what would happen in the arena, Farinas was slower to react than usual, but his body moved, and the spear whistled past, closer than usual, and the crowd roared as Videric ran forward, now holding his sword and shield.

Videric attacked fiercely. It was the only thing that would have moved Farinas into the kind of contest the crowd demanded, a fight that would allow one of them to be considered worthy to live. Eventually, the years of training took over and Farinas went from the defensive to the attack.

The first time he drew blood, he clearly saw Videric's smile and nod of approval. The crowd, experienced and skilled in reading the gladiators, realised what was happening and the roars were of approval and blood lust; knowing they would see a real fight, to the death.

Videric's spear lay in the sand, and they fought with swords and shields. Both men were bleeding from numerous cuts but the first cut that went deep was from Videric's sword. He was reading the crowd and responding to signs of restlessness. The deeper cut drew more blood, but it reawakened the crowd's interest and prompted Farinas to respond. He ran in fast, stabbed under Videric's sword arm and backed away. The crowd groaned as Videric dropped his arm as though it was lifeless, at the same time he brought his shield across, and prevented a second sword stroke from reaching his body.

Videric flexed his fingers and kept a grip on his sword, quickly raising it to ward off another attack. Farinas slowed his attacks enough to give Videric time to recover, but not enough to arouse the crowd's suspicion, until Videric was ready to attack again. The fight continued, but their bodies ached, and their vision blurred. The weight of the helmets, added to the effects of their injuries and blood loss, caused disorientation and affected their concentration and focus. Neither could go on much longer, and the crowd was roaring its demand for a bloody climax. A lot of money was riding on the outcome.

Farinas could do nothing now but defend himself from Videric's determined onslaughts. Suddenly Videric raced over to his spear. Thrusting his sword in his belt, he snatched up the spear and ran back. He stopped, again with his right foot forward and Farinas knew to twist to his left, but he didn't. Somehow, he managed to stop the automatic reaction, and he twisted to his right, accepting the fact that the heavy spear would certainly kill him.

The spectators were on their feet, but the spear flew past, and Farinas was still standing. Videric had known what he would do, even before he decided. He'd spared the younger man. As Farinas hesitated, stunned by his reprieve, he heard Videric's voice over the roaring and screaming of the crowd.

"Attack, Brother! Attack!"

It was the desperation in Videric's voice that got him moving. If he didn't make a good fight of it, neither would live. He ran towards Videric and felt his sword batter the shield before the blade slid off and stabbed Videric's thigh. He collapsed in the sand but kicked out and knocked Farinas backwards stopping his charge. Videric got up and ran at Farinas lying in the sand. Farinas raised his shield and Videric's leg buckled, and he crashed onto it, then rolled over, losing his sword. Farinas got up and Videric struggled onto one knee, the blood from the wound in his thigh pooling in the sand beneath him. He drew the short dagger from the baldric and the men clashed.

Farinas struck downwards with his sword, aiming for Videric's helmet, but Videric twisted to meet the blade and it sank into his neck and slid into his chest. By this time the spectators were in a frenzy, screaming for whichever gladiator they had their money on. Farinas stood dazed by what had happened and watched Videric sink to the bloodied sand. Farinas bent and pulled Videric's tight-fitting helmet off and saw his friend's smile.

"We gave them the best fight ever," he whispered, before taking his last breath.

Farinas bent over his friend and wept. He felt no physical pain, despite the many deep cuts and bruises, and as he knelt in the sand, he wished the crowd would demand his death too. He knew he couldn't live with what he had done.

After the outcome was declared, Farinas collapsed beside Videric and both men were carried from the arena.

Chapter 22

Ten days later, and Farinas stood in the gladiator's cemetery on a barren slope, in front of Videric's engraved memorial stone. Videric had paid into the gladiators' burial fund, and his friends and supporters had paid handsomely to have a block of the finest marble carved in his memory.

The fight had been as savage and skilful as the crowd had hoped and both friends had fought better than they had ever done before, guaranteeing life for the survivor. By the time the fatal blow came, both men were badly injured and losing enough blood to satisfy even the most blood-thirsty members of the baying crowd.

Farinas had tried not to think of his opponent as his mentor and friend, as he fought with every trick he knew. He remembered little of the contest but knew his friend had worked throughout to save his life, at the expense of his own. He tried not to think further, but he remembered watching his friend draw his last breath.

Since being carried from the arena to the wild acclaim of the crowd, he'd been wandering in a dreamworld induced by the poppy and other herbs mixed by Elekos and the best medics in Trimontium, as they fought to repair his body and save his life, to provide entertainment in the arena again.

Shaking his head to dispel the memories, he knelt on the grass and read the inscription through tears. It memorialised Videric's achievements in the arena and the fact that Videric had fought as a *rudiarius*. Everyone who read the inscription would know that, as a free man, he had chosen to fight in the arena. They would know everything carved on the stone, including his killer's name – Leo Africanus Murmillo.

His thoughts drifted back to a grave site on a hill above Theveste. There he had said goodbye to his mother, under a burning golden sun in a cloudless blue sky. On the damp, cold hill above Trimontium, he shivered and longed for that place and that warmth.

A hand on his shoulder roused him to the realisation that he was still in considerable pain, now aggravated by the cold and dampness.

"You must come back to the school." It was Atticus, a fellow gladiator who fought as a *dimachaerus,* who had come to take him back. He was aware of the other gladiators' concerns. No one wanted to kill a comrade, but it was a risk they accepted. It also prevented deep friendships from developing among the gladiators. Videric and he had been the exception. They had been friends before they became gladiators. "You had no choice, and you gave him an honourable death." Atticus repeated what he had already been told, many times. Knowing it was true, didn't help him to accept what he had done.

Atticus helped him back to the school and led him to Gallio's office. The school's owner himself came and helped Farinas to a divan. He threw a blanket over his shoulders and poured wine. Farinas shuddered uncontrollably and held the goblet with two hands as he drank the warmed honey-sweet wine.

He expected no apology from Gallio. To offer one, would imply fault on the part of the official who had demanded the *non missione* ruling for the contest. It would also raise the question of Gallio's acceptance of the condition. Farinas understood his need for funding. Shivering from pain and cold, Farinas cared nothing for that. He just wished Videric had killed him.

Gallio's voice broke into his thoughts. "I understand how you feel…" He broke off, noting his gladiator's anger, then continued thoughtfully. "Well, no, I don't, but I do know you need time to recover. You will not fight in the next games –"

"Your sponsor won't like that!" Farinas interrupted, displaying some of the bitterness he felt.

Gallio shrugged, ending the conversation. They drank in silence, as warmth returned, and the shivering stopped. Eventually, Gallio stood and lifted a package from his desk. "Videric left instructions. This is for you."

Farinas shook his head. He couldn't take much more. Videric in his last days, had thought of him, his killer, with kindness, for he knew his intention would have been kind. Slowly he unrolled the wrapping and gazed at a heavily embossed gold armband. Despite his pain and sorrow, Farinas smiled. It was so like

Videric to bequeath him this. Extravagant and expensive, it had not really been Videric's style, but it was a symbol of the good times they'd shared.

Videric had only worn the wide gold, Herakles knot armband for ceremonial parades in the arena. It had his name inscribed on it, and an image of Mars riding in his chariot, drawn by the dogs of war. They'd reminded Farinas and Videric of Madray and Guyar, the hounds that had guarded them on their journey through Gaul with Pelias and Teo.

The armband had been a gift from a lady friend; a symbol of their love she said, despite being the wife of a high-ranking officer in the legion. Fortunately, the officer had been posted back to Rome, and his young wife returned with him, leaving a relieved Videric who had no wish to anger yet another husband, especially an officer in the legion.

Farinas ran his fingers over the heavy gold and tried not to think of Videric marching proudly in the arena, wearing the armband. Gallio waved him away, and he stumbled out into the corridor with the bundle clutched to his chest.

Ruaraidh was waiting to lead him to his room. After helping him onto the bunk, he placed the bundle on the table and handed him a beaker of the drink that Farinas knew would help him to sleep. He breathed in the smell of warm honey and cloves mixed with other herbs and spices he didn't recognise, but he knew the mixture came from Eithni.

"I hope she's added her blessing," he whispered.

"Of course, you have the blessings of many," the lad replied, leaving him to drink and sleep. In this way, his body slowly healed but his mind remained troubled. Life went on as it does unless the gods decide otherwise and it seemed the gods wanted Farinas to live, at least for the present.

Gallio kept to his word, and Farinas was not entered in the next games, but this just increased the demand for him to make an appearance. He wasn't afraid. He didn't care if he lived or died, but he had no heart for the contests. He'd had a lot of time to think, sometimes befuddled by poppy and other medicines, sometimes more clear-headed than ever. He knew the crowds had acquired a taste for blood, and the gladiators' skills were being largely ignored in their lust for blood and death.

Eventually, he returned to the arena. As a slave, he had no choice, but his bitterness increased when he learned that Wilbeorht Stanier had blocked his being awarded the *rudis*, fearing he would leave the school. Gallio managed to remedy that by arranging a special ceremony on his return to the arena, awarding him the *rudis,* 'for his long and glorious career as a gladiator'. With the crowds cheering, the music playing triumphantly and the award a done deal, not even Wilbeorht could withdraw it.

Farinas appreciated the steps Gallio had taken, and he accepted the award, but he cared little for it, or the fact it made him a free man, although he always carried the small wooden sword, ready to produce it if his status as a free man was questioned.

The spectators welcomed Leo Africanus back, but he felt only contempt for them, knowing that when a younger, better fighter came along, these admirers would turn on him. There was no longer any sense of victory or honour in the arena, and he felt no connection with the other gladiators, Videric had been his only friend. When he wasn't fighting or training, he was drinking.

It got so bad, even the local ladies gave him a wide berth in the wine shops and taverns, although the Aquilla Alba was more forgiving than most. He frequently missed training, consequently spending time in the punishment cell, as he sweated the wine out of his pores, seemingly determined to kill himself, one way or another.

"Wake up!" Farinas heard the voice through a fog of wine and ale, vaguely aware of the cold stone beneath him and the bulk of the tavern behind him.

He rolled over. "Fuck off and leave me alone." He'd been wakened many times by guards from the school and dragged back to be locked in a punishment cell until morning. This time though, the voice was followed by a torrent of cold water over his head and face. On a winter's night in Trimontium, a skin of cold water was neither refreshing nor welcome.

He tried to lash out but found himself tangled in his cloak. He'd passed out on the steps of the tavern, not an unusual occurrence recently, and his fist connected with the doorframe.

"I'll kill you…" he reached for a weapon that wasn't there. Weapons were kept secure in the armoury.

"Didn't you hear the alarm?" Farinas wondered why Ruaraidh was in the settlement, annoying him. "They've opened the gates for latecomers, but they'll lock them again soon!"

He struggled to sit up, dimly aware that something was seriously amiss. He automatically checked the gold armband under the sleeve of his tunic. He never removed it and always feared it would be stolen, especially in situations like this one.

"Get up!" Ruaraidh was becoming even more insistent, and Farinas shook his head and wiped his face with his cloak. He remembered being thrown out of the tavern, but nothing else. It was dark, and the town should have been quiet, but he was beginning to realise it wasn't and he moved back against the wall as he became aware of people running past him.

He wondered briefly if he was still asleep, in the middle of a drunken dream. Some people were carrying babies and children. Others were herding animals and pushing carts. There were shouts of alarm, cries of children and babies, and the sounds of panicked animals. A man dragging a donkey stumbled over Farinas and cursed him before getting up and following the others.

"What's going on? What alarm?" He stood up, mainly to avoid being trampled on, and propped himself against the wall. At Ruaraidh's urging, he staggered out of the alley to see people from the settlement heading to the fort. In the distance, he saw a few gladiators who'd missed the curfew, hurrying through the gates into the school.

"What's happening?"

"The insurrection! It's finally happening. Caledonii have attacked the Great Wall in the south. They killed the governor and his guards, as well as Roman soldiers."

"The governor? Wilbeorht's dead?"

"No! you idiot! The Governor of Britannia! The emperor's representative! He was inspecting the legions along the Great Wall! The Romans will likely push the tribesmen back to the north. No one wants to be caught in that retreat." Ruaraidh's voice rose as his impatience grew.

Farinas could see the local townsfolk hurrying through the gates and into the fort, and he shook his head, trying to make sense of the situation. "They're taking refuge in the fort…with the Romans?"

"They can't be seen to side with the rebels. Not here…in a Roman garrison town."

Suddenly trumpets sounded from the battlements of the fort, and the main gates opened. In perfect formation, ranks of legionaries and auxiliaries marched out onto the paved road leading south to the Great Wall.

Armour and weapons glinted ghostly in the moonlight, and the ground trembled under the thunder of marching feet. It was an impressive sight and Farinas tried to shake off the effects of the rough ale he'd drunk, as they watched the Power of Rome in action, marching out to support the legions in the south…and destroy the rebels.

"Go to the school!" Ruaraidh yelled. "Anyone caught in the settlement will be taken for a rebel. Rome will be looking for revenge. Killing the governor is serious."

"Do I look like a fucking Caledonii rebel?" Farinas growled.

"Maybe not, but I do," he snapped, "and I'm not waiting to be taken." They watched the last of the fleeing townsfolk frantically rushing to the fort before the gates closed.

"We'd best go to the school." Farinas staggered into the middle of the road, but Ruaraidh turned away.

"Not me. I'm going north. I'm from one of the northern tribes. They'll take revenge on us all."

"Gallio will —"

"Gallio won't be able to protect me." Ruaraidh gave him a push. "Go on! Get into the school. Who knows how far the ordinary Roman soldier will go for revenge when his brothers are being massacred in the south and he sees every tribesman as an insurrectionary?"

After the confusion and noise, an eerie stillness had fallen over the settlement, with only the occasional bark of a fox and the cries of owls breaking the silence. The frosty night air was slowly clearing Sigdan's head, and he was beginning to appreciate the danger, especially for Ruaraidh. The lad was dressed warmly, as for a journey and he was carrying a bulky sac with the now empty waterskin attached to it. He had delayed his escape to find Farinas and warn him.

"Go on! Get out of here!" he shouted.

Ruaraidh turned to run, just as the smaller gate opened, and a column of auxiliaries marched out of the fort. They avoided the main Roman Road and headed into the narrow streets of the settlement.

"Wait!" Farinas pulled Ruaraidh back into the shadows. "If you go into the open now, they'll see you." Ruaraidh watched the soldiers moving closer. "They're looking for rebel sympathisers or any fleeing from the south. They're scared and likely to kill on sight."

"We can explain —"

"You can," Ruaraidh answered, slipping back into the alley.

Farinas watched as the column of men split up. Some began searching the perimeter, while others moved through the narrow alleys. He hoped Ruaraidh wouldn't try to run, not yet. In the moonlight, any sudden movement would be picked up.

Two soldiers were heading for the tavern. Hoping to distract them and give Ruaraidh time to escape, Farinas staggered off the road, sat down against the tavern wall and closed his eyes. He heard the soldiers approaching, then he was kicked viciously in the ribs before being seized and dragged upright by the auxiliaries. "Doesn't look like a rebel," one growled.

"I don't care what he looks like, Basilius. We're takin' him in." This one was looking for trouble, and he thought he'd found it.

"Wh…what's going on?" Farinas mumbled. The soldiers had never bothered him before. Whenever he'd passed out in the settlement, they just left him to be taken back to the school. Tonight, the atmosphere was very different. The threat of an insurrection had become real, and it changed how the Romans viewed the natives.

"Name and business in the town!"

"Who the fuck are you? I'll report you. I'll —"

"You'll shut your mouth."

"I need to get back." Farinas tried to shake off the hand clamped to his shoulder, but he stumbled and fell against the wall. "I'll be locked out —"

"Locked out?" The auxiliary named Basilius, peered into his face and laughed. "Hey, Titus, we've caught ourselves a famous gladiator." He turned back. "You're Leo Africanus, aren't you?"

Farinas nodded and tried to find his *rudis*. His fame would see him right with the soldiers and the wooden sword would prove he was a free man. Ruaraidh could escape, while he kept them talking about his exploits in the arena. He'd earned many a drink in the tavern that way.

Chapter 23

Unfortunately, Farinas hadn't realised how much things had changed since Videric's death and now, with the news of the uprising terrifying the soldiers, escape was not going to be easy, for either of them.

Basilius was delighted with their catch. "Titus! Come and meet Leo Africanus!"

As Farinas hoped, the auxiliary named Titus, turned back, but the response was not what he had been expecting. "Leo Africanus!" Titus spat on the ground at Farinas's feet. "You're the whoreson that lost me my bet at the last games…a draw was no good to me." He carried on into the alley, calling back as he went. "You've been useless since the contest between you and your mate! Sodomites, were you? Can't get over killing your lover?"

Farinas ignored him. He'd heard the accusation before, but he paid attention when he heard scuffling sounds followed by a cry of pain. Titus emerged from the shadows, dragging Ruaraidh out of the alley. "This your new catamite then?" He threw Ruaraidh to the ground. "A bit younger this one, isn't he?"

Farinas lunged at Titus, trying to protect the lad.

"Get back!" Farinas heard the panic in Basilius's voice, as Titus brought the flat of his sword down on Ruaraidh's back.

"He's not a rebel!" Farinas insisted. "He's from the gladiator school."

Titus was not to be stopped. The Romans lived uneasily with the 'civilised' Caledonii, but no one knew how many rebels there were between the two walls, just waiting for something like the attack on the Great Wall to give them the incentive to go on a murderous rampage.

Ruaraidh was curled up, trying to protect himself, as Titus vented his rage and fear on him. "Bastardin' Caledonii, barbarians like you are killing our brothers in the south, but I can make damn sure, you won't be killing any of us here!"

As Farinas tried desperately to reach Ruaraidh, Titus changed his grip on the sword, and his time Farinas saw the edge of the blade coming down. Hungover or not, he acted instinctively, breaking free and lunging at Titus. The force of his attack pushed the auxiliary against the tavern wall. He rebounded and fell to the ground. There was a stunned hush as they watched a stream of blood glistening black in the moonlight, flowing out from under him,

"You've killed him." Basilius drew his sword and stepped back, watching Farinas with renewed terror. He could imagine it all; hordes of barbarians overrunning the fort, torture, death…

"He's not dead," Farinas insisted, trying to calm the situation. Titus struggled to his feet, and they saw the sword had sliced into his body, just below his breastplate. "The cut's not deep," Farinas pointed out. "A flesh wound. Take him back to the fort. The *medicus* will deal with it."

"I'll have you crucified for this, you bastard," Titus vowed, pressing his tunic over the wound.

"You fell on your sword," Farinas pointed out, but he knew the situation was serious; one soldier was wounded, and one was panicking. Farinas bent and pulled Ruaraidh to his feet while trying to convince the auxiliaries to leave. "Get your friend to the fort before he loses too much blood. It needs to be cleaned and bound, to stop the bleeding and prevent the wound from festering."

"You're both coming with us," Titus snarled, but already he was swaying and struggling to stay on his feet. His friend sheathed his sword and supported him while watching Farinas. "I need to get you to the *medicus*, Titus. Don't worry. These whoresons aren't getting away. One of our patrols will bring them in." He put his fingers to his mouth and gave a piercing whistle. This was returned, then quickly followed by shouts and the sound of running feet.

Farinas threw Ruaraidh over his shoulder and ran. Gallio was governed by Rome just as everyone else was, so the school could no longer provide protection. Their only hope was to avoid the patrols and get out of the settlement. As he ran from the soldiers responding to the whistle, a dark hooded figure separated from the shadows and beckoned him to follow. The figure looked sinister in the moonlight, but, with no other options, he followed.

The figure was leading them away from the settlement, towards the gladiator school, when a loud cry went up. They'd been seen. It was only a matter of time before they were caught. Farinas was strong, but weeks of drinking had taken a toll on his fitness, and he was burdened by Ruaraidh.

"Put me down!" Ruaraidh gasped. "No point in us both being taken."

"Be quiet! You're only here because of me." Farinas staggered on, following the dark figure into a grove of small trees bordering the perimeter of the compound. Here they stopped, and Ruaraidh slid to the ground, still clutching his bundle, as the figure pulled at the undergrowth under a tight thicket of brambles, revealing an opening into a dark tunnel. Moving closer, Farinas could see the brambles had been trained to make a canopy over a ditch dug into the hillside; together they formed a tunnel…a low, narrow tunnel!

The figure turned and he recognised the old druidess, Eithni. Her bright eyes twinkled in the moonlight. "What're you waiting for?" she grumbled, indicating the tunnel. "An invitation from the Arch Druidess herself?"

As the sounds of pursuit came closer, Farinas shoved Ruaraidh into the tunnel. Eithne was examining the big gladiator. "Best take that fancy cloak off. The tunnel wasn't made for a big bruiser like yourself. Roll it into a tight bundle and push it in front of you."

Farinas threw off the soft leather cloak with a red felted lining and rolled it up. Eithne prodded him. "Get on with you, lad. The gods will protect you and I'll be behind you to poke you with this dirk if you stop, or if you fart in my face. I could get drunk from the alcohol fumes coming off you!"

Farinas took a deep breath and forced himself into the darkness. The space was tighter than he had imagined, and he felt panic rising. He was reminded of the first time he'd worn the *cassis crista*. Breathing deeply, he pushed under the tightly meshed, thorny branches. A prod from Eithne, who had closed the cleverly camouflaged entrance, spurred him on, and he pulled himself forward on his belly.

The structure had been built for the smaller Caledonii, and he could see Ruaraidh scampering forward on his hands and knees, while Eithne frequently poked him to make him move faster.

Despite deep breathing, and the threat of Eithne's dirk, the darkness, and the closeness of the tangled roots, were affecting him. He imagined being stuck there, unable to go forward or back. His breathing quickened, sweat, thick with the smell of stale alcohol seeped from his body, and he gasped for breath.

Eithne sensed his fear, and he felt her hand patting his leg. "Not long now, lad," she murmured. "Stay calm." He grunted, choosing to believe her. Slowing his breathing, he forced himself on. 'Not long now', he kept repeating in his head. 'Not long now'.

Just as he felt his breathing quicken and panic beginning to take hold, he heard Ruaraidh hammering on an obstacle ahead. Slowly, light began to filter in, followed by a welcome blast of cold air signalling the end of the ordeal. Farinas took great gulps of the air and dragged himself out, panting and shivering as the sweat dried on his body.

Gods! Eithne was right; he stank!

They found themselves in another dense thicket of brambles. Eithne slid the cover back into place over the mouth of the tunnel. "Stay low!" she hissed, leading them into a clearing.

"Our thanks, Mother. We owe you our lives," Ruaraidh said, and Farinas nodded. Neither Ruaraidh nor he would have survived the night without her help.

"Aye well, mayhap you'll return the favour one day. Maybe not to me, but to one of my kind." She grinned and Farinas recognised another reference to the druids.

"I would be honoured," he replied, bowing as he would have done to a great lady, which he realised, she was.

"If we had more time, I'd maybe let you honour me here." Eithne's cackle and shameless wink made her meaning clear, and he could only laugh. The old woman grinned. "You'd best be on your way. Dolts they may be, but it won't take them long to work out where we are. You've caused quite a disturbance, and they're terrified of the barbarian hordes they believe are pouring across the wall in the north."

Ruaraidh had fallen on the ground, in pain from his beating but determined to carry on. Farinas dropped to the ground and crawled out of the shelter of the trees. He looked downhill to the compound that housed the school. The gates were barred and there was no movement. It seemed even the gladiators were keeping their heads down.

To the left of the compound, the massive bulk of the fort was illuminated by torches and braziers on the perimeter walkway. Below that, soldiers and civilians moved about among horses and carts, and farm animals. Shouted commands, rising about the noises of confused civilians, carried to Farinas, watching from the hill.

Spreading out from the fort, the houses and businesses of the native settlement were eerily quiet and empty. Nothing was moving except groups of auxiliaries searching the settlement and rounding up a few stragglers. Of more concern were the auxiliaries searching the undergrowth as they moved, slowly and methodically, towards where they were hiding.

"Will you come with us?" he heard Ruaraidh asking Eithne. "You're in danger too."

She shook her head. "I'm needed here. Injured tribesmen will be returning soon. They'll be named traitors to Rome. Traitors to a foreign country!" She spat on the ground in disgust then added, "I'll help where I can." She helped Ruaraidh to his feet. "No need to worry over Old Eithne. There are sacred places everywhere. The gods look after their own." She handed Farinas a roll of linen. "Bind the lad's ribs, when you're safely away."

He shoved the linen into the pouch on his belt and threw the cloak over his shoulders, grateful for its warmth. "I will, Mother and my thanks."

"Stay with Ruaraidh," she told him. You've got the brawn, but he knows the land...and the people. He'll see you right. Search out the ancient track over the top of the hill. It'll lead you north. Best to head west too...less Roman patrols that way. Stay away from the Via Regia...You'll be less likely to meet anyone in authority on the local pathways."

They nodded and Farinas pulled a few coins from his pouch and pushed them into her bony hand. "To help those escaping from the south."

Eithne nodded, and the coins disappeared. "The gods go with you," she said quietly, "yours and mine," before turning and disappearing into the bushes.

Chapter 24

Farinas took Ruaraidh's pack and helped him to his feet. "Seems you and me have a way to go. Think you'll manage?"

Ruaraidh gasped and pressed his hand to his ribs. "I'll manage. Remember you're old and not so fit —"

"That right?" Farinas grinned and set off, keeping low to the ground, and using the whin and bramble bushes for cover. As his head cleared, he felt surprisingly cheerful, considering that his lucrative career as a gladiator was over, and his only refuge was the barbarian land beyond the Antonine Wall, far from any semblance of civilisation. "I don't suppose there's any tiled baths or underfloor heating where we're going?"

Ruaraidh shook his head, saving his breath for walking. Farinas slowed his pace, but he knew their future depended on getting as far away from the fort as possible, as fast as possible. "We'll stop soon, and I'll bind your ribs."

"I'm fine," Ruaraidh gasped.

The going got easier as they crested the brow of the hill and headed down the other side. When they found the ancient track they followed it, heading northwest.

At the first stream they came to, Ruaraidh checked his cuts and bruises, which were colourful, but not serious. He washed the blood away and Farinas bound his chest tightly with the linen strip.

"I owe you," Farinas admitted gruffly, as they ate the bread and cheese Ruaraidh had brought. "If you hadn't come looking for me, you'd have got away, and I'd have been taken with the other drunks, and now I'm eating your food."

"Don't worry about it," Ruaraidh smiled at Farinas's discomfort. He wasn't used to being in anyone's debt. "I expect things will even out on the way." He paused. "Unless there's somewhere else you want to go to?"

Farinas thought about that. He could never imagine returning to Theveste and there was nowhere else he wanted to be. He had no idea where they were going, and he decided, he wasn't much concerned. He shook his head. "I'll come with you, if you don't mind."

That decided, they filled the waterskin and moved on, although, unless the Romans decided to send out the cavalry, which was unlikely, they were far enough ahead that they weren't worried overmuch about pursuit from Trimontium.

Farinas forced the pace as much as he dared but eventually, he slowed down. "You needing to rest?"

Ruaraidh shook his head, and they struggled on until they came to a pool just off the track. "I give in!" Ruaraidh gasped. He staggered over to the water where he drank and splashed his face.

"Thanks be to the gods!" Farinas groaned. "I was wondering how long I could keep up with you." He doused his head and face in the cold water. "Any more food in your pack?"

"None. We'll need to find a settlement before nightfall."

Tired and hungry, they headed off again, stopping only when they came to a fork in the track. "Which way?" Farinas asked.

"We need to head west, avoiding the old Roman forts, then north across the Antonine Wall." Ruaraidh checked the sun. "We should go this way," he decided, leading the way. "It's a three or four-day march, I reckon to the wall."

What about the garrison troops along the wall?" Farinas asked.

"There's none," Ruaraidh told him. "We sent them away a long time ago...well maybe not that long ago... but it's been abandoned. When I left, the settlements were still there. It's mostly local Caledonii but there's veterans from the legions and freed slaves, with their families."

They trudged on with Ruaraidh collecting leaves and plants on the way. "Food," he explained showing Farinas a handful of greenery. "It's not the best time to be looking. Too late for fruits and berries, and too soon for the spring plants. We'll need to buy some."

Farinas agreed. He didn't think he could go far on a handful of greenery, but since he'd eaten more than half of Ruaraidh's food, he couldn't complain.

Using the sun as their guide, they kept heading northwest, skirting any signs of Roman fortifications which were mostly in ruins, and straight, well-used Roman roads. As the sun moved towards the horizon, they stopped at a stream to drink, and share what they had foraged.

"We need hot food," Farinas grumbled, "and beer to wash the dust from our throats."

Ruaraidh refilled the waterskin and agreed. "We might be able to buy what we need from one of the settlements, but they're still very Roman, so be careful what you say."

"I'll leave that to you," Farinas decided. "I hope we find one soon. It's getting dark." As they continued, they caught up with a group of villagers, carrying farm implements, coming from a field bordering the track.

"*Salvete, amici*," Ruaraidh called out, while Farinas kept his head bowed and tried not to look too intimidating.

The group stopped, and a man who was slightly older than the others stepped forward but kept his eyes lowered. The greeting was not returned and Ruaraidh continued. "Is there anywhere we could get food and a bed for the night?"

"Tavern's ahead." The man joined his companions, and they trudged off along the track.

"Surly bunch," Ruaraidh noted.

"Or like dogs that have been kicked too often," Farinas suggested. It was more than tiredness from a hard day in the fields. There was a dull hopelessness about the people dragging their feet in the dust ahead of them. They reminded Farinas of slaves he had seen before he joined the gladiator school. "At least we know there's a tavern close by."

The track led them past the ruins of a stone villa. Beyond the ruins, they could see a collection of roundhouses badly in need of repair. Much of the building material from the villa could have been used to repair the dwellings but it seemed like no one cared very much.

As they passed the ruins, the man they'd spoken to, stopped and indicated a paved road leading into the trees. "The tavern," he said, before following his companions making their way to the roundhouses.

The road was wide, but the paving stones were cracked and overgrown with small plants, and the branches of trees bordering the path formed a dark tunnel over their heads. There was nothing to welcome the weary traveller but, as the building came into view, Ruaraidh gave a sigh of relief. "It's a *mansio*."

"It was a *mansio*," Farinas corrected him. "Now it's a run-down tavern."

The gates had fallen off the hinges and the gardens were overgrown with native trees and brambles. The fountain was dry and cracked and full of dead leaves. Most of the windows had lost their glass, but there was an appetising smell of cooked meat and spices coming from the open door.

"Think it's safe?" Ruaraidh asked.

"There's hot food!" Farinas replied. "We're staying!".

"Don't draw attention to yourself," Ruaraidh advised quietly, glancing at the large, dark-skinned, richly dressed figure beside him.

"I can't help looking the way I do," Farinas pointed out, but he drew his cloak round himself and pulled his hood up. "Right, let's get food and beer, or whatever passes for beer in this establishment."

They walked into what had once been an elegant, tiled entrance but now served as a drinking and eating place. Sturdy wooden tables and benches replaced couches that would have greeted the weary traveller looking for a room for the night, and a meal in one of the dining rooms, probably after enjoying the bathhouse and a relaxing massage.

"Not the type of customers you'd expect to find in a *mansio*," Ruaraidh noted.

"A bit rough," Farinas agreed, "but so is the establishment."

"Keep your cloak around you. Our clothes don't fit with the company, and we don't want to display our wealth." Farinas had never considered himself to be wealthy, but he recognised the sense in Ruaraidh's warning as he examined the other customers.

Six men were sitting on benches at one long table. Their thick woollen trousers and tunics were serviceable but well-worn and filthy. The cloaks thrown on the floor or over benches were of the same rough material and condition. Their beards glistened with grease from large haunches of roasted meat taken from a decorated, terra-cotta platter in the centre of the table, and each had a glass beaker in front of him, brimming with beer. Farinas wondered how long the Roman tableware would last.

The men displayed daggers or short swords stuck into broad leather belts reminding Farinas he was without a weapon of any kind and that he would have to remedy the situation soon.

Conversation stopped as the newcomers entered, and the stares directed their way were openly hostile.

"*Salvete*." Ruaraidh's voice broke the silence, but there was no reply from the men, who returned to their eating and drinking, snuffling, and grunting like so many pigs at a trough.

"What can I get you?" The voice came from the side of the room where a long wooden counter had been set up. A tall, thin man stood behind the counter. He looked as surly as the villagers they'd met, but he was offering sustenance.

"Beer and hot food." They walked over to the counter.

"And wine if you have it," Farinas added.

"Sit. I'll bring it over." The man was nervous, and Farinas wondered why, although the way he kept watching the other customers suggested they were the reason for his unease.

They sat at a small table in a corner of the room, and the tavern keeper brought them a jug of beer, a flagon of wine and two glass beakers.

"Surprisingly good," Ruaraidh decided as they washed the dust of the road from their throats.

"The food looks good." Farinas had been eying the roast meat enviously. The gladiators' diet included little in the way of meat, but he enjoyed it whenever possible.

"Don't stare at them," Ruaraidh hissed. "They look even less friendly than the villagers."

"But better dressed and fitter than the villagers we've seen," Farinas replied quietly, "and they're armed."

He turned his attention to the room and saw that underneath thick layers of dust, there were brightly coloured mosaic tiles and murals. Statues standing by the entrance had been toppled from their plinths and broken. "You wouldn't happen to have a weapon in that pack of yours?" he whispered.

Ruaraidh shook his head. "You know they keep the weapons locked up. As soon as word came of the insurrection, the school was locked down. I was lucky to get out with a little food and a few possessions."

They sat silently, considering their position, but they forgot their problems when the innkeeper brought a steaming platter of roast meat and vegetables to their table.

Sitting back later with their beer, Ruaraidh pulled out a drawstring pouch and carefully considered its contents. "I'm not sure we have enough for a room, not if we want another meal, sometime soon." His words were accompanied by a warning glance which Farinas took time to interpret. Eventually, he realised Ruaraidh was trying to give the impression that they were poor, despite their clothing.

"We can ask," he replied, not mentioning his own, quite heavy coin pouch. "But we might have to sleep outside again."

The tavern keeper overheard and came over. "You can sleep in the back," he offered. "You need have no fear. Our friends here will ensure you are not troubled during the night." The sullen glance he cast at the group, indicated that they were not friends, and their services were not wanted.

One of the group laughed and called over. "That's right, Adair. We'll see your guests aren't disturbed."

It was not ideal but, in their position, it was the best they could hope for, and they followed the tavern keeper into what had once been a very fine room, now overlaid with a film of dust and grime.

Looking around at the neglect and damage, Farinas questioned whether they'd be more comfortable sleeping outside.

Chapter 25

Palettes lay on the floor and Adair indicated a pile of rough woollen blankets. "Help yourselves," he muttered. "The latrines are out the back."

"Do we need to take turns on guard?" Farinas asked.

"No," Adair shook his head. "Oswy was right. He and his thugs will make sure you aren't disturbed."

"Oswy?" Ruaraidh asked.

Adair glanced uneasily at the door. "He used to work at the Camulosessa Præsidium, a Roman fort north of here. Says he was a Roman legionary, but he wasn't… They moved south years ago. He probably worked in their kitchens or cleaned out the stables." The man seemed quite surprised by his outburst and quickly changed his tone. "I'll see you in the morning, *Domini.*"

He left and Ruaraidh and Farinas visited the outhouse and settled for the night. "Do you think we're safe?" Ruaraidh asked.

"I expect so, although Adair doesn't seem happy with whatever arrangement he's made with Oswy," Farinas said, pulling the blanket over himself and preparing for his first sober sleep for a while. "We need weapons," he decided, and Ruaraidh nodded in agreement.

Sometime later a scream pierced the night, followed by loud laughter and the sound of furniture being knocked over. "None of our business," Farinas grunted, pulling the blanket over his head. They lay quietly until a roar of anger erupted, followed by loud sobs.

"We'll never get any sleep with that going on," Ruaraidh muttered, sitting up.

"Go ahead. I'll sleep just fine."

The sobs continued and Ruaraidh got up. "You're going to ignore that?" Farinas shrugged but he was beginning to feel uncomfortable, picturing what might be going on in the tavern.

"Well, it doesn't look like you're getting any sleep," Ruaraidh pointed out.

Farinas groaned. "It's you that's keeping me awake," he complained, but he got up and followed Ruaraidh to the door. "Go on then."

Ruaraidh pushed open the door and they went through to a scene of drunken revelry. Benches and tables were overturned, glass and pottery shards littered the floor, and five men were sitting on the benches, laughing, and calling encouragement to Oswy who had cornered a young girl.

She was clutching her torn tunic around her, and a bruise was beginning to show on her face. Despite this, her eyes gleamed with defiance. and she snarled as she faced the man looming over her.

"What d'you want?" one of the men demanded, noticing Farinas and Ruaraidh.

"It's hard to sleep with the noise," Ruaraidh said.

"Too bad. Have a drink with us or get out!"

"I don't think so," Farinas stepped forward and pulled the *spatha* from Oswy's belt. That got his attention.

"Bastard!"

Farinas made a few elaborate passes and twists with the sword, indicating a skill they had not expected. When one of the men lunged with his dagger, Farinas brought the flat of the blade down on his wrist, easily disarming him. His scream of agony was met with more drunken laughter.

"Hey, Oswy. He knows how to use that sword better'n you do."

Oswy turned in a drunken fury, but even in his condition, he recognised danger when he saw it. "What d'you want?"

"Some peace and quiet."

"Looks like you came to the wrong place, then."

"Maybe not." Ruaraidh had retrieved the dagger dropped by the man nursing his bruised wrist, and now he stood beside Farinas, watching the others.

The girl had taken advantage of their intervention to move away from Oswy. She was standing by the door watching them and making no move to leave. "That's Leo!" she suddenly exclaimed. "Leo Africanus!" You'll no' beat him, you prick. He's a gladiator. I've seen him fight at Trimontium."

Oswy looked at the figure holding his sword. "A gladiator! So, you took advantage of me. If I'd known what you were, I'd have been ready for a real fight."

"You!" the girl standing forgotten by the door, laughed. "You carry a big sword but you're no man enough to use it. Touch me again an' I'll kill you!" She pushed open the door and hurried out into the night.

Drinks were poured, the man with the injured wrist was given a dirty rag to bind it, and Oswy held a beaker out to Farinas. "Have a drink and I'll have my sword back."

Farinas refused the ale and held onto the sword. "You can have it when we leave."

Although familiar with that type of weapon from the arena, he would have little use for it on the journey north. He needed a shorter weapon like the knife Ruaraidh had acquired, easier to carry and better suited to close fighting, for tonight, keeping the sword might prevent an ill-advised attack from Oswy.

"Maybe we can get to sleep now," Farinas grumbled, as he and Ruaraidh left the drinkers and returned to their palettes. They were soon asleep and, although both woke often during the night, there were no further disturbances.

Farinas woke early the following morning, with his head unusually clear.

"You're awake then?" Ruaraidh was waiting with his pack already fastened, ready to move out.

"And hungry."

"We could buy food from Adair before we leave."

Farinas considered. "Might be best but we leave as soon as we can. We don't want any more trouble."

They went into the tavern, but Adair was nowhere to be seen, and the room was empty. After leaving a few coins in a jug on the counter, along with the sword Farinas had taken from Oswy, they made their way outside into the sharp morning air. It was a refreshing change from the stale atmosphere inside the tavern.

"Let's follow the track to the settlement. We might find food there," Farinas suggested. "It's not far from the track we were following."

On the way, they met the group of villagers they had followed the night before. None responded to their greeting, just trudged on, looking as miserable and downtrodden as they had before, and Farinas and Ruaraidh continued on their way, happy they would soon be leaving the depressing settlement.

They had almost reached the cluster of roundhouses, when a blast of heat hit them, and they heard the ring of metal hitting metal. "That's fortunate." Farinas stopped. "You go ahead and buy the food. I might find a serviceable weapon here."

He entered the forge and found a massive figure wearing a leather apron and gloves, shaping a piece of hot metal. He took a few moments to become aware of his visitor, and Farinas looked around. The forge, unlike the tavern and the roundhouses, was in good condition. The floor had been swept, and tools, household, and farm implements, as well as a few weapons, were neatly displayed on the walls.

Eventually, the smith noticed Farinas standing by the door. "You'll be the gladiator," he said, wiping his forehead with a rag.

"Word travels fast."

The smith nodded. "Ælfræd, the smith."

"Farinas, retired gladiator."

"It's nice to hear o' Oswy bein' bested. Don't happen often…in fact never."

"I expect you'd be a match for him," Farinas noted, but Ælfræd shook his head.

"Any attack on Oswy or his men means misfortune fallin' on the settlement. When they first came here, Silas the pig man, tried to stop them taking one o' his beasts. His house burned to the ground that night. Family was lucky to get out alive, wife and three babbies and his old mother."

"So, they do as they please?"

"Not much we can do. I've kept them away from the weapons, but I've a daughter to think o'. Adair pays them to leave his customers, an' they take what they want from the rest o' us."

Farinas couldn't imagine living like that, but he had only himself to consider. Then he realised…and now... Ruaraidh.

"They're too cowardly to do anything about it." The voice, full of disgust, came from the living area at the back of the forge, and the girl from the night before came through. "There's plenty able-bodied here, but they won't take them on."

"Was that what you were doing at the tavern?" Farinas asked, and her face coloured as she glanced at the smith.

"It wasn't what you think, Gladiator!"

"None of my business." He dismissed her and turned back to Ælfræd. "I have need of a weapon, short and sharp." He examined a particularly well-made short sword discovering it was a Roman *gladius* that had been expertly mended.

"Most o' these were left behind by the Romans," Ælfræd explained. "They were damaged or broken, and I repaired them. They're strong and sharp. I do good work. Mostly farm implements now though."

It was the girl who lifted a short dagger from the rack on the wall and handed it to Farinas. "Similar to the *pugio* but slightly longer. It's sharp, an' there's a leather sheath." She lifted a sheath from a pile and placed it in front of him.

He hefted the weapon and made a few passes with it, enjoying the feel of the hilt in his hand, and the balanced way it handled. This was no repaired weapon, and he turned to Ælfræd with a smile. "Nice work."

The smith grinned, as the young woman snatched the dagger from him, and placed it in a sheath. "Are you buying or just puttin' on a show?" Her attitude was annoying, but he ignored her and glanced over at the smith.

"My daughter, Sgathaich. She forged the dagger. It's no' a mended one."

Farinas understood. She felt he had dismissed her skill, but she was selling. He was buying. It was a business transaction, and he could do without the insolence. "I'll take the dagger," he said, and picked out a bronze sheath decorated in the Roman style, as well as the plain leather one.

She named a price, and he haggled it down, but not by much. They both knew the weapon's worth, and he knew how fortunate he was to find it in that decaying village. He was just as surprised and pleased when she handed him a sharpened razor, similar to the ones they'd used at the gladiator school. He'd been beginning to think he'd have to grow his hair and beard like a barbarian.

It was a shock to Farinas to realise he was thinking like a Roman. He had once ridden with his uncles. If he'd not been captured, he'd be one of those bearded barbarians.

"Well, d' you want them?" Sgathaich was growing impatient. He nodded and paid.

As he was fitting the sheath on his belt, Ruaraidh returned with wheat pancakes. He handed the lad the leather sheath. "So, you don't accidentally stab yourself," he told him. "You can get a fancy one when you can handle the blade better."

"I did well in training," Ruaraidh complained but seemed pleased enough.

"Your training's over, lad," Farinas explained. "Get used to real life."

They went outside and sat on a bench where the heat from the forge took some of the chill from the air. Farinas was in no hurry to move on, but he had no wish to spend another night in the tavern. Life on the road might not be so bad, he thought, enjoying the pancakes, and realising there would be no exercises, no commands to be obeyed and no screaming spectators to please.

He understood that even after winning the *rudis* and becoming a free man, he'd never really been free, not like this. It was a situation he was finding hard to get used to.

Chapter 26

They were finishing off the food when Farinas overheard a conversation between the smith and his daughter. He'd obviously caused a problem between them.

"You told me you were going to help Maetta with her handfastin' gown," the smith said.

"I did," Sgathaich answered. "But Oswy sent for her, to serve them."

"So, you went in her place!"

"I can stand up to him—" Sgathaich declared but her father wasn't pleased.

"How is that so? You came in with a bruise on your face. You lied to me. You said Maetta's hound jumped on you in play."

"Oswy would have done worse to Maetta!"

"It's no' your place to defend everyone!" The smith roared, and it was apparent they'd had this conversation before.

"Someone has to!" she shouted back at him.

"Why does it have to be you?" He was pleading now, but her answer silenced him.

"Because no one else will!"

"If the men had half her spirit, they wouldn't be living like beaten curs," Farinas remarked, as a young man hurried past them into the forge.

"He seems upset," Ruaraidh noted.

The young man was demanding a sword, which the smith was unwilling to provide.

"Calm down, Alwin. You're no swordsman."

"Out of my way!" There was the sound of metal crashing to the floor.

"Just tell me what's happened, lad," the smith was saying, as Ruaraidh stood and went back into the forge, leaving Farinas to eat the last pancake and wonder if Ruaraidh's concern for others would lead them into troubles that were none of their business. He listened as the smith continued arguing with the lad. "You'd be no use with a sword, Alwin. What's happened?"

"They came in the night for Maetta. I tried to stop them…I did…but they knocked me out…I've only just come round. Maetta's gone. They've taken her an' I have to bring her back."

"You'll get yourself killed too," the smith told him, but it seemed the boy was in no mood to listen. Farinas heard scuffling and the lad, Alwin came out carrying a sword. Farinas stuck his foot out and tripped him. He took the sword from him, and Ruaraidh came out and helped Alwin onto the bench.

"What are we going to do?" Ruaraidh asked.

"What we decided earlier. We're getting as far away from here as possible. This is nothing to do with us. Oswy only has five men. The men here should be able to deal with them."

"You heard what the smith said about Oswy taking it out on the settlement—"

"Why can't they just kill Oswy and the others?"

It was Sgathaich who answered. "They're no' fighters." She and her father had come out, and she spat on the ground in disgust.

"We never had to be, when the Romans were here," the smith explained.

Farinas remembered how well the settlement and surrounding areas at Trimontium were governed, and how much happier the people seemed. "Seems like law and order went with the Romans."

The smith agreed. "Aye well, maybe it's time we did something about it."

"Past time!" Sgathaich snarled and Farinas was in total agreement with her. She looked ready to kill Oswy and his gang single-handedly. "They'll use Maetta, then kill her. Remember what they did with Rosamunde when they came here? No one helped her!"

"Are there any men who would fight?" Ruaraidh asked.

"Well, I would…I mean I've kept them out of the forge. There was no way they were gettin' weapons from me," the smith said. "Then there's Alwin here. He's Maetta's brother. There's only the two o' them now."

Sgathaich continued. "Maetta and Caratacos are to be hand fasted. He's strong. He'll fight… Matugenus is a veteran, served out his time with the legions, then settled here…and I think Silas would—"

The smith sat on the bench. "Silas tried it once. He wouldn't risk harm to his family again. He'd need to be sure we could get rid for good."

"We're wastin' time talkin'." The boy got to his feet but then hesitated, clearly unsure of his next move.

"Going off in anger'll only get you killed, Alwin. We need to prepare," the smith explained.

"We need to kill them!" Sgathaich growled. "Every last one of the whoresons, then we stick their heads on poles, as a warning to others!"

The smith looked shocked by his daughter's outburst, but Farinas thought she had the right idea. "Learn from the Romans; public crucifixion usually works," he suggested. "And it stops others."

"I'm done talkin'." Alwin stopped his pacing. "It's time to do somethin'!"

Listening to the discussion, Farinas was beginning to see why nothing had been done about Oswy and his gang, and it didn't look like that was going to change anytime soon.

He got to his feet. "Seems like you need to get as many as you can behind you, lad." He handed the sword back to the smith. "Gods be with you." He looked at Ruaraidh, still sitting on the bench "Well? Ready to go?"

"Go? Aren't we going to help?"

"Why? It's their problem, nothing to do with us."

"You've never really had anyone to care about except your mother and Videric, and he never needed looking after," Ruaraidh said. "We help others and others will help us."

Farinas shrugged. Talking wasn't helping and he was anxious to be on the move. He'd never had time like this to just sit and…well just do nothing and it was making him restless. He needed to be active...or drinking.

"You need to gather people you can trust," Ruaraidh was saying.

"They can come here, and I'll sort out weapons." The smith seemed ready for action, but Farinas had little faith in the villagers they'd seen so far.

"I'll go and get the men," Sgathaich offered, turning and running back towards the field. The smith and Alwin went into the forge. "I'll stay and help," Ruaraidh said as he followed them in.

Farinas listened to the sounds from inside the forge, but he was done sitting around. He could set out for the north, but Ruaraidh was the one who knew where they were going, and Ruaraidh wasn't going to leave without helping the villagers. He was also surprised to realise how much he would miss Ruaraidh's company. He sat warming himself against the forge wall thinking about the situation and trying to decide what he should do. It was a new experience. Until now, he'd lived his whole adult life obeying orders. The immediate problem seemed to be the young woman held by the gang, but Ruaraidh couldn't take them on, and no one else was moving very quickly so, until she was rescued, they were going nowhere.

He thought about the smith's daughter. She seemed to have some spirit and he wondered if she was managing to recruit others. Maybe, if he helped her, they could leave. Sighing, he folded his cloak and shoved it under the bench then set off after Sgathaich.

Chapter 27

Farinas met Sgathaich and the few men she'd managed to persuade to join them, just beside the field they'd been working in. They made a sorry-looking bunch, and he wondered how she'd managed to persuade them to join her. They'd be more of a liability in any rescue attempt, even with serviceable weapons provided by the smith.

Sgathaich stopped beside him, and they watched the others trudging past. "Leaving?"

He ignored the question and the sneer that accompanied it. "What did you tell them?"

"That Oswy and his men had taken Maetta an' we needed to get her back, afore they killed her."

"That wasn't too clever. Anyone likely to have gone to warn Oswy?"

This didn't seem to have occurred to her and she frowned before answering. "Ida, she services the gang for food for her family." She made no move to pass but pointed in the opposite direction. "North's that way."

Farinas couldn't believe how useless they were, and he made up his mind. Unless he did something, there was no telling when Ruaraidh would agree to move out. "I'm in no hurry so I thought I'd go and get Maetta. They're likely to kill her, while your menfolk talk." He made to move on, but she stopped him, and he saw a spark of something in her eyes, shame at his view of her neighbours, or determination, he wasn't sure which, but she stepped off the track into the bushes.

"Follow me," she snapped. "They won't expect anyone to come this way."

Farinas followed Sgathaich through the bushes to the back of the tavern, where there was a separate building, a villa that would have housed special guests when the *mansio* was being run properly. This was why they'd not heard Maetta being brought in during the night.

Under a window at the back of the villa, Sgathaich moved the bushes aside and revealed a trapdoor. They pulled it up and went inside. Farinas closed it and followed her down a set of stone steps to the cellar.

He peered into the gloom, fearful of stumbling and alerting the gang. The top part of the walls was above ground, and a few shafts of light filtered in. The parts below the ground were covered in wine racks, and the floor was littered with smashed glass and pottery. Moving as quietly as possible, Farinas followed the girl up another flight of stairs to a door.

Sgathaich stopped. "I'll go alone. Best they don't see you, and Maetta'll trust me. She'll come with me—"

"If she can walk." Farinas wasn't sure rescuing an injured woman would be so easy, and Sgathaich's face clouded over as she realised what he was implying.

"I'll come for you if I need you," she finally decided.

"Or scream," he advised, thinking of the things that could happen. She hesitated, then nodded, opened the door and slipped through.

Farinas waited, slowing his breathing, and listening for any signs of a disturbance, imagining what could be happening behind the door. It was quiet at first, then he heard voices, hushed and urgent, becoming louder as they came closer. Taking a chance, he opened the door and saw Sgathaich coming towards him carrying a lighted torch. She was followed by Adair the tavern keeper, carrying Maetta. Farinas breathed a sigh of relief. Crossing the cellar would be simpler if they could see what was underfoot.

Maetta's face was swollen and covered in bruises. Her dress was torn and bloodstained, and she lay still in Adair's arms. Farinas let them pass, then closed the door and followed. Carefully picking their way through the glass and pottery shards, they crossed the cellar to the steps. Farinas moved in front of the others, leading them to the top where he opened the trapdoor and stepped outside.

He'd underestimated the thugs, or one of them at least. He was waiting for them with a wolfish grin on his face and a sword in his hand. "Think we're all as thick as Oswy?" he grunted, waving the sword. As well as underestimating the gang, Farinas realised they had weapons he'd been unaware of.

Farinas had been telling everyone it was time for action, not talking, so he acted. Instead of drawing his own weapon and stepping back, as expected, he darted in and pulled the man by his tunic until they were face to face. The sword was virtually useless at such close quarters, even if the brigand had been skilled in its use.

It was a matter of a heartbeat for Farinas to draw his dagger and force it in under the man's ribs. He felt the blade slide in, meeting little resistance until it reached the heart, a quick thrust upwards, and the man slumped forward with a gasp. It was a fatal blow that Farinas was well-practised in, and he let the body fall to the ground. He wiped the dagger and slid it into its sheath. It had proved itself to be sharp and well-crafted.

He realised that killing him hadn't been any harder than killing condemned felons in the arena; easier than in most cases...he'd deserved it.

Taking the dead man's sword, he thrust it into his belt, thinking to give it to the smith for the rebellion, then looked around, not wanting to underestimate the rest of the gang, but there was no one else about. It seemed that this man alone had been made suspicious by the news Ida had brought from the fields, and he'd come outside to investigate, or perhaps he'd been sent by Oswy. If so, the brigands' leader would be expecting a report.

Farinas turned to the others, gazing at him in horror. They didn't seem so used to killing. Sgathaich had dropped the torch which lay guttering in the wet grass. Her face was as white as Maetta's. "You've killed him," she said. "He's dead."

"And we're alive," he answered. So much for her fierce fighting spirit; he was realising it had never been tested. Adair looked equally shocked, and Farinas just knew the rebellion wasn't going to go well. "I've killed better," he said. Remembering Videric, he added, "much better."

They set off in the direction of the settlement, keeping a lookout for Oswy or his men, knowing that the dead man would be missed, and the alarm could be raised at any time. Sgathaich stumbled alongside him. "That's one less for you lot to worry about," he pointed out, thinking it would cheer her up. It didn't.

They were approaching the track leading to the forge when they heard a shout. Turning, they saw Oswy and his men stumbling out of the building behind them. Clearly hungover, they were getting in each other's way, rubbing sleep from their eyes, and squinting in the sunlight. One had his wrist still wrapped in a rag and looked even worse than the others. Oswy bent to examine the dead man, and after exchanging a few words with the others, he led them forward.

After Sgathaich's display of frustration at the villagers' inaction, Farinas might have expected her to stand with him, but he realised he could expect no help from her or Adair. He stood aside and urged them on to the forge, then barred the way with the sword. It didn't feel comfortable, and it certainly wasn't as well maintained as the swords he was used to, but he reckoned the weapons he'd be facing, wouldn't be any better. Mostly he was wondering how he'd got himself into this situation. He decided Ruaraidh and his kind heart were to blame.

Oswy and his four followers approached but none seemed anxious to close the distance between themselves, and a man they now knew as an experienced fighter and killer.

"You killed Udell, you bastard." Oswy had drawn his sword from his belt and was waving it around. His men stumbled out of the way of his weapon and stood at a safe distance.

Farinas checked out the opposition, as he had done so many times in the arena, deciding he had little to worry about, but knowing to expect the unexpected. As the gang advanced, Oswy moved slightly behind the others, a typical bully and coward.

Farinas moved fast before they could gather their wits. Using the sword, he slashed right and left, bringing down the two leading men. The others quickly retreated to be stopped by Oswy. Farinas was hindered by the fallen men, neither was dead, and he stepped back, knowing they still posed a threat.

He'd been lucky to take two down. He'd acted fast, while they were deciding what to do. It was a tactic that had saved him in the arena many times. Oswy and the other two were more cautious. They realised he was at a disadvantage, but they'd seen their comrades cut down in a heartbeat and they were taking their time deciding whether to attack or run when they were distracted by a sound from their rear.

Farinas looked beyond them, to see Ruaraidh crashing through the undergrowth, followed by three men. Perhaps he'd underestimated the villagers. There was a moment of stillness as each man summed up the situation. The three thugs still standing, turned to face the new threat. One of the wounded men tried to stand, but he was bleeding badly from a sword slash beneath his ribs, and, as Farinas moved forward, he fell to the ground in a pool of blood.

Farinas backed away and looked up. He recognised Alwin and supposed the other young lad was Caratacos, betrothed to Maetta. He was sure neither were fighters, but they seemed comfortable with the long knives they carried, presumably knives they'd used in hunting. The fourth man was older and carried his sword, a Roman *spatha*, with pride. He alone seemed eager to engage, and Farinas thought he must be Matugenus who had been a Roman auxiliary. Military men never lose their aura of discipline and pride, and the veteran took in the situation immediately and advanced on Oswy. In backing away from Farinas, he had brought himself closest to the men Ruaraidh had brought.

The two raised their swords and they clashed, but there was little in the way of a fight. The old soldier had skill and ability with his weapon, which was clean, sharp, and familiar. The ruffian was no match for him, and soon the inevitable happened, his sword went spinning into the bushes, he fumbled at his belt and pulled out a dagger, but before he got close enough to strike, Matugenus struck, piercing his chest.

As the man fell to the ground, Alwin and Caratacos ran forward and attacked, shouting encouragement to each other. There was no finesse, no display of skill. Fuelled by anger after months of frustration and humiliation, the two lads forced their way to the last two men standing and savagely attacked at close quarters with their hunting knives.

Ruaraidh who had been prepared for a more even fight, looked on in horror as the two slashed and stabbed until the last man fell in a bloody heap on the ground. The two lads then turned their attention on the two brought down by Farinas, dispatching them with the same ferocity and savagery.

As the men's cries and pleas for mercy died in gasps and moans, the two lads gazed at the bloody scene, shocked by what they had done.

"All dead?" Matugenus calmly asked.

"Five here, one back there," Farinas told him.

"Aye, that's the lot." He nodded wiped his sword on one of the dead men's tunics and sheathed it.

"Thought you'd left," Ruaraidh said.

"I've no idea where we're going," Farinas replied. It was partly true, but they both knew it wasn't the whole truth.

They were recovering from the fight when the smith appeared with another man. "Seems like they started without us, Silas," Ælfræd said, surveying the bloody scene.

"Started and finished," the other man noted with considerable satisfaction. Although both men looked slightly shocked by the sight of so much blood, they soon rallied. "Your work, Gladiator?" Ælfræd asked.

"Can't take all the credit," Farinas answered. "Matugenus and the two lads here settled the score for the settlement."

The two lads were beginning to recover from what they'd done, and at his words, they appeared reassured that their actions had been justified.

"Well done, lads," Ælfræd congratulated them and looked at the man who'd come with him. "Mayhap you could gift them a nice pig for the handfastin' feast, Silas."

Silas looked none too pleased at the suggestion but decided to make the best of it. "S'pose I can spare one, now those bastards won't be stealin' any more o' my beasts."

Their attention was drawn back to the carnage before them, and they looked at the bodies. "What'll we do with 'em," Alwin asked, trying not to look too closely at the bodies.

"Let the others see 'em. They'll no' believe it otherwise," Ælfræd answered, seemingly over his initial horror at the killings. "Show them we don't need to live like beaten dogs."

"We'll go and get the others." Caratacos seemed eager to be away from the scene of so much bloodletting, and he and Alwin left.

Matugenus gave a brief salute which Farinas returned, then he marched off into the trees.

"It's late to be setting out," Ælfræd told Farinas and Ruaraidh. "Come back to the forge for a bite to eat. You can stay at the tavern another night."

"What about the bodies?" Ruaraidh asked.

"Don't you worry 'bout them." Silas grinned. "I've a herd o' hungry pigs that lost their shelter when these bastards set fire to their home." He strode off. "I'll go and give them the good news," he called back. "A feast's on the way! I'll be back with the horse an' cart."

Farinas and Ruaraidh walked back to the forge with Ælfræd. Farinas thought of what Silas had said and shuddered. It seemed that life in the countryside could be more brutal even than life as a gladiator. At least a gladiator got a decent burial and a memorial stone when he died.

Ælfræd took them to the living space behind the forge where Maetta was being looked after by Sgathaich, whose fighting spirit was no longer in evidence. Maetta was conscious and the two girls looked up, their eyes going to the door as they entered. "Alwin…Caratacos?" Maetta tried to sit up, and Ælfræd moved over and calmed her.

"Hush, lass. They're safe. They've gone to tell the others. Oswy and his gang are dead."

She sank back on the palette, and Maetta looked questioningly at her father. "The gladiator here, Matugenus and the two lads did for them. It's over," he told them.

"Caratacos and Alwin killed them?" Sgathaich whispered in disbelief, her eyes widening as she spoke. Farinas understood. If he hadn't witnessed the fight, he wouldn't have believed the lads capable of the killings either, but their frenzy had been fuelled by fear as well as rage. He'd seen it in the arena.

"They were angry at what had been done to Maetta and the others," Ælfræd explained, excusing the lads' uncharacteristic behaviour, as he set about preparing food.

"What happened to the folk you brought from the field? Farinas asked Sgathaich.

She shrugged. "They left to tell Matugenus what was happening. I suppose they went home...or back to the field."

"It's lucky someone told Matugenus," Ruaraidh said. "He's not forgotten how to fight."

"What happens now?" Adair asked.

These people really hadn't learned to think for themselves, Farinas decided. First Rome, then the gang had ruled their lives. He hoped Ruaraidh wasn't planning on taking over as their headman.

Ælfræd shrugged his shoulders "Well get the folk together and decide." He turned to the tavern keeper. "You should clean your place up. It used to be a decent tavern. We'll meet there."

Adair nodded and Sgathaich got up. "I'll help Adair." She followed him outside, smiling at Farinas as she passed, and he wondered, just for a moment, then shook his head. They were moving out, and she wasn't really his type.

Ælfræd served a hot vegetable broth to Maetta, leaving the others to help themselves.

They sat at the table enjoying the broth and talking about what had happened. They seemed doubtful about what to do next and Farinas hoped someone would take charge. Eventually, the broth and the conversation finished, Ælfræd offered to put them up for the night.

Farinas shook his head. Although a lot had happened, it was not long past midday, and he was anxious to be on the way. "We need to be moving on. We have a-ways to go yet, I think." He looked to Ruaraidh, not sure if the lad wanted to stay.

Ruaraidh smiled. "We do, and there's still a good bit of the day left. The broth will keep us going." Ruaraidh got up and Farinas reckoned the lad realised he'd pushed his luck enough, seeing as Farinas had been the one risking his life to help the village.

"I'll get my cloak and we'll be off, "Farinas said.

"My thanks," Ælfræd said. "Without you, we'd still be in the hands of Oswy and his thugs." He shook his head in wonder. "They've been here so long, it's hard to believe we're finally free o' them."

"You'll need strong leaders to make sure it doesn't happen again," Farinas reminded him. "Without Rome's laws and the legions to enforce them, the countryside will be full of lawless bands, looking for an easy billet."

"Aye well, Matugenus is a good man...military experience...and Silas. We'll see what happens when our neighbours get together."

"The young lads did well too," Farinas reminded him as they collected their belongings, "Gods be with you," Ruaraidh called.

"And with you both." The smith's blessing followed them as they walked down to the north road.

Adair came running out of the tavern with a package of food. "For the journey," he said, shoving it into Brude's pack. "Thanks to you, I may be able to run a successful business." He grinned. "I'll put a sign out on the road, showing where it is...for travellers."

"Good luck," Ruaraidh answered, grateful for the food. "We'll look out for it if we pass this way again."

Chapter 28

They joined the North Road and continued their journey, but Ruaraidh was still concerned about the village, and Farinas was worried he'd talk him into staying. He didn't want to live like that, although he wasn't sure that where Ruaraidh was taking them would be any better.

"The smith's going to need the gods' help getting those folk to do anything worthwhile," Ruaraidh pointed out. "They'll be taken over by the next gang that turns up looking for victims."

"There are some good people. They just need a leader, someone to organise them." Farinas wasn't sure this was true, but he wanted to put as much distance as possible between them and the settlement before Ruaraidh decided they needed to stay and help.

"I don't know if there is anyone who—"

"They'll have to sort themselves out. We've done what we can." Farinas insisted. "It's nothing to do with us."

"You said that before," Ruaraidh reminded him with a grin, "and look what happened."

"Aye well, nothing would have happened, if you'd kept out of the argument at the tavern," Farinas pointed out.

This far north, they had little fear of pursuit, but they picked up the pace to keep warm. They had food, and they were armed and free. Life seemed good, and Ruaraidh sang a marching song he'd learned from the legions. Farinas soon joined in, then their feet were moving in time to the beat, eating up the miles.

When they eventually stopped at a stream, they drank and washed the dust from their faces before enjoying the food Adair had given them. Farinas ate the vegetables then picked out a piece of meat and examined it, wondering if it had come from one of Silas's animals.

"Don't think about it," Ruaraidh advised, although he shared his apprehension. "I doubt that Silas's beasts often enjoy human flesh." Farinas didn't hesitate for long. He was hungry. The food tasted good, so he ate it.

They carried on walking, but now they were anxiously looking for somewhere to spend the night. This far north, the days were shorter and the nights colder. They had no food left, and no way of knowing how they would get more. As the sun sank towards the horizon, the air cooled and promised a frosty night. They picked up the pace, and Farinas finally thought to ask where they were going although it didn't seem very important.

"I'm going home," Ruaraidh answered. "They'll welcome you too," he added.

"Where's home?"

"The land of the Vacomagi, beyond the Antonine Wall. My people are warriors. The Romans were never able to defeat us, though they had many camps in the area, and tried often."

"How did you come to the gladiator school?" Farinas asked.

"My father was killed in a raid on a neighbouring tribe, just after I was born. My stepfather bred hunting dogs. And I grew up helping with the pups. The dogs had been popular with the Romans but when they left, it was hard to sell them . After my mother died of a fever, my stepfather decided to take our last litter to the Romans. We travelled all the way to Trimontium without any luck. There he sold them to whoever would take them... then ... well then, he sold me."

"He sold you...?"

Ruaraidh shrugged. "He had nothing left to get us back home." He smiled. "I was lucky. I was better fed at the school, learned about gladiators and fighting, and now I'm going back home with the famous Leo Africanus."

Ruaraidh laughed then suddenly stopped and sniffed the air like one of the hounds he'd bred, sensing prey. "I smell smoke."

Farinas sniffed appreciatively and grinned. "I smell cooking."

They left the track and pushed through a wild tangle of briars and branches into a clearing where the ruins of a Roman villa stood. Huge stone slabs, lumps of marble, plaster, bricks, and broken tiles littered the clearing. Beyond the ruins, they could see smoke rising into the sky and they followed a narrow track to a cluster of roundhouses. Unlike those in the last village, these were in good condition, and each had smoke rising from its neatly thatched roof.

A few people were outside tending to animals in pens. Others could be seen moving inside the houses. Children, dogs, and chickens were generally getting underfoot, but it seemed a happy place, and they hoped for a warm welcome or at least a share in the food they could smell cooking.

"You do the talking," Farinas told Ruaraidh, hoping the villagers would recognise his accent, and find him less intimidating.

As they approached the cluster of buildings, hounds appeared from the shadows, circling them silently, until a tall, well-built man came from the biggest roundhouse and whistled. The dogs retreated and lay, quiet but watchful, behind him.

They stopped a respectful distance from the man who was dressed in woollen trousers and tunic, with sturdy leather boots. He looked to be someone in authority, probably the headman. He was above middle age, with a tidy grey beard and a lined face. His expression was hard to read, but he didn't look displeased to see them, or surprised.

Ruaraidh made a small bow, and the man inclined his head. A hush had fallen over the place, even the young children had stopped playing and were watching, as older villagers came out to view the newcomers. It appeared that the village, so far off the Roman Road and not very close to the ancient tracks, received few visitors.

"Welcome," the head man said. "They are docile unless commanded otherwise." His lips twitched as he observed them watching the hounds, and Farinas relaxed.

The people he could see were mostly women, standing protectively beside the children. The men, he was sure, were watching from the shadows, armed and ready, and he realised why this village had not been taken over as the last one had. Farinas nodded his understanding, and the atmosphere seemed to lighten, but only slightly.

"We were hoping to buy food and maybe stay the night," Ruaraidh spoke, and the headman nodded.

"Come with me."

He led them to the biggest roundhouse in the clearing. There was a long table with benches set alongside it, and he invited them to sit. The entrance darkened as five men entered and sat beside them. Farinas threw back his hood, and let his cloak fall open.

"You're the ones that killed Oswy and his men," the headman said. "The gladiator and his *servus*."

Ruaraidh looked surprised and glanced at Farinas. There was no point denying it; Farinas had made a career out of being famous. "Ruaraidh is no *servus,* " he answered quickly. "We are both free men." That wasn't strictly true. Farinas had his *rudis* as proof of his status. Ruaraidh was still a slave, but until he was caught, he was a free man. "We helped the villagers," he added.

"I am Divixtus," the headman said. "It was well done. We will be able to trade with them now. We have heard their smith does excellent work, and we are sadly lacking in such goods."

"And his daughter," Farinas agreed, placing his hand on the hilt of the knife. He hesitated, seeking permission which Divixtus granted, with a nod. Farinas took the knife from the sheath and slid it, hilt first across the table. Divixtus examined the knife and passed it to his men who examined it and returned it.

"His daughter fashioned it," Farinas explained, "and they repair swords and other items left behind by the Romans."

"We should trade before they get taken over by another band," one of the men said.

"You should hand-fast the daughter, Sigurd and then we'd have our own smith," another said. Farinas relaxed as he felt the tension easing in the good-natured laughter at Sigurd's expense.

"An alliance might not be a bad idea," Divixtus, said, amid the laughter, and it seemed he was seriously considering the possibility of making alliances to strengthen the two villages.

Just then, servers came in carrying platters of food and mugs of ale. The food was delicious, and the conversation ended as they attacked the food, but soon Divixtus stated the obvious. "You'll be heading north."

"To my home beyond the wall," Ruaraidh answered. "I am of the Vacomagi."

Their information-gathering methods were such that they already knew who he was, but Farinas offered anyway. "Farinas, once known as Leo Africanus, gladiator and *rudiarius*." He wondered if they'd been tracked throughout the day. The thought did not trouble him. He appreciated the methods they used to maintain security. "Have you news from the south?" he asked, wondering just how good they were at gathering information.

"Well now," Divixtus said, clearly wondering what to tell them. "The rebels had initial success at the Great Wall. I believe they managed to kill many soldiers, as well as the governor, but they were soon captured and executed. A few stragglers managed to head north, but our information is, that the rebels have been killed and are no longer a threat."

They must have looked doubtful because Divixtus laughed and nodded. "I expect that's what the Romans want us to believe."

One of the men added, "The bastards are already sending legions north. Those beyond the wall are in for a seriously hard time."

"We'll stay out off the Roman Road," Ruaraidh said, while Farinas was thinking that life outside the gladiator school was looking more and more dangerous every day.

"We're heading to Clotagenium tomorrow." Divixtus, broke the sombre silence, adding. "It's a settlement that grew up around the Roman fort. The fort's been abandoned, but the settlement's still there. It's a good size and, first day of the month, there's a market. Ride with us," he offered. "It'll take you nearer home."

That sounded good, Farinas hadn't walked so much, since his days chained to Videric and Cináed. He decided he'd had enough, but he wanted to know the cost; there always was one. "In return…?" he asked.

"In return," Divixtus smiled, "you ride guard, display your weapons, and be prepared to defend the carts."

Farinas looked at Ruaraidh who was grinning, evidently, he had walked far enough too. "Agreed!"

More beer was drunk, and they talked until it was time for the men to return to their homes. Sigurd brought furs and laid them out against the back wall. Farinas and Ruaraidh rolled up their cloaks and put them under their heads, looking forward to a peaceful night, warm, dry, and undisturbed. It was not to be.

Shortly after they lay down, a shadow blocked the doorway and Farinas slid his knife out from under his cloak and stared into the darkness. He didn't really fear an attack, but he had learned to be cautious. Across from him, he sensed rather than saw

Ruaraidh preparing to deal with any intruders. A soft giggle broke the silence, and a gentle voice hushed the first.

Farinas lay back and felt a cold body sliding in beside him. A gasp from Ruaraidh let him know, he too had a visitor. He slid the knife back under his cloak and, as the girl settled herself beside him, he hastily slid the gold armband off, and placed it inside the folds of his cloak. It was a habit learned in the less-than-trustworthy, brothels of Trimontium.

It had been many days since such an encounter, mainly due to his drinking, and he was happy to oblige the young lady. She was energetic and less schooled than his usual 'ladies of the night', but that only added to the attraction. Her expressions of delight had been unsophisticated and genuine. Neither of them had any complaints when they finally fell asleep.

As dawn broke, the two young ladies slipped out of the roundhouse. "I could settle here," Ruaraidh murmured, gazing after his bedmate.

"There'll be other women," Farinas told him, slipping back into sleep until roused by the early morning sounds. Cocks crowed and pigs grunted, reminding them of Silas and his hungry beasts, dogs yelped and barked, and children cried, shouted, and laughed. Two young lads brought in thick wheat pancakes drizzled with honey, and mugs of ale.

"We leave soon," one told them. They seemed interested in Farinas's dark skin and curly hair, more obvious now it wasn't covered by the cloak. Farinas supposed they'd not seen so many dark-skinned people, as those living near forts did. The Roman army had soldiers from all over the empire, of every race and colour.

He smiled, knowing how his teeth gleamed in the poor light, and the boys laughed. The youngest ran his fingers through his thick curls and the older boy, perhaps his brother, smacked his hand away.

"He's young and an idiot," he apologised, dragging the youngster away.

"He's curious," Farinas said, "This food is delicious, thank you."

The older boy made a clumsy bow and dragged the younger boy outside, as Ruaraidh laughed and wolfed down the food.

“Your night-time activities have given you an appetite.”

Ruaraidh nodded, but he couldn’t help smiling with considerable satisfaction. Farinas grinned back.

Chapter 29

They dressed quickly, and Farinas slid the armband on under his tunic, fastened the sheathed knife onto his belt and threw his cloak over his shoulders. Outside, they watched the wagons being loaded with pottery and jewellery that had been crafted in the village, leather goods and freshly baked bread. There were cheeses and honey. Oxen were brought and yoked to the carts, and men they'd eaten with the night before, rode up leading two horses.

"These horses do you?" one of the men asked, and Farinas nodded, making himself known to the bigger of the two beasts.

"I'd do better without the saddle," Ruaraidh advised. "I learned to ride on hill ponies, no saddles."

"Saddle's fine for me," Farinas said. The saddle was like the Roman cavalry saddle he'd become used to with Libertas.

"Romans left a lot of equipment behind," Sigurd explained, as he checked the saddle. "We mend what we can. We use a lot of their stuff too."

"Aye," another added. "Trenus over there has a tiled floor in his roundhouse."

There was laughter from the men and Trenus, who was holding their horses, joined in. "You'll see," he said. Your women will be wantin' one soon."

"Right, time to be moving." Divixtus rode to the front of the line of wagons, and they mounted.

Two women armed with long sheathed knives, climbed onto each of the wagons, and Divixtus led the little cavalcade out, escorted by armed horsemen.

They could see why their presence was welcome. There was a wealth of goods in the two carts that would attract the attention of the many bands of desperate men roaming the countryside now that there were no soldiers requiring their services, or anyone to impose law on the land.

Farinas rode tall and felt a little of the pride he'd experienced when riding Libertas into the arena. He pulled his cloak to the side, displaying his knife, prepared, but hoping he'd not need to use it. He'd had enough of killing.

Occasionally they would see movement in the trees bordering the track, which had been broadened to take a cart and outriders, and two or three of the riders would investigate then return, having displayed their alertness and willingness to fight off any marauders.

They arrived at the market just before midday. "This used to be the legions' training area," Trenus explained, as they dismounted, and the women set out their wares in the wagons. The Roman walls were in disrepair and the ruins of the fort towered over the settlement and marketplace.

They took the oxen and horses to a row of pens and settled them with food and water. "They held games here with gladiators when the Roman Emperor, Antoninus Pius died," Sigurd told them. "Tribesmen from the north even came to watch and later they joined in the festivities."

Farinas looked to the north, where great snow-capped mountains rose into the air. He imagined hordes of naked tribesmen charging down the slopes to attack the wall, and he wondered what they were doing now, and what he would do once he got to the north.

"That's where you're going." Divixtus had seen him looking to the hills and recognised his unease. "Unless you'd like to stay with us. Carssouna and Dagvalda are looking for mates." He smiled. "I believe you impressed them last night."

Farinas and Ruaraidh had seen the glances the girls had been casting in their direction and knew their bedmates had been talking about them. He laughed and shook his head. "I thank you for the offer," he replied. "Carssouna is very beautiful and …accomplished, but Ruaraidh is keen to return home, and I think I should go with him."

Ruaraidh nodded. "I've been away too long."

"Well, if you choose to return, you will be welcome, although I doubt the maids will wait long for mates," he added. "Take a look round our market," Divixtus advised. "We have goods from foreign lands brought in by the river." He pointed to the river they could just see through the trees. "The *Abhainn Chluaidh*, the Romans named it the Clota."

"I was thinking," Ruaraidh said. "We could journey part of the way on the water. There must be traders who've come here by boat and would be happy to return with a couple of passengers."

"There are a few I'd trust." Divixtus nodded. "Old Uilleachan has a good-sized boat, and he's done the trip many times. We could ask him if he could take you to his harbour at *An t-Àrchar*."

Ruaraidh seemed delighted, not so Farinas. "My experiences with boats haven't been fortuitous," he said, remembering being chained to the ship while it rolled and bucked in the storm. "I was once attacked by pirates," he told them, adding for effect, "during a storm."

Ruaraidh rolled his eyes and pointed to the calm narrow stretch of water in front of them. "Does that look like a dangerous sea, full of pirates?"

"No," he agreed, "but it could change farther on."

Ruaraidh nodded. "It does, but only far beyond where we would be going."

Divixtus saw how unhappy Farinas was and hastened to reassure him. "Don't worry, these people are seafarers like their grandfathers and great-grandfathers were, even before the Romans came, and they build good boats. You'll be fine. Sigurd will take you to Uilleachan."

Sigurd was happy to take them to the shore and they followed him to where they could see a fire burning. As they got closer, they saw an old man wrapped in a blanket, sitting on the grass outside a makeshift shelter. Young boys were stacking full sacs inside the shelter. The old man waved a wineskin at them and called a greeting.

"Uilleachan," Sigurd called and returned the greeting. Old Uilleachan was very drunk.

Sigurd and Uilleachan struck up a conversation in the old language. Farinas imagined they were bargaining over their passage. The old man frequently drank from the rapidly emptying wineskin and examined them through eyes that were none too clear.

"He can't sail a boat in that condition, can he?" Farinas desperately hoped Ruaraidh would agree, but he just smiled and dropped his pack on the grass.

"Lots of experience," Sigurd finally offered. "He's sailed the strait of *Coire Bhreacain* and escaped the clutches of its whirlpool."

Farinas wasn't sure he needed to know what a whirlpool was. The name was descriptive enough, but he had to know. "Will we be going near there?"

"Not unless the ship's master gets blown way off course," Sigurd laughed. "Don't worry."

The old man suddenly waved his wineskin at them and shouted something. Sigurd explained. "He wants an amphora of *mulsum* from each of you. He acquired the taste from the Romans." He listened again, then added, "And honey, quite a lot, so he can get his daughters to brew his own *mulsum* at home. I can sell you the honey," he added, smiling happily.

One of the young lads came over and held his hand out. "How much?" Farinas asked, and Sigurd named a reasonable amount, especially when he considered how much he used to spend, dining with friends at Trimontium. Sigurd spoke to the lad, presumably explaining where he could buy the honey, and handed over the coins. The lad ran off in the direction of the market.

"When do we sail?" Ruaraidh asked.

"At nightfall. Uilleachan is staying overnight, but one of his ships will leave later today." Farinas breathed a sigh of relief. Whoever the ship's master was, he had to be better than the drunken old man.

"Best buy warm clothing," Sigurd advised. "It'll be cold on the water, and it's even colder where you're going. Your fancy cloaks look warm enough, but you need something to keep out the rain. They get lots of that in the north."

Heeding Sigurd's warning, they bought woollen leggings, socks, and heavy tunics with long sleeves. They were also lucky to find a wagon selling cloaks that seemed to have been copied from the Roman *saga*. These were thick and warm and would keep most of the rain out. They would make good blankets on cold nights and be big enough to wear over their other cloaks. They bought plain sturdy fibulae to fasten them.

Knowing there would be no Roman bathhouses where they were going, Farinas purchased a rough towel, goats' tallow soap, a strigil, and a small vial of oil. The merchant handed him a canvas sac to put everything in.

They bought plenty of food to keep them supplied on the voyage and refilled the water skin then they headed back to where they'd left Uilleachan. He seemed not to have moved since they left, although the empty wineskin suggested otherwise. He was pulling the stopper from a fresh one, as they approached. He shouted something, and Ruaraidh interpreted. "We're to leave now."

A young lad came and lifted their packs and bundles of provisions and carried them to the shore, where he splashed into the water and waded out to the nearest boat bobbing on the waves. Their belongings were placed inside, and the lad returned.

"Couldn't we just walk?" Farinas made one last plea, but Ruaraidh laughed. "It's fine. They come here regularly and there's been no drownings yet."

"Yet," he groaned.

The old man spoke to Ruaraidh, and Farinas waited to hear what other bad news there was. "This boat will take us to a bigger one waiting just by *Alt Chluaidh*. We need to go now, or we'll miss the tide."

Ruaraidh was sitting on the grass removing his boots, socks, and leggings. Resigned to his fate, Farinas sat and did the same, then they rolled them in their outer cloaks, and they were ready to go.

They said goodbye to Uilleachan and followed the lad out to the boat. The water was icy and there was an undignified scramble as they tried to get into the small boat without overturning it or getting soaked. The old man gave a drunken cheer and waved his wineskin, in acknowledgement of their achievement.

They dried their legs with their cloaks and pulled on the new, warm socks and leggings, then laced their boots. Wrapped in his new cloak, Farinas silently thanked Sigurd for his warning about the cold but he also wondered how it could get any colder, and if it did, how he could survive it.

The lad rowed the little craft downriver in a smooth motion and Farinas relaxed when Ruaraidh pointed out a ford, opposite a hill the lad named, *Dun Buic*, knowing the water was still quite shallow. Past *Dun Buic*, the bulk of a huge hill loomed up ahead of them. *"Alt Chluaidh,"* the lad explained when Ruaraidh questioned him. "There's a fort on it, *Cair Brithon,* Fort of the Britons." Its craggy sides looked impregnable, and it commanded the land and river approaches. Now it looked peaceful, with several boats of different sizes, anchored in its harbour. The lad rowed over to a fair-sized boat, and again with difficulty, they managed to scramble on board. It had a flat bottom and two sets of oars, but a rolled-up sail was waiting to be raised on a central mast.

They sat on wooden benches along the sides and huddled into their cloaks, already feeling the wind lifting the waves and setting the craft to bobbing on the water. Farinas gripped the sides and clung to them, until his knuckles turned white, desperately hoping the little boat wouldn't bring on his seasickness.

The ship's master and two young men were at the front dealing with ropes and the cargo that looked like wineskins, and sacs of vegetables and grain.

"At least you're not having to row this time," Ruaraidh reminded Farinas. He seemed delighted to be on the river and was in good spirits. Farinas wasn't.

The ship's master overheard and walked to the stern. "Welcome, did I hear we have an experienced oarsman on board?"

Farinas's heart sank, and he really, really didn't want to be there. "It's a woman!" he gasped.

"You don't like women?" she asked.

"If she wasn't good, she wouldn't be the ship's master," Ruaraidh reassured him, but he couldn't imagine it. In his world, women didn't sail ships, even small ones, but, he reminded himself, they weren't blacksmiths either.

"Ruaraidh and Farinas." Ruaraidh made the introductions and the woman nodded. "Criosaidh, ship's master. You do as I say while on this boat, understand?"

They nodded. Criosaidh was tall and slim but had curves where Farinas liked to see them. She was dressed in a long woollen tunic over leggings and her hair was hidden under a close-fitting cap. He imagined her taking her cap off and letting her hair tumble over her shoulders; the gorgeous red hair, women here were known for. It was the first pleasant thought he'd had in a while, and it took his mind off his seasickness. He also realised they were using a common form of Latin, like the one he'd grown used to in the south.

"This the gladiator?" she was asking Ruaraidh.

"That's him," Ruaraidh answered. "Leo Africanus."

"Doesn't look like a gladiator," she said, and Farinas thought she looked disappointed. He didn't think his drinking had affected him that badly.

"He doesn't like boats," Ruaraidh explained his un-gladiator-like attitude.

"Or women in charge," Criosaidh noted.

"I can talk for myself." He interrupted their conversation, sounding childish even to himself. He thought of the blacksmith's daughter and reckoned he'd need to get used to women who had more to offer than their oiled and perfumed bodies.

"Best you don't. Just sit quietly. Let us get on with sailing the boat unless you want to row."

"No, I really don't," he assured her.

She turned to the lad who'd brought them. "Right, of you go, Dàibhidh. Tell our gran'faither, we left on the tide wi' the two passengers."

The lad climbed into the small boat and rowed back upriver, as Criosaidh called out orders to the two men at the front of the boat. Criosaidh noticed Farinas's white knuckles as he gripped the sides of the boat. "Stop worrying," she said. "I'm the best ship's master on the river."

"And we're the best oarsmen on the river," one of the oarsmen called back. "Me an' my brother, Torcall." Criosaidh laughed but didn't deny his claim.

They raised the sail, and Criosaidh settled at the stern, between Farinas and Ruaraidh, steering. They were glad of the wind now as the boat sped across the water. With luck, this voyage would be short. Ruaraidh passed him the wineskin and he drank, surprised, and pleased he'd not felt sick. He was ready to eat when Ruaraidh shared out the food they'd brought.

Criosaidh and the men ate but remained alert, and Farinas felt safe on the water with them, even though they were now sailing in a much wider and deeper stretch of water than before. "This isn't so bad," he said, and Ruaraidh nodded.

"Better than walking."

"Aye," Criosaidh agreed. "Only one thing can improve the voyage. Pass over the mead, Torcall."

The honeyed drink was passed around then Farinas leaned back, watching the stars sparkling in the night sky. The river glinted in the starlight and the hills loomed as dark shadows ahead. Thinking of the hills and the journey ahead reminded Farinas of Cináed and he remembered he had spoken fondly of Caledonia. He hoped he had survived but doubted it. Farinas fell asleep, smiling as he remembered a guard telling him, being on a boat was like being rocked in a cradle. He'd never thought so before.

Chapter 30

Farinas woke to the sound of Criosaidh ordering the sail to be lowered. She had moved forward, and the brothers were pulling on the ropes and stowing the sail. The lads then raised the oars and ran them into the water.

A faint light appeared on the shore ahead and as it grew, people appeared from the darkness and stood on the shore. "The voyage is over," Ruaraidh remarked softly. "No pirates and no storms."

"It wasn't so bad," Farinas admitted. "But I'll still be happy to feel the ground steady beneath my feet."

People waded out and guided the boat onto the beach and unloaded the cargo. Ruaraidh and Farinas climbed out and hurried up to a blazing fire; the light they had seen earlier. They sat as close to the flames as possible, drying off from the spray and getting warm.

Platters of food were brought, and those who'd been unloading the ship joined them beside the fire. The food was plain, but it was hot and delicious. They discussed the cargo and the trip to market, then, after a polite interval, they questioned the visitors.

"You'll be heading further north?" one of the villagers asked.

"Aye, Vacomagi land," Ruaraidh answered. "My people live there."

"This is Damnonii land. We're at peace with our neighbours," another said.

"For now," a voice added, and this was followed by laughter.

"Shouldn't be any problems on the way. Just head east to the village of Tairbeart Loch Laomainn, from there, head north to A' Chrìon Làraich then northeast into Vacomagi land. It borders the land of the Venicone, but we haven't heard of any trouble," Criosaidh told them,

"How far?" Farinas asked, hoping for a short walk.

"Two or three days," Criosaidh said. "Depending on how fast you walk."

"Three, maybe four days then," Farinas decided and got an appreciative laugh.

"You're welcome to stay and rest a while, if you wish," one of the women offered, but Ruaraidh was anxious to move on, and Farinas made no objection. The sooner they were on their way, the sooner the journey would be over.

The brothers, Dùghlas and Torcall brought them full waterskins, slices of porridge, oatcakes, cheese, and bread for the journey. The cold porridge didn't look very appetising, but Farinas knew he'd eat it if he was hungry enough. He turned to Criosaidh, smiling. "I'm sorry I doubted your seamanship."

Criosaidh laughed. "You'll find the women in the north as good as the men, in most things."

He nodded. "I've been finding that out," he said, smiling and for a moment he regretted not staying. He really would have liked to see her hair…tumbling over her bare shoulders…

"Ready?" Ruaraidh was waiting. The look he gave, said he knew what Farinas was thinking.

As they set out, frost glittered in the early morning sunshine and crunched under their feet. "Not far now," Ruaraidh called, then raced ahead, leaving Farinas struggling through dense springy heather and leathery bracken. Fortunately, Ruaraidh's burst of speed didn't last long and Farinas soon caught up. They trudged on for a few more miles then Ruaraidh stopped and pointed to a cluster of houses below them. "That'll be Tairbeart Loch Laomainn," he said. "We head northeast now."

"Is there no flat land in Caledonia?" Farinas grumbled. They were surrounded by rocky hills, split in many places by rushing burns and waterfalls. He thought they would look better in sunlight, but so far thick grey clouds had hidden the sun.

"Not a lot, but we were glad of the mountains and bens when the Romans came," Ruaraidh told him. "Aye and we might be needing their protection again," he added, as they carried on, avoiding the village. People going about their business stopped to watch them. They seemed curious but showed no signs of hostility.

They had to change direction often, to avoid foaming streams tumbling over rocks and pebbles, or they crossed them, stepping from boulder to boulder. Once when Farinas slipped, he was shocked by the cold. "Melted snow from the hills," Ruaraidh told him, pointing to the still snow-capped rocky peaks. Farinas had thought Trimontium the coldest, the wettest place on earth. Now he knew he'd been wrong.

When they came to the hamlet Criosaidh had mentioned, the people were anxious to talk, visitors being rare, but Ruaraidh avoided too much conversation, wanting to put as much distance behind them as possible, before nightfall.

They eventually stopped just after mid-day, but looking at the dark clouds gathering, they hurried the meal, deciding the cold porridge could be left to last, hoping they might not need it at all. Farinas had often enjoyed hot porridge, especially with fruit or honey, but the plain, cold slices weren't something he would eat, given a choice.

As they moved on, the sky turned darker, and the wind blew stinging rain in their faces. They clutched their cloaks tightly and fought their way through wet vegetation that clung to their legs, often tripping them. Eventually, through the dark and rain, they saw a figure ahead, herding a few sheep along the track. They caught up with him and helped him as he struggled to pen the beasts, then followed him to a small stone and peat shelter.

Inside it was dark, with a stone bench along the wall, covered with a palette of heather and bracken. A few thin blankets lay at the bottom of the makeshift bed. The man who was bent over and moved awkwardly, blew on the embers of a fire set in the middle of the floor, and broth in a pot hanging over the flame heated up.

He spoke in a language Farinas could not understand. It bore no resemblance to any he'd heard, but Ruaraidh was able to understand enough to carry on a conversation, telling him their names and where they were from. "His name is Dànaidh," he said. "He lives here. There's a small village nearby. Dànaidh looks after the village beasts and helps with the planting and harvesting. The villagers give him food and drink, maybe a few coins."

"Doesn't look like they give much." Farinas had been noticing that the basic dwelling lacked anything to make it comfortable.

"Don't think they talk much to him either. He's so pleased to have our company." The old man grinned and nodded constantly, as Ruaraidh translated. "He has Faileas for company."

"Faileas?"

"Shadow." Ruaraidh laughed. "The big dog in the corner."

Farinas only then noticed a dog that had been assisting with the sheep. It was grey and so quiet it blended into the shadows. He kept an eye on the huge beast, but it seemed happy to lie quietly and watch them from big orange eyes. The old man threw down some meat for the dog, and he ate it while keeping his gaze fixed on the visitors. Farinas thought the dog probably ate better than the old man.

Ruaraidh and Dànaidh spoke some more and then Ruaraidh explained. "We can stay here tonight. We'll share our bread, and he'll share the broth and he'll take us to a safe crossing over the river in the morning."

"At least it's dry, and the broth will be warm," Farinas said, relaxing by the fire, as the wind whistled outside. "How far do we have to go? Does he know?"

"If we cross the river above the falls and go north, we'll avoid straying too far into Venicone lands. He's not sure what kind of welcome we'd get…seems a bit suspicious of them.

"Not very friendly, then, these Venicone?"

Ruaraidh shrugged. "I don't remember any trouble with them, but things change quickly in the hills. I seem to remember the Romans used a harbour on Venicone land, to supply their soldiers in the north."

They ate the broth and bread, then Dànaidh and Faileas went out to check on the sheep, while Ruaraidh and Farinas wrapped themselves in their heavy cloaks and lay close to the fire. It wasn't comfortable, but it was warm and dry; both had slept in worse places.

In the morning, Farinas gave Dànaidh some coins for his hospitality, and to take them across the river. He wasn't sure how much to give, but apparently, it was more than enough. Dànaidh left and returned with a bowl of hot porridge which they enjoyed by the fire and a parcel of buttered oatcakes. They put half the oatcakes in their packs for the journey and gave Dànaidh the porridge slices, knowing he could heat them up later.

Outside, the sun was shining, birds were singing, and raindrops sparkled; life looked good again. Farinas was beginning to see that his mood often depended on the weather. He found this quite troublesome, given the type of weather they'd been experiencing.

In the light, Dànaidh looked older than they'd thought. He was bent over, and when he walked, he leaned heavily on a gnarled stick, but his blue eyes twinkled, and his long grey hair was tied back with a strip of undyed, braided wool. When he laughed, which he did often, it was obvious he had lost more teeth than remained, but he was remarkably cheerful. As they followed him to the river, he whistled happily. Faileas trotted along, happy to stay close, or sometimes he would wander off into the undergrowth, but he and the old man always seemed connected in some way.

Not long after setting out, the river widened, and the waters roared. "*Eas Dochart,*" Dànaidh told them proudly as they passed the falls. The water foamed as it rushed over stones and forced its way between boulders. A little further on, where the waters were calmer, Dànaidh stopped and pointed. He spoke to Ruaraidh. "He says the river's shallow here, but watch out for the rocks, we might slip, or maybe the spirit of the glen will give us a wee push if we don't leave an offering."

Dànaidh's head was bobbing in agreement, and he pointed to a tree whose branches hung over the water. There were offerings hanging from it; not the fine linen and silk offerings they had seen in rich garrison towns, but strips of undyed wool. As they stood looking at the offerings, Dànaidh caught Ruaraidh by the arm and offered him the braided wool he'd been wearing in his hair.

As the wind caught his hair and blew it around his face, the old man smiled, and happily accepted the coin Ruaraidh handed him. Farinas wondered how many of the offerings had been bought from the old man. Still, he'd not been slow to ask the gods for help on his voyage from Gaul, so he had no issue making an offering to these local spirits, and he was happy to improve the old man's life even in a small way.

Dànaidh was pointing up the hill and talking to Ruaraidh. "He says there's a good path along the side of the hill just behind those trees, going towards *Obar Pheallaidh*. We can follow it, but not for too far or we'll be on Venicone lands. We need to go north just beyond the Three Sisters." He explained. "It's just three big boulders." He looked at Dànaidh who was nodding and smiling. "Dànaidh says, you look big and strong but you've not to move them, or you'll set an evil spirit free, to wreak havoc on the world."

"He didn't say that!" Farinas laughed, and Ruaraidh grinned.

"Aye, he did!"

As the breeze dried their cloaks, Farinas and Ruaraidh splashed through the river, taking care on the rocks and pebbles. On the other side, they turned and waved to Dànaidh, waiting to see them safely across. Faileas wagged his tail and seemed to be grinning.

"This country of yours would be fine if the sun shone more," Farinas remarked as they made their way through the line of trees, onto a pathway running along the side of the hill. "The streams and pools are beautiful."

"All the rain makes them so," Ruaraidh pointed out. "Wait until you see it snow-covered, with the sunlight shining on ice sticks hanging from the trees."

Farinas shivered and laughed. "Don't think I'm ready for that."

"Some places seem gloomy, no matter the weather. Farther north, near where I lived, is the place the Romans call Mons Graupius. It's where they massacred us. The only time the tribes joined under one leader, Calgacos to face the Roman army in battle. The very stones seem to carry our sorrow." His mood lifted slightly. "At least it taught us never to fight the Romans that way again."

Farinas remembered his fellow slave and his stories of Caledonia. "Cináed mentioned that."

"What did he say about it."

"He said they didn't talk about it." Farinas laughed. "He was big and bad-tempered. We knew not to mention it again."

Walking was easier on the pathway that seemed to have been made for horses and carts. They stopped to eat the buttered oatcakes, sitting on a rock, and watching the waters tumbling over the pebbles in the stream below.

As they continued their journey, Farinas found himself shivering. He pulled his hood low on his forehead as the wind strengthened and blew icy rain into their faces. "I could do with less rain," Farinas grumbled.

"Aye, well, it's only going to get worse," Ruaraidh warned him as they reached the Three Sisters Dànaidh had told them about, but they hadn't been prepared for their size. "Dànaidh must have thought you looked stronger than you are," Ruaraidh laughed. "Only a god could move these."

They moved out of the shelter of the boulders and Ruaraidh led the way uphill, away from the track. "We start walking north now, uphill into the wind," he warned.

Unable to see much in front of them, they struggled on, battling the wind and rain until Ruaraidh stopped.

"What now?" Farinas asked, hoping they could find shelter and eat, preferably something hot and greasy. He was discovering he wasn't nearly as fit as he thought he was.

"I'm just trying to make sure we haven't strayed east into Venicone lands," Ruaraidh said. "It's probably best we avoid them."

The wind had dropped, but the sun was sinking behind the hills, and it was bitterly cold. Moving was the only thing that helped keep them warm and they were continuing the climb when the sound of voices, low, and muted by distance, carried through the stillness. Remembering Dànaidh's warning about the Venicone, they stopped and listened. The voices were coming from the west and seemed to be heading in their direction.

The Three Sisters would have provided a handy hiding place, but the hillside before them was bare of anything but small rocks, low vegetation, and a few stunted trees. "If they're Venicone, they should keep to the track below us, heading towards the coast," Ruaraidh explained. As the voices grew louder, they scrambled up the hillside hoping to find some cover.

After being brought down again by the tangled heather, Farinas thought the sound of his breathing must be echoing across the hillside. Struggling to his feet, he wondered how long he could keep to the pace set by Ruaraidh. A little further on, Ruaraidh stopped behind a tree, gasping for breath, and Farinas slipped in behind a similar, stunted tree. Neither hid them completely but their lungs were burning, and their legs ached.

Looking out they saw a group of hunters with arrows stuck in their belts. They were carrying bows and each hunter carried his kill, but two were carrying the carcass of a sheep strung on a pole between them. It looked as though they would pass by, lower down the hillside, and Farinas drew back with a sigh of relief, then Ruaraidh tapped his arm and pointed.

"Romans," he whispered.

Farinas peered out from the tree and carefully examined the hunters. In the gathering gloom, it was difficult to make out details, but they seemed to be Caledonii; small and wiry under rough woollen cloaks and leggings, hair and beards blowing wildly in the wind. Alerted by Ruaraidh, however, he examined the two bigger men more carefully. Their clothing was better quality and included Roman military cloaks and boots. Their hair was very short, under close-fitting woollen caps, and they had no facial hair. Instead of the bows and arrows of the tribesmen, they carried *lancea,* light, throwing spears that Farinas had seen the cavalry at Trimontium using.

This was more serious than a group of weary hunters returning home.

Chapter 31

As Farinas shifted position, he startled a small, ground-nesting bird, that flew out from among a group of rocks near his feet, and its cry alerted the hunters. Farinas knew the Romans would be raising their spears, and the tribesmen knocking arrows, ready to take down their prey.

There was a moment when the hunters hesitated, seeing the men, then Ruaraidh took off up the hill. "Run!" he roared, but Farinas was already close behind him, trying to dodge between the few small trees there were, hoping the failing light would spoil the hunters' aim.

They could hear the arrows and spears, but the hunters had aimed for the bird, before registering Farinas and Ruaraidh, so they fell in a cluster behind them. The hunters could either aim again or give chase.

"The village can't be far away." Ruaraidh panted. "Unless we lost our way."

"You go on," Farinas said. "No point in us both being caught." Ruaraidh hesitated. "Go on! Find your people."

"I'll wait for you, so you better keep up, Old Man." Ruaraidh began to run, as the voices came nearer, and Farinas followed him, determined not to hold the lad back.

Then, as they neared the top of the hill, a lone figure appeared, riding a small hill pony. His cloak covered himself and much of the pony and they were so still, they seemed part of the landscape. The rider turned and signalled, and two more riders appeared, similarly cloaked, followed by a band of riders. They spread out on the hilltop, gazing down on the hunters and their prey.

Farinas followed Ruaraidh, not knowing if they were being driven into a trap. He tried to move his cloak to ensure he could easily free his knife from its sheath, but it was impossible to move the sodden material and continue climbing, so he gave up. He'd think about fighting later when he was warm and dry.

Ruaraidh called out to the riders, but they made no reply. Under their cloaks, they seemed slim but well-muscled. They had the pale skin of the Caledonii and long hair and beards. Still and silent against the lowering sky, they reminded Farinas of scenes of barbarians painted on Roman frescoes. These were the men so feared by the mighty Romans.

Ruaraidh called out again, as they came closer and the rider in the middle replied. "Come on!" Ruaraidh called, as the riders moved apart, allowing them to stumble through between them. The line of horses closed again, still making no sound but continuing to face the hunters, whose voices rose in a defiant bellow, followed by silence.

Farinas collapsed behind the line of ponies. "What's happening?"

"These are Vacomagi," Ruaraidh told him. "The hunters are Venicone. They've collected their spears and arrows and left."

"Just as well," Farinas said. "I couldn't run up hill any more. I was getting ready to charge them."

Ruaraidh laughed. "Me too." He became serious as he continued. "That sheep they killed, do you think it was one of Dànaidh's?"

Farinas had wondered the same thing, but he tried to be hopeful. "There must be other sheep in these hills, and he had Faileas for protection."

Before they could say anymore, the riders turned their ponies and headed in single file through the bracken, onto a track heading north. Ruaraidh and Farinas followed, taking care not to get too close to the ponies, as clumps of mud and vegetation were thrown back at them by their hooves, but at least they appeared to be with friends, and safe.

They followed the horses until it became fully dark, and Farinas was wondering how long it would be before he collapsed when they saw lighted torches ahead. Before long a cluster of roundhouses appeared, nestled in the shelter of a rocky crag. They crossed a small stream then passed through a gate in a wooden palisade, with torches on the gate posts.

Inside, the roundhouses looked strong and well-made, and smoke rose from the thickly thatched roofs. Behind the houses, there rose a tall stone tower. It had a sturdy wooden door, but in the flickering torchlight, it was hard to make out details. Those who had gathered to watch their arrival looked curious rather than suspicious or hostile.

"Take care of the ponies!" The leader of the horsemen called, and a group of young people hurried over and led the ponies away. The horsemen dispersed, and the leader led Farinas and Ruaraidh towards a man waiting outside the largest building. This building stood in the middle of the village. The only square building in a village of round houses.

The man was above middle age, but tall and still strong, with long grey hair and a beard. His tunic and leggings were of thick wool, and his cloak was leather, lined with fur. His wide, gold torque was as beautifully decorated as Farinas's armband, but in the style favoured by the Caledonii, having patterns and designs but no figures. He was very obviously a person of authority, surely the headman.

Farinas was impressed by their security. The riders had been dispatched quickly to deal with strangers on their land.

He tried to keep his gaze fixed on the headman, but it was drawn to the warrior at his side. Tall and with the pale complexion of the Caledonii, she was beautiful by any standards, but her glorious russet hair arranged in thick glossy braids, and startlingly green eyes, were what drew his attention. That and the long sword with a carved, horn pommel, hanging in its scabbard from a chain link belt at her waist.

There had always been tales of the Caledonii women among the legions. They were known to be as aggressive and dangerous as the men, and there was no doubt, this was such a warrior. As they approached, she took a step forward and hefted the sword with the familiarity of a seasoned combatant. Farinas smiled, truly the women of the Caledonii were extraordinary, as well as beautiful.

Ruaraidh it was, that brought him out of his wonderment with an elbow in his ribs, and Farinas quickly returned his gaze to the headman, who was openly amused by his attraction to the woman. "Welcome, strangers. If you come in peace."

Farinas realised Ruaraidh was not having to translate for him, as he had expected, this far north. They were speaking the language developed by locals and legionaries throughout the empire. It was similar enough to the language spoken in the taverns and shops of Trimontium, that Farinas could understand most of what was being said. He had been surprised to see any

Romans this far north, but these people had clearly had dealings with them over many years, possibly through trading.

"We thank you for your welcome," Ruaraidh replied, "and wish only peace and prosperity on you and your people."

"You have travelled far?"

"From the town of Trimontium."

"A long journey." He showed no surprise at the information, appearing to recognise the name of the town, although it was so far to the south.

Ruaraidh added. "I am Ruaraidh, my mother was Flòraidh of the Taexali. My father was Fearghas, and my foster father was Horus... both Vacomagi, from a village farther north —"

"Your foster father," the headman thought for a moment then asked, "did he breed hounds?"

Ruaraidh nodded. "Aye, my lord. I went with him to Trimontium to sell a litter... While there, I was sold to the gladiator school."

The headman nodded, then turned his attention to Farinas.

"My name is Farinas from Theveste in Tripolitania, by way of Gaul and Trimontium."

While they were speaking, a woman, much younger than the headman, more of an age with the warrior woman, came from the house. She spoke quietly as though fearful of interrupting. "The food is ready, my lord." She was small and slight, with long fair hair and deep blue, almost violet eyes, she could be considered beautiful, Farinas thought, but she lacked the spirit of the warrior woman.

The headman nodded dismissively. "Aye Eithrig, we will question our visitors first. See to the food." He led the way into the building, as the young woman entered one of the roundhouses.

The heat inside was welcome, and they hung their heavy cloaks on pegs on the walls, then sat at a long table set up on a dais at the top of the room, opposite the door. To the side of the dais, a haunch of meat was cooking, and Farinas found himself changing his view of these wild barbarians. So far, they appeared civilised and hospitable, though he had no doubt of their prowess in battle.

As well as the leader of the horsemen, the headman and the warrior woman, a man with long white hair and beard, most certainly a druid, was sitting waiting. Hanging from his leather belt was a knife in a bronze sheath, and pouches to hold his magical powders and herbs. His staff, carved with druidic symbols and topped with a silver acorn, stood against the wall behind him. Here it appeared, druids were more openly recognised than in the south, where Old Eithni had worked mostly by candlelight, or firelight in woodland groves outside the settlement, and the word, 'druid' was never mentioned.

They sat and beer was poured, as the headman continued the questioning. "These men…were they hunting you?"

Farinas was content to slake his thirst and let Ruaraidh answer. Ruaraidh shook his head. "No, my lord. They came upon us by chance. They looked to have been returning from a hunting expedition."

"What do you think, Corentyn?" The headman turned to the leader of the horsemen who nodded.

"Aye, so it seemed. They were Venicone with two others who looked to be auxiliaries. They wouldn't have noticed these two if they hadn't startled a bird out of cover."

"So, there's no danger?"

"Shouldn't think so, but I'll set extra lookouts."

The headman nodded. "Send in the unit commanders."

"Aye." Corentyn got up and went outside. Servers took the meat away and Farinas hoped they would soon bring it back to the table. As they waited, a man and a woman came in and joined them at the top table. They helped themselves from the jug of beer as the headman introduced himself and the others at the table.

"I am Laeomann, *ceann-cinnidh,* or headman of this village. Corentyn who has just left, looks after our security. My daughter Keitha, and Cairistìona, are unit commanders along with my son, who's out guarding the pass. Torcadall leads the spears. We are Vacomagi and Quistaghyn is our druid. He is our wise man, and he deals with matters concerning the Otherworld, and its effect on us."

As each was named, he or she nodded, and Farinas realised the beautiful young warrior was the headman's daughter. There was an element of suspicion and wariness in the looks the warriors gave the strangers, as was to be expected. In the silence that followed, Farinas raised an issue that had been concerning him. "We didn't expect to see legionaries, this far north."

It was Quistaghyn who answered, and he seemed well-versed in the history of their land and the Roman occupation. "Romans recently set up a temporary camp at Carpow, above Uisge Dhè, where the River Earn meets the Tay. It's on Venicone land and there's a harbour close by where Rome has berthed ships in the past. There's a Venicone village, named Clatchard on a hill near the harbour. The Old Ones lived there many years ago and some Venicone have built a village on the ruins."

Laeomann was nodding. "Aye," he agreed. "The hunters will have come from around the south, with auxiliaries from the camp at Carpow."

"The Romans haven't bothered us for a long time, but if there's trouble, they're a bit too close, so we set extra guards and keep alert," Cairistìona added.

"We're always on our guard." The way Keitha added this information, it sounded like a warning, but the meat was brought in on large platters with slabs of bread, and conversation stopped as everyone helped themselves to hot greasy, delicious food.

The meeting hall was bigger than the village roundhouses and because it was square, unlike the other houses, the chief and his advisers sat on a dais in front of benches where, Farinas thought, villagers would sit in meetings and maybe at social gatherings. There was none of the clean marble and plaster he'd become used to. The walls were rough wood and clay, and the floor was beaten earth. The smoke from the fire rose and spread through the thatched roof.

"The smoke kills bugs and beasties that might live in the thatch." Cairistìona had been watching him, in a way he was used to. He had seen the same look on the faces of his many female admirers in Trimontium.

He smiled at her. "I'm glad of its heat. I'm not used to the cold here."

"Cold! Wait 'till it snows," Torcadall roared. "Your piss will freeze hard, as soon it hits the air."

"Told you," Ruaraidh laughed. "This isn't cold."

"Aye, so everyone keeps telling me," Farinas smiled, appreciating the growing feeling of acceptance from the company.

"You're from Caledonia, aren't you?" Cairistìona asked Ruaraidh.

"Aye, I'm Vacomagi too, but from further north."

"His foster father was Horus. He went from village to village selling his hounds," Laeomann explained.

"I remember," Torcadall said. "Some of our hounds are from his litters, good strong beasts they are."

"Do you know what happened to him?" Ruaraidh asked, and there was some discussion, but no one really knew, just that he'd stopped coming to the village.

"You'll not be from round here," Torcadall said to Farinas.

"I expect you can tell by my curly hair." This raised a laugh and Farinas continued. "No, I'm from Africa Proconsularis, a long way from here, across land and seas."

As they finished eating, the platters were cleared away and Farinas realised that others had been coming in to sit in the main part of the hall. They looked like warriors, fit men, and women, from youths to much older veterans. They were relaxed, talking quietly together, and many had brought mugs of beer, but mostly they were studying Farinas.

Farinas decided there was nothing aggressive, or even suspicious in the glances cast his way. Black skin and hair were bound to be a source of curiosity, in a land of milk-coloured, generally red- or fair-haired people. He prepared for questions although, so far, the courtesy shown to guests seemed to be keeping the villagers' curiosity at bay.

Then a voice called from the hall. "You look like a Roman officer." Farinas heard Ruaraidh draw in a breath, but he smiled and prepared to tell his tale, or at least as much of it as was relevant, and hoped he would be accepted.

Chapter 32

"I'm not Roman," Farinas began, "although I was born in Theveste, a Roman garrison town far across the seas, in a place the Romans call Africa Proconsularis. My people, the Imazighen call it Alkebu-lan. In my country, the sun is a red-hot ball in a blue sky…warming the land…every day. Here, I've almost forgotten what it looks like." He paused for laughter then continued.

"I am named for one of our great heroes, Tikfarin. The Romans named him Tacfarinas. He had been an auxiliary, but returned to the desert and led a rebellion against the Romans, using tactics learned from them, long before I was born. My uncles and I carried on this rebellion, fighting the Romans from our desert home. During a great battle to seize a wagon load of Roman gold, they were killed, and I was wounded and captured."

There was a stirring of interest and Farinas paused, ignoring Ruaraidh's knowing smile. He *would* have fought in great battles against the Romans if he hadn't been captured first. He took a drink and felt the audience's interest rising.

"I was sold to the owner of a gladiator school at Trimontium, another Roman garrison town. For the last ten years, I fought in the arena, as Leo Africanus." He paused and looked for any signs of recognition, but apparently, his fame hadn't spread that far north. He was pleased, however, to observe a definite look of interest in Keitha's eyes, as she raised her head to examine him, or perhaps, like Criosaidh, she was thinking he didn't look much like a gladiator.

"So, why did you leave?" a voice called out.

"Things changed. The crowd wanted killings, blood, not skill. I had to fight a comrade…to the death." He stopped, remembering brief moments of the last fight with Videric. He finished that part of his tale quickly and with a minimum of detail. When he paused for breath, someone at the table refilled his cup and handed it to him. He drained it and continued.

"After that, I found it hard to fight and kill, just to please folk who would turn on me, when they found another favourite."

A voice broke the silence that followed. "What did you do?"

"As soon as I recovered from near-fatal injuries, I drank…a lot." There were cheers and mugs were banged on tables. When there was silence, he carried on. "I was no use to anyone, but Ruaraidh here kept me right. He'd wake me in the morning with a kind word…and a bucket of freezing water, so I would be in time for morning training sessions."

There was more laughter, and then Farinas became serious. "You'll know that Caledonii raiding parties attacked the Great Wall, killing the Roman Governor and many of the soldiers." There were nods at this, and he wondered if any from here had taken part in that raid.

"Ruaraidh knew the Romans, including those at Trimontium, would be out for revenge. He left the gladiator school before the great doors were locked, to return to his home here. Finding me asleep at the door of the tavern, he invited me along. We had a minor disagreement with two soldiers who were determined to take us to the fort in chains. Swords were drawn. Blood was spilt…not ours," he added to more laughter and cheers.

"A local druidess helped us evade the soldiers and get out of the settlement and we made our way north. We've fought our way through lawless lands, battled brigands, sailed on a moonlit river, and climbed the highest, craggiest mountains I've ever seen to reach the beautiful land, Ruaraidh often spoke of."

He paused for effect, then continued. "I've never been so bloody cold and wet in my life, climbed so many inhospitable, dangerous mountains or been bitten by so many nasty flying creatures." He waited for the laughter to die down. "But we have been welcomed and fed wonderful food everywhere on our journey… and the women we have encountered, have been very beautiful."

There were more cheers, and the audience appeared to have enjoyed his tale. As he sat down, he glanced at the headman's beautiful young daughter, who looked even less impressed than she had before.

"You're a fighter, then?" Cairistìona asked, and Farinas recognised the spark of interest in her eyes. She was slight but muscled in a way the southern women hadn't been. Her skin was light, and her fair hair shone in the firelight. Her inviting glances would have sparked a similar interest in Farinas, had the red-haired Keith not been sitting nearby.

He smiled at the young woman and answered her question. "I fought in the arena, which is not the same as fighting in battle. We fought against selected opponents, and usually one-on-one, although not always."

"What weapon did you fight with?" Torcadall asked and seemed disappointed when Farinas told him his weapon had been a sword. "Pity," he answered. "We can always do with another spear."

"Maybe we should see how he does in a real fight." Keitha spoke sharply, and Farinas chose to think she was showing a spark of jealousy. Cairistìona smirked and the conversation was interrupted when Corentyn returned and reported all well with the sentries.

"How about you, Ruaraidh?" Torcadall asked. "What were you training with?"

"Sorry," Ruaraidh smiled. "I hadn't been training for long, and only with wooden practice swords."

"You are welcome to remain here." Farinas realised Quistaghyn had stood up. The only interest he had shown, had been at the mention of the druidess, but now he was talking, and the hall was silent. "We are at peace with our neighbours and hope it will remain that way, but we can always use strong willing workers. You are welcome." He bowed solemnly and sat down.

"We could use another spear, should you decide to change weapons!" Torcadall called out. "We're always preparing for the next fight."

"I can always do with another straight, strong weapon in my unit," Cairistìona shouted over the laughter, then smirked suggestively at Keitha, who got up and walked out of the hall.

"I think she likes you," Ruaraidh whispered to Farinas.

"I know," Farinas said, "but it's the red-haired one I like, Keitha."

"That's who I'm talking about." Ruaraidh slapped Farinas on the shoulder and laughed at his puzzled expression.

The atmosphere lightened after the questioning, and Farinas relaxed and joined in the drinking, but he had become used to waking with a clear head and drank sparingly.

When Keitha returned, he frequently caught her glancing his way, but couldn't tell if this was caused by attraction or suspicion. Back at the taverns in Trimontium, he would have had no doubts, but it seemed that not all Caledonii women were impressed by a famous black gladiator.

Ruaraidh was approached by a few people who remembered his foster father and his hounds, and Farinas was happy the lad had been accepted so readily back into the tribe.

During the evening, Farinas was approached by Corentyn who looked almost as out of place as he did. He was less robust and smaller than the others. His eyes were dark brown, in striking contrast to his thick curly hair, which was so fair, as to be almost white.

"Are you sure you weren't followed or tracked here? The Romans aren't known for allowing runaway slaves to stay free for long."

Farinas thought about that, and about the soldiers they'd seen with the hunters. "I'm sure we weren't. I'm a free man." He took his *rudis* from his pouch and showed it to Corentyn. "This will prove it to any Roman."

Corentyn nodded. "I came from Cornouia in the south. I recognise the symbol of a *rudiarius* but what about Ruaraidh?"

"Caelus Gallio Flavius, the owner of the Gladiator School, is a fair man." Farinas thought back to his last meeting with Flavius. "He knew Ruaraidh was from the north, and he would have understood our reasons for leaving. He would not have reported him."

"And you saw no sign of pursuit from the fort?" Corentyn continued. "You did spill Roman blood," he reminded him.

Farinas had wondered about this, but he told him what he believed. "We headed west, as the druidess advised, and stayed off the Roman Road. The Romans had more to concern themselves with, than us." He smiled and answered truthfully. "It wasn't really a fight. The auxiliary kind of fell on his sword…he was barely injured, and it wasn't something he'd want to boast about."

Corentyn smiled. "When I ran from Roman rule in the south, I found a home here where I don't need to answer to Rome. I look out for the village's safety." He returned to the information

Farinas had given him. "You probably weren't followed this far north, but I've posted extra guards, just to be sure."

That night, after Laeomann and his advisors left, and others still sat drinking, Ruaraidh stopped on his way out, to talk to Farinas. "There's an old couple living in the village who knew my father. They've asked me to live with them to help with their beasts." He looked worried, and Farinas realised the lad felt responsible for him.

He was quick to reassure him. "I'm pleased, Ruaraidh. I'm fine here." Ruaraidh left, smiling, and Farinas thought about what he had said. He did feel comfortable in the company of the Caledonii, finding them not much different to the gladiators he'd just left. Not so well dressed perhaps, although their weapons, their gold and gemstone jewellery, and their hospitality were a match for any he'd seen in the south. He felt he could fit in.

While others still drank, he wrapped himself in his cloak and lay against the back wall. Lulled by the voices and warmed by the fire, he fell asleep feeling more secure than he had since leaving Trimontium.

Once again though, his sleep would be interrupted.

Chapter 33

Farinas had no idea how long he'd been sleeping when there was a sudden loud banging and shouting outside. The excited baying and barking of the hounds added to the confusion, and Farinas sat up to see others who had slept there, men and women, staggering to their feet, anxiously reaching for weapons.

The door was thrown open, crashing against the wall, and a warrior stood, framed in the doorway, with hair blowing wildly in the wind, making an image to terrify anyone.

"Where is he?" The voice was loud and rough, and Farinas hoped whoever he was looking for, was safe elsewhere. The hounds had lain down again, apparently recognising the newcomer, and realising he was no threat.

The bellowing voice matched the image framed in the doorway. "Come out, Leo Africanus!"

Farinas felt sudden panic. Had someone followed him from Trimontium? How had they got past the guards?

All around, men and women were grumbling and settling back down. Like the hounds, they clearly recognised the voice and were happy to know they weren't the target.

"Farinas," the voice roared. "Come out into the moonlight so I can see you." It ended with a roar of laughter, and Farinas stumbled to the doorway. "You've grown," the huge warrior roared, and Farinas found himself staring into deep blue eyes, in a pale face surrounded by long red hair.

It was the grin that stirred his memory. During the hardest times on their journey, Cináed's grin, because it was so rare, cheered them up. Now the mouth was surrounded by a thick beard and moustache. The red-haired barbarian seized him and crushed him to his chest.

"Cináed, you'll break my bones!" Cináed released him and stood back laughing. "You escaped from the sea!" Farinas gasped.

"Aye, I did! The pirates —" Cináed's account was interrupted when the man nearest the door kicked it, sending it crashing into

Farinas's back with a solid thump. "Have your reunion somewhere else, Cináed. We're trying to sleep."

Cináed kicked the door back then drew Farinas outside and they walked a little way in the moonlight.

"Corentyn's had me out watchin' the pass into the village. Our relief told us about a gladiator from Trimontium. I wondered how many black gladiators there could be and decided it had to be my old friend." He examined him and grinned again. "Leo Africanus! You're no' a boy though."

"I always hoped you'd escaped," Farinas told him. "It didn't seem possible."

"The pirates pulled me out of the sea, and we managed to get their ship back to land. I just travelled north from there. The man sent to relieve me on sentry duty, told me your story...." he hesitated. "Videric was it?"

Farinas nodded, unable to talk about it.

"An' the Romans call us barbaric…" Cináed muttered.

"It's good to see you," Farinas told him. "You've grown too."

A figure appeared from one of the roundhouses, "You're wanted, Cináed. Get your arse in here."

"We'll drink to our survival soon, but I've to go and report." He clapped Farinas on the shoulder and walked off. Farinas crawled back under his cloak, hoping for dreams of red-haired maids and warm sunshine, not pirates and stormy seas, or dying friends.

When he woke again, the fire flickered low in the hearth, and the air was thick with smoke and the smells from bodies, lightly pickled in mead and ale. The three large hunting dogs lying by the door also added their aromas to the mix. Farinas wasn't troubled by the rich mix of smells; he'd experienced worse. He was however concerned about one smell, his own. He'd become used to being cleaned, oiled, and perfumed in the marble bathhouse at the gladiator school. Here there was no evidence of any bathing facilities, although everyone had seemed clean enough.

He got up quietly, grabbed his pack, crossed to the door, and opened it. The sun had yet to rise above the snow-capped mountain peaks, and a cold wind brought fresh smells of frosted heather and gorse. He wondered if he'd ever get used to such changing weather. Leaving his heavy cloak to dry, he took his lined cloak and slipped outside.

He breathed in the crisp, fresh air and looked around. Some animals were penned up, while others grazed on the hillside. A young lad, perched on a rocky outcrop, was keeping watch over the animals and the approach to the village. Behind the settlement, towering over everything, was the tall stone tower-like structure that he had seen the night before. It dominated the landscape and looked impregnable.

Carrying his pack, Farinas went through the gates, nodding to the guard, and followed the stream downhill from the settlement until he reached a place where a rough barrier of rocks formed a pool of crystal-clear water. The pool was in a small valley, and the tree-lined sides, sloping gently on either side, sheltered it from view.

He almost turned back, remembering Ruaraidh telling him the water in these streams was melted snow, but surrounded by the stale odour of his body, he decided he'd better get used to the cold.

He wiped the armband and carefully wrapped it in his cloak, then removed his sweat-stained clothing, rolled it up and put it in his pack to deal with later, when it was warmer perhaps.

He oiled his body and scraped away as much of the dirt as he could. A skilful slave would have done so much better. He shaved his face, fearing a serious injury as the razor shook in his trembling hand then, after soaping himself, he plunged into the water, roaring as he came up into the frosty air. Swimming took a little of the bone-numbing chill away, but the pool was too small to allow a decent swim, so he quickly made his way out and grabbed the rough towel.

Standing in a patch of sunlight trying to rub some heat into his frozen body, he heard smothered laughter and saw a group of young women, including Cairistìona, carrying baskets of clothes, coming to the pool. They were openly eyeing his naked body and calling out comments in their own tongue. It was clear from the laughter and hand gestures, that the comments were complimentary.

Farinas was used to such attention from the arena, although he had never been fully naked there, and he responded to the admiration as he always did, smiling and bowing, before dressing in clean clothes. He fastened the belt, adjusted the dagger, and pushed the armband, wrapped in the towel, into his pack.

With a dramatic flourish, he threw his cloak back over one shoulder, picked up his pack and left, smiling broadly as he passed the young women. He was disappointed not to see the green-eyed maid, Keitha.

Once out of sight of the women, he slid the armband back on his arm and pulled the sleeve of the tunic down. The armband had become his talisman and his connection to Videric, making him feel as if his old friend and mentor was with him, sharing his experiences. Without it, his arm felt bare.

As he neared the settlement, an arrow whistled past his head, sending him diving into the bushes beside the path. Peering out, he saw the arrow pinning a hare to the ground. The laughter this time was less admiring and more mocking, as Keitha casually approached and removed the arrow from the dead animal.

"Did I startle you?" Keitha replaced the arrow in her belt and watched as he untangled himself from the thorns. Before he could respond, an alarm sounded out over the still air, harsh and loud.

"Back to settlement!" Keitha shouted. "Run!"

Chapter 34

Farinas tore free of the briars and followed Keitha. An alarm in any form was not to be ignored, and he realised this was serious. In the village, armed warriors were already answering the call. Keitha grabbed her sword and a pony's reins from a young lad who had served the meal the night before, and joined others, lining up behind Laeomann.

The young women who had been at the pool ran into the roundhouses and reappeared, armed and ready to fight. There was no laughter now. Youths, still too young to be warriors, were harnessing ponies to small lightweight carts. Ruaraidh was among them, but he broke away and ran to join Farinas, as he hurried to the meeting house. There Farinas threw his cloak and pack into a corner. "You can't fight," he told Ruaraidh. "You've no experience."

As they hurried outside, Ruaraidh explained. "I've to stay with the carts. We'll wait until we're needed; to bring back the wounded and—"

Farinas interrupted. "I'll need a sword."

"I'll bring one." Ruaraidh turned and ran.

Beasts were being driven into the broch, the stone tower behind the village. It had great wooden doors, but no windows or arrow slits. A roof covering had been pulled back and already Farinas could see children looking over the parapet at the top. It looked impregnable and provided an excellent watchtower. Chickens scratching in the ground were shooed inside by small children, as they themselves ran inside. Any boar near the roundhouses were being driven into the woods.

Men and women too old to fight, and those who were ill or infirm were slowly climbing stairs inside. These led to the top of the structure where they, and the babies and young children would be looked after. An elderly woman was standing outside, gathering the people in. Farinas saw the timid young woman, Eithrig, with an older woman carrying a babe, hurry into the broch. Eithrig appeared to be the only woman of that age, not preparing to fight.

Lookouts were galloping through the stream and shouting the warning. "Armed men from the south, coming up the glen!"

There had been no panic. Everyone appeared well drilled in what to do, and they did it without fuss. As those remaining behind made their way into the broch, the others lined up in front of the carts.

"Who's attacking?" Farinas asked one of the men, as they ran to line up.

He shrugged. "No clan banners, but there's two Venicone villages in the south. A friend would have sent riders on to alert us, especially as it's still near dark," he explained. "You fighting?" he asked.

Farinas nodded. He hadn't given it much thought, but he knew he couldn't stay behind sheltering in the broch. Ruaraidh joined him with a sword. He had chosen well. The sword, a Roman *gladius*, felt well-balanced and settled easily into his grip.

The weapons he could see were mainly swords and a few battle axes. They all looked to be in good condition. One unit of men and women carried spears. Farinas had refused a shield. He wasn't sure how he would manage with an unfamiliar sword and shield, in this type of fighting. He felt comfortable with the sword and the shorter dagger he wore on his belt. Some of the Vacomagi carried rectangular shields with bronze bosses and tribal designs, and others fought without shields, like Farinas.

Standing waiting for the signal to move out, Farinas noticed the small group of riders at the head of the column. They were the men and women he'd met the night before; Laeomann and his daughter, Keitha, and the unit commanders. Quistaghyn and Corentyn were also mounted and waiting with them.

As the column shifted and formed, Farinas stood at the back with Ruaraidh, then the riders moved out, followed by the foot soldiers with the carts bringing up the rear. Just then a rider rode along the column and joined the group at the front.

"What's Cináed doing?" Farinas asked.

Ruaraidh looked puzzled. "He's Laeomann's oldest son, Keitha's brother. Didn't you know?" Farinas shook his head, but he realised Cináed hadn't been lying when he'd said he was a kind of prince in his own land.

Ruaraidh continued. "Laeomann's woman, the mother of Cináed and Keitha, died after Cináed was captured. Laeomann took two other women after that, but both died before giving him any children. I suppose he wanted more children, in case Cináed never came back, or something happened to Keitha."

Farinas realised why the young woman, Eithrig had stayed behind in the broch. "The young woman with the baby?"

Ruaraidh nodded. "The Lady Eithrig. She's from the Votadini tribe. I expect he thought he'd have more luck with a younger woman…and maybe one not of our blood. They have a son."

They were talking to hide their nervousness, but silence fell as the column stopped its slow move down the glen and a discussion took place at the front, presumably about where the encounter would take place, and where best to draw up the battle lines.

Suddenly, with none of the warnings and posturing that usually heralded a tribal battle, a horde of tribesmen charged out of the tree line on their right. Screaming battle cries and waving swords and axes, they gave Laeomann and his advisers no time to plan tactics or organise formations.

Ruaraidh and others of his age hurriedly grabbed the horses' reins and led them back to the waiting carts, as the riders dismounted and faced the enemy. Laeomann's force hastily formed ragged lines, and, with no further warning or command, Farinas was caught in an uphill scramble towards the enemy.

Despite the surprise attack, there was a discipline, similar to that shown at the settlement. Everyone knew his or her position in the lines. Farinas followed the man beside him who was also armed with a sword, as Torcadall's spearmen led the charge.

The sound of clashing steel let them know the leading forces had engaged, then the enemy streamed through the gaps in the lines, and they were in the midst of a brutal fight for their lives.

The men beside Farinas hacked their way back to the rear of the column and formed a defensive line in front of the carts, preventing the Venicone from getting behind, and surrounding them. Farinas went with them, with no real sense of how the battle was going. Deafened by the roars of battle cries and the clash of weapons, he found himself engaged in hand-to-hand fighting like nothing he'd ever known. With no time to employ the tactics he'd used in the arena, he hacked and thrust, depending on brute force rather than skill and expertise, trying to survive.

Realising how difficult it was for him to distinguish friend from enemy, he concentrated on fighting off his attackers. He stood out enough for the Vacomagi to recognise him and for the enemy to target him. The noise of weapons clashing, screams and roars of men, and the general confusion, was something Farinas had never experienced before. He recognised that this was not his type of fight, and he was beginning to panic when a voice cut through the sounds of battle.

"Leo Africanus!"

Farinas sensed rather than saw Cináed, fighting his way through the battling tribesmen to take up a position behind him. "Don't let the bastards get past!" he roared, strengthening the resolve of those around them. Back-to-back they fought, then Cináed roared his battle cry.

"*Buaidh no Bàs!*" (Victory or Death!)

Despite the horror surrounding him, Farinas felt his strength returning, knowing his back was covered. Remembering something one of his fellow gladiators had often declaimed in the amphitheatre, he found his voice and roared,

"*Ego sum mortiferer!*" (I am the destroyer)

It was only after the battle he appreciated that screaming in Latin may not have been advisable. In the heat of the battle, however, it served to raise his spirits. He heard Cináed's roar of laughter, then together they repeated the Roman battle cry.

Sometime later, there was a shift in the battle, a sense that something had changed. The attack seemed to have slackened, and Farinas dashed the sweat from his eyes and looked up, as a hush came over the battlefield. Farinas watched as the woman who had been standing at the doors of the broch, rode past the carts and into the middle of the battle. Wielding a sword, she fought her way to Laeomann, screaming his name. The two came together, as a group of Vacomagi formed a defensive barrier, and the woman passed on her news then slid down from the pony.

Laeomann grabbed the reins and mounted the pony. He gave a signal, and a unit of warriors broke away and followed him to the waiting ponies and carts. The ones in front mounted the loose ponies, the others got into two carts, and they followed Laeomann back towards the village. As a significant part of the Vacomagi force left, the fighting carried on with renewed energy.

The woman who had brought the message to Laeomann now stood in his place with drawn sword, and Farinas saw Keitha, bloodied but seemingly unhurt, move to stand and fight beside her.

Farinas had no idea of time, but as the sun rose in the sky, he knew he'd never fought so long and so hard. The contests in the arena had been short with rest periods between. This was relentless, and as the ground underfoot became mired in blood, he sensed the tide of battle moving against the depleted Vacomagi force. Bloodied and exhausted, still they struggled on. When he stumbled and had to be pulled to his feet by Cináed, he knew he was not going to survive many more onslaughts.

His vision was blurred by sweat, and he could feel blood from a glancing blow to his head running down his back. His arms ached from slashing and stabbing with a sword that felt heavier each time he raised it, and his legs trembled so badly he knew he would soon fall and be unable to get to his feet.

Cináed, sensing his weakened state, tried to encourage him. "We're beatin' the bastards, Farinas. Stay strong!" Then he was twisting away, slashing at a screaming enemy who fell face down in the mud.

Suddenly, in the midst of the carnage, a horn sounded. Not the alarm Farinas had heard earlier, but a deeper longer note. The enemy horn blower, stationed high on the hill above the battleground, repeated the call, and the enemy began to withdraw. The Vacomagi gathered their strength for a final push, and soon the enemy force was in full flight.

"Look!" The cries alerted everyone to the sight of Laeomann's force returning. When the enemy commander had seen the force returning, he had sounded the retreat.

"What's happening?" Farinas asked Cináed.

"The treacherous bastards! They must have sent a force through the village to attack us from the rear. Now the Venicone have seen our unit returning, they know there's no reinforcements coming."

Afraid to relax completely, they watched as the two Vacomagi groups came together, but it was soon obvious that something was wrong. In the hush that hung over the scene of carnage, Keitha's scream of anger and loss chilled everyone.

"Laeomann's missing," Cináed muttered, then he was running, pushing past others, as the cry rose above the battlefield.

"Laeomann's dead."

Farinas gazed over the scene. He had fought and killed, but never like this. There were so many bodies, so many injured and so much blood and gore. Listening to the cries of agony, he found himself trembling and he sank to his knees in the blood-soaked mud.

Chapter 35

Farinas knelt in the mire, thanking the gods for his survival. Others were beginning to come back from their battle lust and were desperately searching for family and friends. The enemy tribesmen were disregarded at this point; their cries for mercy ignored.

A young woman Farinas recognised from the pool, was struggling to assist an older man to his feet. He was bleeding from a sword slash to his thigh, and blood was streaming down the woman's arm from a gash in her shoulder. Farinas got to his feet, stuck the sword in his belt and went to help. They joined those taking the wounded to the carts, now drawn up as close as possible to the battlefield. When each cart was loaded, it was driven back to the village. No one knew exactly what had happened, only that Laeomann had been killed fighting a rear-guard action.

As the carts left with the wounded, the dead were being laid out for their last journey home. The unit leaders had mounted, ready to move out and Corentyn was talking with Keitha and Cináed. Carrion crows, hawks, and buzzards circling overhead added their shrill screeches to the sounds of the dying.

The stench was much worse than any Farinas had noticed in the arena, where blood and body fluids soaked into the sand to be raked over between contests. Here it was almost a physical thing, catching in his throat and choking him. In the midst of it all, he looked for Ruaraidh and sighed with relief as he saw him helping to load the injured into the carts.

Eventually, when the Vacomagi were accounted for, and the uninjured and walking wounded were gathered beside the unit leaders, Cináed rode slightly ahead of the mounted group and faced them.

"The bastards attacked with no warning. They killed Laeomann in a cowardly attack from the rear. That is not our way!" There was a roar of anger that seemed to silence even the birds, then his voice carried through the stillness. "Kill the treacherous whoresons! All of them!" No one moved. This was not their way either, but Cináed dismounted. "They killed Laeomann!" Heads were bowed in sorrow, but still, no one moved but Quistaghyn.

He moved away from the body he had been administering to and raised his voice. It carried clearly to everyone, and they listened. "We are few in number. If we are to face Rome, we cannot be massacring each other. Let them come for their dead and wounded. That has always been our way." He placed his hand on Cináed's arm. "It is what he would have done."

Cináed slowly calmed and gave a brief nod. "Bring one back to be questioned," he ordered, and Corentyn seized a young Venicone warrior, slumped in the mud but conscious and not badly injured. He bundled him into a cart and ordered it back to the village.

Farinas had expected a slaughter. Living with his uncles and then the Romans for so long, he accepted killing as part of the struggle, but he could see the sense of saving lives...if they would come together to fight the Romans. He helped load the dead and wounded, then the foot soldiers marched back. As they approached the village, a flock of black birds circled above, a portent of even more bloodshed and death.

Inside the village, older folk who hadn't fought were looking after those returning, exhausted, bruised and battered. The seriously hurt were in the broch being tended to, and the youngsters were caring for the ponies. Above it all, was the sound of quiet weeping and stifled sobs.

Farinas and Ruaraidh went to find Bearnais and Artair, the couple who had taken Ruaraidh into their home. They were tending the minor wounds of neighbours, returning from the battle. Artair handed them mugs of ale.

"This is Farinas, the gladiator who came with me from Trimontium," Ruaraidh said.

"Just as well you told us," the old man muttered. "We'd no' ha' known otherwise.

There were some smiles and Bearnais glared at her husband, who grinned back at her. "Go on wi' you, Old Man, bring me some hot water. The gladiator looks hurt."

Despite his protests, she bathed his head wound which had stopped bleeding, then gently removed his tunic, revealing a sword slash across his back. "It's no' deep but it could putrefy," she said as she cleaned it with wine and water, then placed a wad of moss over the wound and secured it in place with strips of cloth.

"What happened here, Artair?" The young lad who'd spoken had a bandage around his head but looked well recovered from his injury.

Artair settled down with a mug of ale to tell his tale, and Ruaraidh translated where necessary, for Farinas.

"Well, they treacherous whoresons, were gonnae storm through here and take you lot from the rear," the old man explained. "But our young un's were keepin' watch from the top of the broch an' saw them coming. Mistress Foirbeis who was in charge of the broch, rode off to warn Laeomann." His voice broke here and Bearnais took up the tale.

"Old Mother MacRiada led those of us that were able —"

"An' willin'," Artair interrupted.

"Aye, an' willing," she nodded. "She led us up the hillside above the entrance to the glen, an' we rolled big boulders down on them."

"We held them up, 'til Laeomann and his unit got here," the old man continued. "But we had to watch those *luchd-brathaidh* kill Laeomann."

Laeomann leading the frontal assault had been an easy target for the Venicone spearmen. The villagers watching from the hillside had seen the spear lodge in his chest. Their cries of anguish were the last sounds he heard. Laeomann's men had attacked the remainder of the badly disorganized band with ferocity and savagery, fuelled by grief and a desire for revenge.

"When Laeomann's unit came back to the battleground, the enemy knew their reinforcements wouldn't be coming," Ruaraidh told them. "They ran away."

"Aye. We knew they wir cowards, attacking wi' no warning, then coming through to attack from the other side. That's no' how we fight." The old man shook his head in disgust at the thought of the enemies' treachery. There were conventions and they were usually adhered to by the local tribes. He got up and others moved away to help with whatever needed doing in the village.

Ruaraidh got up too. "They'll need help building a pyre," he said.

"I'll wash and mend your tunic," Bearnais told Farinas. "Come back for some food later," she called after them.

Farinas went to the meeting house and put on a tunic then joined Ruaraidh, cutting and stacking bracken and heather for the funeral pyre, while others cut peat.

They stopped as Laeomann's body, washed and dressed in fine clothes, was carried out of his roundhouse on a board which was laid across two flat rocks beside the stream.

Two men with drawn swords, positioned themselves at his head and feet, as his family surrounded the body. They remained there for only a short time; there was serious work to be done and preparations to be made. As the family moved away, other families brought their dead out and laid them in front of the *strykin beuird,* bearing the body of their headman.

"The peat will make it burn hot and long." Farinas turned and saw Cináed, standing above him, looking over at the bodies.

"Your father, Cináed, I am truly sorry. He was well loved."

"Aye, he was. He was a great leader. I doubt I'll do so well."

"You'll learn," Farinas said, then remembering the feeling of terror as he fell to his knees during the fighting, knowing he was an easy target, added. "I owe you my life, today."

"You fought well," Cináed acknowledged, then added, with a small smile, "for a gladiator." He threw his arm across Farinas's shoulders. "I'm meeting my unit leaders later, to hear their reports. The prisoner's being questioned. We'll decide what to do when we know more."

When the piles of peat and vegetation were considered high enough, Farinas and Ruaraidh returned to Bearnais and Artair and they sat down to a meal of oats. There hadn't been time for much hunting to restock after the hard winter, but Farinas was glad of what there was. They spoke of the people who had been killed. Bearnais and Artair had known them all, and their parents and often their grandparents. They wondered at the enemy; what tribe they were and why they'd attacked so unexpectedly. The grain store was practically empty, and the beasts were lean with little meat or fat on them. It hadn't been a normal raid.

As they were finishing, a message came for representatives from the families to go to the meeting house. "You go, Ruaraidh," Artair said. "I've heard enough war talk in my lifetime."

Farinas and Ruaraidh went together to the meeting house. The Lady Eithrig, now widowed, sat on the dais, flanked by Cináed and Keitha. Corentyn and the unit heads sat with them. Representatives of each of the families were sitting on benches or standing wherever there was space.

As the meeting house filled up, it was Quistaghyn who stepped forward out of the shadows and walked to the front of the dais. He pounded his staff three times on the floor, but there was no need. A hush had fallen over the room as soon as he appeared.

"Our first business before the gods is to commend the spirit of our headman, Laeomann to them, as he journeys to the Otherworld. With him, we commend the spirits of those who died alongside him today."

He appeared ready to continue but Cináed interrupted him. "Thank you, My Lord Quistaghyn. There will be time to mourn our people when we have avenged their deaths."

This was taken up by a voice from the assembly. "Aye! We're wastin' time talkin'. It's vengeance our dead want, no' words!" There were shouts of approval and it was evident the druid felt that he, or perhaps the gods, had been disrespected. Facing Cináed's anger and grief however, he bowed and retreated to a chair at the side of the dais.

His leaving was barely noticed, as Cináed spoke. "The prisoner has been questioned. He is Tadhg, son of Tàmhas, the headman of Hillfoot, a Venicone village. The attackers were from Hillfoot and Clatchard, two villages southeast of here. They sent envoys to the Roman camp at Carpow, and they've made a treaty with Rome."

There were roars of anger at this news and Cináed waited until it had died down, before continuing. "This attack was their way of persuading the Romans that they would be useful allies."

"That didn't work very well fur them," a voice called out and there were some growls of anger.

"Why go crawling to Rome, now?" another asked, and it was Cináed who answered.

"It has to do with the killing of the Roman Governor, Caerellius Priscus by northern tribesmen, at the Great Wall—"

There was a stirring among those gathered and a voice interrupted. "Aye, we know about that but it's nothing to do wi' us. The legions leave us alone. Have done fur years."

Farinas saw Cináed glance in his direction. He nodded and Farinas joined in the discussion. "That may have been true in the past," he agreed, as the villagers turned to listen to him. "It's different now. When we left Trimontium, Ruaraidh and I, the Romans weren't treating it as an ordinary attack by a few tribesmen. A representative of the emperor was killed. Rome will have no choice but to retaliate. Not to do so would imply weakness and invite further attacks."

"We heard of the fighting," Cináed added. "Some Carvetii came here from Luguvalium, looking for refuge. They'd decided the only way to escape Rome's retaliation was to cross to one of the islands in the north. We sent them on their way with food and warm clothing."

The druid stepped forward. "My information is that the emperor, Commodus, is sending a general to quell, what the Romans are calling an uprising. He has stated his intention to re-occupy the wall built by Antoninus, south of here on Damnonii land. From there he will proceed north. This occupation will be extensive. Reprisals will be brutal."

The druid was indeed well-informed if his information was correct, and Farinas had no reason to doubt it. It certainly caused uproar in the room. Farinas waited until there was silence then added. "In the south, tribes made treaties with Rome and lived in peace with them. Some may seek to do so here, but Rome is vengeful. She only makes peace from a position of strength.... after she has destroyed her enemies. She considers all Caledonii to be her enemies now."

Corentyn added. "The Venicone that attacked us may have thought to win favour with Rome and avoid any involvement in a coming war. They are our concern for now – not Rome."

There were murmurings throughout the room, rising steadily to a demand for vengeance. One old man, whose son had been injured, called out above the mutterings. "If the Venicone get away with this attack, others will try."

Cináed waited for the roars of agreement to stop, then continued. "We lost good warriors today, including Laeomann. Not to exact revenge will show weakness to other tribes, but also to Rome!" He waited for the cheers to die down then continued. "However, we cannot afford more deaths like those of today."

"So! What are we goin' to do?" Cairistìona glared at him. Her brother was lying wounded in the broch. "Just talk?"

"What Cináed said is true. We cannot afford more battles like the last one," Quistaghyn stood and spoke with authority, but even the druid faced opposition.

A warrior with old scars, and a few new ones, jumped to his feet, looked ready to storm out. "So, they get away wi' it? Others'll see us as weak." The speaker was clearly well-respected, and his words were greeted with murmurs of approval. The scars spoke of old battles, and the bloody linen bands wrapped around his head and one of his arms showed he'd fought that day.

Cináed smiled at him but quickly took charge. "Sit down, Goraidh, you'll get your chance to show you're not weak." Cináed knew how his people felt and he knew he had to take charge if he wanted to be accepted as the new headman. He spoke with confidence and silenced the objectors.

"We will take a small warband to attack Hillfoot, the village closest to us. The prisoner has given us some useful information —"

"How do we know he speaks the truth?" a voice called out.

"He spoke the truth…eventually." Quistaghyn spoke quietly, but no one disputed his words or enquired into the manner of the questioning, and Cináed continued.

"We hit Hillfoot hard and fast, in the night. We get out before they can raise the alarm and call on reinforcements from Clatchard."

There was silence as they considered this. "How do we do that?"

"That is what I will decide with the unit commanders and my advisers, but we will only be taking a small force, so tend to your families, eat, rest, and recover from today's battle. It was hard on everyone." He stopped and looked around the gathered villagers, then told them what they needed to hear, from their new headman.

"Our dead will be avenged!"

Chapter 36

Cheers followed this announcement, and the villagers, satisfied with the decision, moved out, as Cináed gathered his commanders and advisers to him.

"Stay, Goraidh." Cináed smiled at the grizzled warrior who'd questioned him. "I'm appointing you, unit commander in my place, now I'm the overall commander." There were pats on the back for Goraidh, who joined the others on the dais, looking pleased but uncomfortable in his new position.

"You too, Farinas," Cináed called. "Your knowledge of Rome could be useful." As Ruaraidh was leaving, Cináed walked over and spoke to him. "You did well today, and Bearnais and Artair are better for you being here." Glowing with pride, Ruaraidh was happy to return home, leaving the advising to Farinas.

The Lady Eithrig remained seated, as though unsure what she should do. She was a sad, lonely figure and Farinas had observed no one approaching her to express sorrow at her husband's death. It did not seem as though they were being cruel. It just seemed as though she was overlooked in all that was happening.

She had said nothing during the meeting and seemed unlikely to add to the coming deliberations, but Cináed addressed her civilly. "Do you wish to say something, my lady?"

Before she could answer, Keitha spoke. "You're not intending to take over in Laeomann's place, are you?" Keitha's sharp tone made it clear what she thought of the idea.

Eithrig shook her head violently. "Of course, I am not." Farinas felt sorry for the young widow, alone in a strange tribe.

"You may go," Cináed told her.

Eithrig's eyes shone, and a quick smile lit up her face. "Really? I can go home?" As she saw the others' puzzled looks, her smile disappeared, and her shoulders slumped. "Back to my own people, my family?" she whispered.

"Na bi gòrach, caileag!"

Farinas had no idea what Keitha had said in the old language, but it was clear she had lost patience, and was anxious to get on with the plans for the raid on the Venicone.

"Your son is our brother, the son of Laeomann, our *ceann-cinnidh*. You remain here." Keitha turned away, anxious to continue with the main business, and Eithrig got up to leave. Farinas was sure others must have felt some sympathy for her, but only Keitha spoke.

"Send food and ale," she ordered.

Eithrig hesitated, then, for the first time, Farinas saw a different side to her. "I am the Lady Eithrig. I am not your servant. If you cannot treat your headman's widow, mother of his son with respect; expect none in return." She walked from the hall, and Farinas thought she looked more like a headman's woman than she ever had before.

Cináed shrugged. "She's right, I suppose. If we want food, someone had better go and tell the servers."

"I'll tell them." Goraidh got up and hurried out.

Corentyn drew the meeting to order. "So, Cináed, as overall commander, what's your plan?"

"I don't have one," Cináed growled. "Think fast," he added. "We go tonight."

There was a stunned silence broken by Quistaghyn. "Tonight is too soon."

"And so it will seem to the Venicone," Cináed responded. "They'll not expect it."

"For good reason," Cairistìona protested. "It's madness!"

"That's why you mad bastards are here. A small surprise attack on Hillfoot...in and out hard and fast, before they know what's happening." As Cináed looked around, waiting for ideas, Goraidh returned. "We're planning a raid on Hillfoot," Cináed told him. "Tonight!"

"We only have a few hours 'till darkness," Corentyn reminded them.

"So! Think of something. You're my advisers. Advise!" Cináed got up and paced up and down. "Whatever happens, we're leaving tonight!" he warned. "We need a plan!"

The others looked at each other, wondering what could be done, as Cináed continued. "The prisoner has given us information about his village, the one called Hillfoot. We know where it is, how many houses and how many men and women of fighting age there are. Most important for our plan, we know where the lookouts are set —"

"It's not our way," Keitha said.

"The attack on us was not the way of the tribes," Corentyn pointed out. "We must change our ways...or be wiped out."

"Fire!" Farinas interrupted, and the others looked up. "The Romans loose flaming arrows or spears. If they have thatched roofs, they'll burn fast and cause panic. We can get away while they're fighting the fire."

"Most of the flames would go out before the arrows reached the target," Corentyn said, and the others nodded. If it wasn't raining, it was windy in the north, usually both.

"Aye." Torcadall nodded after a short silence. "Our spears could do it." The others showed some interest then. "Get in closer."

"Maybe. Aye, maybe," Goraidh murmured.

"It could be done." Corentyn was thinking as he spoke, and the others listened to the 'outsider' who'd constantly used his knowledge of Rome's tactics in the south, to improve their safety. "I go in early with a few men to deal with the lookouts. Torcadall follows with a small band of spears and sets fire to the roofs —"

"Archers can cover the spearmen's retreat," Keitha added.

"I didn't know you had archers," Farinas interrupted.

"We don't use them much in battle, but we do use them to kill for the pot," Keitha reminded him. It seemed a long time since he'd seen her arrow, expertly pin a hare to the ground. "I'll lead the archers," Keitha added, and no one argued.

"We'll take one bowman from each unit," Cináed decided. "Chosen by the commanders."

"Don't volunteer yourselves unless you're the best. Our spearmen will be depending on you." Corentyn warned, but he knew they would be going. They wouldn't be commanders if they weren't the best. "How many spears, Torcadall?"

"I can handle a spear," Farinas offered, and Torcadall hesitated. He'd seen the gladiator in battle and knew he was dependable with a sword. He wasn't sure how well he would do with a spear, but if it saved one of his men going, he'd risk it. "Aye. I expect you could hit a target the size of a roof," he said, raising a laugh.

"If you aim for just the main meeting house, we can take fewer men," Cináed advised. "It's in the centre of the village, like here. Setting it on fire will keep them busy."

Torcadall nodded and, as they were considering the plan, the food and drink arrived. "Eat, drink." Cináed interrupted the discussion. "There won't be time later."

As they ate, they worked out the details of the plan.

Torcadall spoke around a mouthful of buttered bread. "I'll take the gladiator and four of mine. That should do it if we only aim at one target. We'll start wrapping the spear points in peat when we're finished here.

"I have shale oil," Quistaghyn offered. This was something none had heard of, and it added to the druid's air of mystery. "When they're wrapped, soak them in it. It will burn well, even if the roofs are damp, but there isn't much, so use it carefully. When we get there, I will light the fire for the spears."

"Where is this place?" Cairistìona asked, swallowing the dregs of ale from her mug.

Corentyn pointed to a piece of animal hide he'd scratched a crude map on. "I've drawn this from information given by the prisoner," he said and pointed out the main features. "Just past the falls, there's a track to the east. We follow it for about an hour until we reach an oak tree in a stand of silver birch at the top of this hill. The track dips down just beyond the trees." He pointed to crudely drawn trees. "That's where Hillfoot gets its name. The second village, Clatchard, is a few miles further east, but we should be away before word gets to them."

He looked around, impressing on them the need for speed, then continued. "After my men deal with the lookouts, we'll wait there to look after the ponies during the attack. All clear?"

The others nodded, and Cináed continued. "The spears will go down here, on foot. This is the target," He pointed to the roundhouse in the centre. "You go in quiet and fast, Torcadall. Don't wait for the fire to take hold. With the gods' help, you'll get out before the alarm is raised." Torcadall nodded, and Cináed turned to Keitha. "The archers will be in position at the top of the hill, ready to shoot down on the village as soon as anyone comes out to fight the fire. This should, gods willing, give enough light to aim by. Remind them to avoid our spearmen coming back."

Keitha gave him a look that said, this did not need to be stated, but said nothing, and Cináed explained. "In the dark and confusion, some might need a reminder that our spearmen will be coming uphill towards them. They could easily be mistaken for Venicone."

He turned to Torcadall. "Remind your men to keep low, as they climb back." Torcadall nodded. "And tell them to ride out as soon as they reach the horses. The archers will follow as soon as they've loosed their arrows; five each be enough?"

Keitha looked at Cairistìona and they nodded. "Aye we can do a lot of damage with five arrows," Cairistìona said.

"So, that's the plan," Cináed looked at each of them. "Any questions?" When no one answered, he sat down and drained his mug. "Right, Corentyn, you and your men leave at the end of the first watch. We'll follow at the end of the second watch, so we attack in the dead of night when there should be no one about."

The men and women, tired and still bloodied from battle, left with renewed energy, to prepare for the raid. Cináed leaned over and filled Farinas's mug. "How will we do?" he asked.

"Fine, unless Corentyn doesn't manage to silence the lookouts before the alarm is raised, or the fires go out, or the spearmen's aim is bad, or the roof's too wet to catch, or they're waiting for us…" He stopped and grinned at Cináed who slammed his empty mug down on the table.

"Apart from that…we'll be fine," he said.

"Aye, we'll be fine," Farinas agreed, sliding his hand over the gold armband, with its image of the god, Mars. "With the gods' help."

He followed Cináed out and went to prepare his spear. Once the spear points were thickly padded with peat, and faster-burning material that would spread quickly to the thatch on the roof, the spear points were left standing in a bucket of Quistaghyn's oil, then Farinas rolled himself in his cloak and slept for the few hours until it was time to move out.

Youngsters brought the horses and assisted the riders with their weapons. Corentyn and his men had left as planned, and Cináed was leading the spearmen and archers. Quistaghyn rode with Cináed.

There was little light from the sliver of moon in the overcast sky, and the horses picked their way slowly down the glen. The friends and family who had come to see the band off, were subdued and quiet, watching them make their way towards the falls, where they would turn towards the Venicone village.

Farinas thought of other journeys he'd made with Videric, and more lately with Ruaraidh. This was the first he'd made alone. He shivered and wrapped himself tightly in his cloak, wondering if he'd ever get used to the cold.

"Least it's dry." The spearman riding close behind had noticed him tightening his cloak. "That should help the fire take hold."

Farinas turned to answer, and Torcadall's voice carried from the front of the unit. "Keep your mouth shut, Lorcan or I'll throw you on the fire." There were a few nervous laughs, quickly cut short, and no more was heard from Lorcan or anyone else.

If the mission had not been so serious, Farinas would have enjoyed the ride. He missed the big horse, Libertas. This pony was small, but strong and sturdy, and plodded on in line with the others. When they came to a pool below a small waterfall, they dismounted and allowed the horses to crop the grass.

"Everyone know what they're doing?" Cináed asked. There were silent nods and weapons were checked. Farinas passed his hand over the armband, asking Mars, and Videric to watch over them, then they mounted for the final stage of the journey.

When his pony stopped again, Farinas looked up to see the riders in front dismounting and gathering beside the oak tree they'd seen on the map. The journey had passed so quickly, he thought he must have dozed. He joined the others and listened as Corentyn gave his report.

"All's quiet," he whispered. "We've dealt with the lookouts, three…dead. Quistaghyn's waiting for the spearmen."

"Leave the horses and go," Cináed ordered the spearmen, who quickly and quietly disappeared into the trees. Farinas handed the reins to one of Corentyn's men and followed them. Quistaghyn was holding a chain with a ceramic pot hanging from it. It glowed red and a plume of white smoke rose into the trees. He handed each of the spearmen a wad of dry vegetation.

"Rub the hafts of your spears," he ordered quietly. "Remove any oil that's dripped down. That oil will burn bright and hot as soon as it meets a flame. If you do get burning oil on you, smother the flame as quickly as you can...if you can," he warned.

When Quistaghyn was satisfied all traces of the oil had been removed he nodded. "Now carry them pointing down, so any oil drips on the ground," he told them.

They moved out onto the track and Cináed approached. "Archers are in place. We need to hurry before we're seen."

Quistaghyn nodded and signalled the spearmen to follow him. Farinas gripped the spear, fearful now of the oil, and followed the druid down the track towards the quiet houses. At the bottom of the hill, he led them into bushes, opposite the central building.

In twos he had them line up, as he held the pot of fire. "As soon as the spear catches fire, move between those two houses, and throw. Do it fast, before the flames come back on you."

He waited until he saw they understood. "As soon as the spear leaves your hand, get back up the hill. Don't wait to see if your aim was true, or if the flame went out. Keep your heads down. The archers will be covering you...but they'll be close. Throw and run!" He looked at Farinas, standing tall above the others. "You'll go with Torcadall. Aim for any patches that haven't caught fire, but don't wait."

There were three pairs, with Farinas and Torcadall placed last. They watched as the spearmen lit and threw their spears. The flames burned brightly and stayed alight although one missed and buried its tip in the ground, still burning.

Quistaghyn hissed his annoyance, but they heard no alarm and Farinas and Torcadall lit their spears, ran forward, and threw. Despite Quistaghyn's warning, they both stood and watched as the spears struck the roof, and the flames joined the others already leaping into the night sky.

"Run!" Torcadall hissed and Farinas joined him in a scramble up the hill, as dogs began barking. At the top, they looked back and saw Quistaghyn calmly standing between the roundhouses. He swung the pot by its chain then released it to land on the threshold causing the heavy wooden door to burst into flames.

Suddenly a scream rose above the sound of the dogs. "Fire! Fire!" People spilled out of their houses, shaking their heads, and rubbing their eyes. By this time, the wind had carried embers to two other roofs that were now on fire.

When Farinas looked away from the burning roundhouses, it was to see the druid standing beside him, watching the scene below, as Keitha gave her command to the bowmen. "Knock! Loose!"

Dark figures silhouetted against the flames, were now falling from the arrows, and there was panic, apart from one warrior who had summed up the situation and was trying to gather others to attack, with little effect.

Farinas watched the archers and then realised the spearmen had left. Corentyn and Cináed were waiting with the horses, as the archers loosed the last of their arrows. Farinas was turning to leave when the first of the Venicone arrows landed behind Keitha's unit. He saw Quistaghyn stagger and fall to the ground, with an arrow in his shoulder.

Farinas ran to the fallen druid and broke the shaft off, as Keitha's archers ran for the horses. Corentyn was urging Cináed to leave, but he and Keitha remained, watching what was happening.

Farinas threw Quistaghyn up on a pony. "Can you ride?"

"I can." A quick nod then, holding the reins in one hand, Quistaghyn turned and rode back along the track.

By now the air was full of panicked cries, and the roaring of flames. A few arrows fell on the hillside, but most of the villagers were concerned with stopping the spread of the fire.

"A rider's just headed out towards Clatchard," Cináed said, as he mounted his horse. "He'll be going to report…maybe get reinforcements. Let's get out of here." They mounted and turned to ride after the others, but Keitha wheeled her pony and charged down the hill.

"No! Keitha!" Cináed roared, but she continued her charge, racing alongside the houses and out into the forest beyond them.

"She's heading after the rider, to stop him taking the news to Clatchard," Corentyn said. He laid his hand on Farinas's arm, to prevent him following.

"We have to leave." Cináed turned once towards the flames, lighting up the night sky.

"Amadan!" He roared the insult after his sister, then turned and followed Farinas and Corentyn,

They rode in silence, soon catching up with the others, and as the sun was rising above the mountains, they reached the village. Corentyn sent men to relieve the lookouts, with a warning to be extra vigilant. "Any sign of anything unusual…raise the alarm. Better a false alarm, than being taken in our sleep," he warned.

Chapter 37

Quistaghyn was taken to the broch to have the arrowhead removed and his wound tended. He was usually the one supervising Mistress Foirbeis and her helpers and providing them with herbal potions and medical advice. Farinas wasn't sure how he would feel being one of the injured.

Mistress Foirbeis had met them and immediately demanded to know what had happened to Keitha. Farinas left Cináed to explain why his sister had not returned with them and joined the rest of the band gathering in the meeting house.

Cairistìona handed him a brimming mug of ale. "Where's Keitha?" she demanded before he had the mug to his lips.

"We saw a rider heading east. Keitha rode after him." Before any asked, he added. "There was no point in anyone going after her." He slumped down on the bench and drank deeply.

"And Quistaghyn?" Corentyn asked.

"An unlucky hit, an arrow in the shoulder. It didn't look bad."

"He did well with the oil and the fire," Torcadall said. "It took hold right quick. The roof was ablaze in no time."

The others nodded and spoke of Quistaghyn and his oil, but Farinas had heard soldiers talk of Greek Fire and knew what it could do. He was glad they'd not had that to use.

"What happened?" he asked, seeing Torcadall applying ointment to Lorcan's forehead, under a patch of singed hair.

"Idiot hung onto his spear too long," Torcadall growled. "Got himself burned."

"Do you think my hair will grow back?" The young lad fingered the singed edges of his hair.

"My grandfather singed his hair like that," Goraidh said, examining Lorcan's hair. "Leaned too close to the fire, cooking a hare."

"So! What happened?"

"All his hair fell out."

"No!"

"Aye, mind he was past his sixtieth year when it happened." Goraidh and the others laughed, as Lorcan anxiously patted his hair.

"How can you laugh?" Cairistìona was on her feet. "We should go after Keitha!"

"No!" The door had opened quietly and Cináed joined the group. He took a mug of ale from Corentyn and sat down. "You did well. Stuck to the plan and no more lives were lost. Keitha should not have gone after the Venicone. It will do no good, and she may have lost her life. No one else is risking their life for her...even if she is my sister." He paused and looked around. "How many times do I need to tell you?" he roared. "We need every man...and woman to fight the Venicone, and later the legions."

There was silence as he drank then leaned forward. "Lookouts are posted. Get some rest but be ready for an alarm. Tomorrow, we pay our respects to our dead and decide what to do next... If there is no attack tonight."

They got up slowly, as exhaustion hit them. "I'll go and see Quistaghyn," Farinas said, leaving Cináed to return to his family. It seemed Quistaghyn was respected, but fear of what he was, kept others from befriending him. As a young boy in Theveste, Farinas had been entertained by visiting holy men, performing magic tricks, some with venomous serpents. It would take a lot of magic to make him fear any magus, druid or other.

He found Quistaghyn lying on a palette at the top of the broch. His shoulder was bandaged, and he seemed well enough, if not very happy. Around him lay the wounded from the battle, and the sick and dying who had been brought up for protection before the battle.

"How are you?" Farinas asked.

"Well, but I need to be home. I need to see to my creatures."

"What creatures?" Farinas asked. "I could look after them."

"No, but thank you, lad. My pets can be dangerous if they don't know a person."

Farinas remembered the desert snakes and decided not to ask what these dangerous creatures were. "Can I get you anything?"

"Yes, my cloak and my staff."

Farinas handed him his cloak, and he threw it over his shoulders then he took the staff and used it to support himself as he got up. "Right. Help me down the stairs." Farinas shrugged and helped the druid to make his way to the stairs. If a druid didn't know how to take care of himself, no one did.

"You should remain here, master." The young girl appeared surprised to have spoken so sharply to the druid, and coloured, as he turned to answer her.

"I am returning home, Moireach. It is the best place to heal, but I thank you for your care and attention." The girl bowed and hurried away to her duties.

The thought of going home seemed to lend strength to the druid, and Farinas was soon helping him into his roundhouse, set at a distance from the others. On a rowan tree behind the house, hung small amulets and strips of cloth. Inside, the house was like the one Bearnais and Artair lived in, but the smoke here had a smell Farinas recognised as cinnamon. He drew in a breath and immediately felt as if he was back home watching his mother comb oil through her hair.

He followed Quistaghyn as he walked to the fire and poked the embers until the flames sprang up and heated a pot hanging over them. Farinas could hear chips and cheeps from creatures hiding in the dark corners but could see nothing.

The druid sank into a large, padded chair by the hearth. He gave a contented sigh and relaxed. "Tell me about Keitha."

"She went after a rider, who rode out towards Clatchard," Farinas said, as he sat down by the fire.

"She's a proud and resourceful lass." The druid smiled. "I expect she'll be fine."

Farinas didn't express his doubts, but Quistaghyn smiled, acknowledging them. He opened a wooden box and took out a gold pin with symbols carved on it. It was like the pins used to fasten cloaks, but larger and more ornate than any Farinas had seen. In the middle was a large amber stone. The druid handed it to Farinas.

"You will need this when you next see Keitha. Until then, always wear it on your tunic." He closed Farinas's hand over the pin and gazed into his eyes. "It is important for you both that you wear it...always...like Videric's armband, until you see her again."

For the first time, Farinas felt the power of the druid and remembered Old Eithni who had something of the same aura. He pinned the *fibula* onto his tunic, under the cloak, and Quistaghyn repeated his instruction. "Remember, you must wear it always until you next meet Keitha."

Farinas thanked Quistaghyn and left him sprinkling dried herbs into the pot of warm water, watched by a long, white furry creature with bright black eyes, and a raven that had flown down from the roof to perch on the druid's chair.

He stepped out into the pale sunlight and walked back to the meeting house worrying about Keitha. The druid's words had given him some hope that she still lived but he knew he was too tired to plan anything. Wrapping himself in his cloak, he placed his hand over the armband and fell asleep, hoping there would be no alarm to disturb him.

When Farinas woke, he joined some of the men and women from the raid, eating a breakfast of oats and dried fruit. They still looked as tired as he felt, and the greetings were subdued.

"Someone needs to do some hunting," Lorcan said. "I'm sick o' oats."

"Be thankful for any food," an older man growled. "I remember when we fought the Romans. We ate —"

"We know, Eòin," Lorcan interrupted wearily. "You ate your shoes!" There was laughter at the familiar story and Eòin scowled at them.

"Aye, you young ones. You think you have it hard."

"At least we lost no one last night," Goraidh said, "not killed anyway," he added, as he saw Cairistìona ready to object.

"The druid seems to think Keitha is alive," Farinas said.

"Really," Cairistìona was watching him. "He said that?"

Farinas nodded. "He said we'd see her again."

"How is Quistaghyn?" Eòin asked.

"He'll be fine," Farinas told him.

"Aye, I expect he will." Eòin nodded. "Quistaghyn's been through hard times, like me."

Farinas stopped listening, as he swallowed the bland porridge, and thought of Keitha; wondering what he could do.

The group had fallen silent when Cináed came in. "There's work to be done," he said, and they looked up, alert and ready. "There's lookouts set, but we need to strengthen defences and prepare for planting. We also need hunters out, before we start eating our shoes like Eòin here had to do." He waited for the laughter to die down, then continued. "See Corentyn about lookout duties and see Cairistìona about getting some hunters together. Hunt on the northern side of the glen…don't go too far. The Venicone attacked from that direction before…they might try again." Cairistìona nodded, and the atmosphere changed, as they thought of that attack, and the death of Laeomann.

"What about Keitha?" Lorcan eventually asked.

"We know that the prisoner, Tadhg, is the son of Tàmhas, headman of Hillfoot. We'll trade him for Keitha."

"That's not where she'll be," Farinas pointed out. "If she's a prisoner, she'll be at Clatchard."

"Aye well, that's the best we can do," Cináed sighed. "I'll not risk more lives." He moved to the door and added. "Quistaghyn's supervising the building of the pyre …I'm thankful we've no more bodies to add to it. It will be lit tomorrow."

He left, and the men and women got ready to return to their duties. Already a group had gathered, eagerly volunteering as hunters.

Farinas collected his pack and went outside, avoiding Ruaraidh who was stacking more dry kindling on the pyres. A plan was beginning to form, although he recognised the unlikelihood of it succeeding, and he wondered at the power the young woman had over him.

Walking past the pyres, he found a quiet place by the stream. It was too shallow to swim but, using oil, he hastily shaved his face. His hair was still short enough to suit his plan. He bathed and dressed for effect. Trying to look as Roman as possible, he wore his costliest linen tunic, fine woollen trousers and the hobnailed *caligulae* he'd brought from Trimontium.

He carefully pinned Quistaghyn's brooch to the tunic and hung the *gladius* in a sheath on his belt. As a sidearm, he added the bronze sheath and dagger that Sgathaich, the blacksmith's daughter had fashioned. Turning his cloak with the red lining outside, he slung it over his shoulder and fastened it with the bronze clasp.

He returned to the meeting house and shoved his pack, with his soiled clothing into a corner. Carrying his rolled-up, heavy-weather cloak, he strode over to the stables and demanded a horse, not a big pony, a horse with a saddle. He had seen a few saddles that must have been captured from past encounters with the Romans, or perhaps just left behind by them when they returned to the south.

The lads in the stables looked surprised at his request, but they had seen him often enough with the unit commanders, and with Cináed, so did not question him. A horse was brought, and he fastened his cloak to the saddle and mounted swiftly. He rode out before anyone thought to stop him.

Chapter 38

Farinas rode swiftly past the lookouts, throwing a confident salute in their direction, and headed towards Hillfoot. Once out of sight of the lookouts, he reined the horse in and moved forward, carefully. Unsure of the land, he had no wish to cause the horse to stumble or fall.

He spoke to the horse in the purest form of the Roman tongue that he could, practising for later. The one he had been using with the Caledonii was a bastardised version of their own tongue mixed with the Roman tongue used by soldiers. A language that developed in local forms, in garrison towns across the empire. For his plan to work, he needed to sound, at times, like a proper Roman.

When Farinas reached the falls, he dismounted and allowed the horse to rest, while considering his plan. Mainly he was appreciating his lack of a plan. His horse whickered softly, and this was quickly followed by an answering whinny. Farinas waited, scanning the track until he saw a rider approaching. He wasn't surprised to see Ruaraidh following him on a small mountain pony. "What are you doing?"

Ruaraidh slid down from the pony. "You can't go on your own. I know these people. No Roman would approach a settlement alone. I'm your official translator. I'll use the official language we spoke in Trimontium with you, and the local one with them. That should convince them." He bowed low, adding with a smile. "*Domine.*"

Farinas didn't ask how Ruaraidh knew what he planned, but he was glad of his company. As Ruaraidh had pointed out, language could be a problem. Still, he tried to discourage him. "You know this will be dangerous."

Ruaraidh nodded. "Less so with both of us," he pointed out. "What's your plan?"

Forced to think of one, Farinas worked things out, as he talked. "I'm a high-ranking officer, based at the Roman camp above the river…?"

Ruaraidh nodded and supplied the information. "Carpow above Uisge Dhè. Will you be able to make them believe that?"

"I'll have to," Farinas said. "Did you know a governor of Britannia was once a man from Tiddis, in my country, Gallio told me... Quintus Lollius Urbicus was his Roman name—"

"Not helpful. They're not going to think you're descended from a black governor nobody remembers."

Farinas shrugged. "I just thought of it. Maybe he's looking down on us —"

"And maybe not..." Ruairidh's impatience was clear and forced Farinas to focus.

"Right," He continued. "We heard of a battle in the area...between our good friends the Venicone and another tribe...and I've been sent to get a report."

"And—"

"I'll think of something, but first we need to get past the village we set alight, without being seen." Farinas realised he was struggling at the first obstacle.

He wasn't familiar with the countryside, but Ruaraidh came up with a plan. "We're supposed to be coming from the Roman camp, so we'll cross the hillside above both villages and ride beyond them, almost as far as the Roman camp. Once there, we turn and approach Clatchard, from the direction of the camp."

Farinas was happy to leave the route to Ruaraidh and he followed him, with no thought to direction, until they crested a small hill and he saw neat rows of tents in the distance. "The Roman camp," Ruaraidh told him. "We'll get down behind the hill and rest the horses. We don't want to be seen by any patrols, or lookouts."

They found a stream for the horses and Ruaraidh handed Farinas a slab of bread and a piece of cheese. "I didn't plan this very well," Farinas admitted, enjoying the food.

"Well, officers have others to do the planning for them," Ruaraidh laughed. They mounted and turned away from the camp, riding towards Clatchard. "You're supposed to be a high-ranking Roman officer," Ruaraidh pointed out. "Start behaving like one. We're probably being watched."

Farinas thought about what he had said and realised the lad's life was in his hands. He straightened in the saddle, raised his head, and barked, in his best Roman tongue. "Did I request your advice?"

There was silence for a heartbeat then a muttered, "No, *Domine*."

They rode on, but now Farinas was alert and searched the trees lining the track until Ruaraidh called out. "The village you seek must be quite close, *Domine*."

He nodded and quickened the pace, anxious to get to the village and do what he could to rescue Keitha, if indeed she was there…and still alive. When they came upon two men standing guard at the entrance to a large cluster of roundhouses, they knew their approach had been noted.

The guards led them to a group of warriors obviously waiting for them. Farinas dismounted and threw the reins to the guard, straightened his shoulders, and strode up to the warriors, hand firmly on the hilt of his sword.

Chapter 39

"Tell them I need to speak with their headman…make it a demand," he commanded. Ruaraidh inclined his head, then relayed the instructions.

One stepped forward. "Who are you, riding in unannounced? We could ha' killed you."

"That would have been unfortunate, for you…and your kin folk." Farinas looked contemptuously at the man, as Ruaraidh translated. He watched the tribesmen, trying to see them through the eyes of a wealthy, privileged and powerful aristocrat. "Supplicants from here, came to our camp to sue for peace with Rome. I expected a better welcome."

The man who appeared to be the headman nodded. "Aye well, you'd best come in."

Farinas threw his cloak back over his shoulder and slid his hand over Videric's armband, hoping his friend was watching over them. He followed the headman into the dark, smoky building and sat on a bench with Ruaraidh standing at his shoulder. The headman and his advisers sat, and servers placed jugs of beer and platters of cheese and rough oatcakes on the table.

"Ask him who I'm speaking to."

Ruaraidh translated then replied. "He's Conn, headman of Clatchard. He wants to know why you travel alone, with no escort."

"I am a representative of our illustrious Roman Emperor. We have many allies in the area and retribution from the camp at …?" He stopped, snapping his fingers and Ruaraidh quickly answered.

"Carpow, above the Uisge Dhè, *Domine.*"

He nodded. "Retribution would be swift and merciless, should I fail to return at the appointed hour." He paused as Ruaraidh translated then continued. "I am here to find out if what we've heard is true. You attacked a neighbouring tribe, hostile to Rome."

The headman drank, as Ruaraidh translated. "He says they've always favoured Rome and they and their kinsmen from Hillfoot did attack a Vacomagi village." Ruaraidh listened then added, "he says there was a raid on Hillfoot last night. It was set on fire and four died, others were injured."

Farinas nodded. "Following the insurrection and subsequent death of the governor, there will be retribution. The emperor's patience with this barbaric land has run out, but he is a fair man. He has no wish to see the Caledonii destroyed. Our allies will be spared."

As Ruaraidh translated, Farinas looked around, hoping but not expecting to see any sign of Keitha's presence. "This hostile tribe. What do you know of it?"

"Its village lies a few hours' ride away, to the north," Ruaraidh translated, and Farinas barked his reply.

"We require as much information as possible."

Ruaraidh spoke then translated. "He knows little about them, except they are Vacomagi. He and the others killed the headman when they attacked their village.

Farinas continued. "We'll be building a fort on the site of our camp. Reinforcements are already on the way by sea. We need the information to deploy our forces in a way that does not cause disruption to our allies."

When this was translated, a long discussion arose, and Farinas decided to move things along. "Details of the Vacomagi? Fighting strength? Allies?"

After a brief conversation, Ruaraidh answered. "He has no further information, only that many were killed."

Farinas stood up abruptly. "This information is useless. I'm wasting time here." Ruaraidh was still translating as Farinas marched outside. "My horse!"

Farinas leaving so abruptly, caused concern among the men gathered with Conn. Ruaraidh was just as surprised, but he grabbed a piece of cheese, before hurrying outside. "He wants to know what you're going to do," Ruaraidh said, catching up with Farinas. "He's anxious to be seen as an ally of Rome. He hopes to get Vacomagi land and beasts from his alliance with Rome."

"Tell him, we're returning to the camp. We'll look for allies who can be more useful to Rome."

Ruaraidh translated, then Conn spoke. Farinas knew enough to understand some of what was said. He kept his expression neutral and waited.

"He has a Vacomagi prisoner, a female who can provide important information. She took part in the raid that set Hillfoot ablaze."

Farinas swung round, hiding his relief. Keitha was alive. "We'll take the prisoner with us. The legate will welcome the information when he lands with reinforcements. He will look favourably on those who provided it."

As Ruaraidh was translating, Conn was signalling and shouting instructions to his men. One left the group and entered a roundhouse opposite. When he came out, he was dragging Keitha.

Her head hung down, but her hair failed to hide the purple bruises on her face. Her tunic was torn and what could be seen of her body was covered in lacerations and dried blood. Farinas struggled to hide his shock and anger, as she was dragged across the rough ground and thrown at their feet where she lay, still and almost lifeless.

Farinas heard Ruaraidh gasp, and he barked a command, fearing his response would alert the Venicone. "Bring our mounts and a pony for the prisoner." Ruaraidh translated for Conn, and soon after a lad appeared, leading the beasts.

"Secure the prisoner's hands with a leading rope; attach it to your saddle." Farinas was careful not to look at Keitha, as Ruaraidh assisted her onto the pony. She hung down over the pony's head and Farinas feared she would fall causing more hurt and injury. Hiding his concern, he mounted his own horse as Conn and the others engaged in animated conversation. Eventually, Ruaraidh came over, riding alongside Keitha and doing his best to support her. Farinas turned his horse, anxious to leave, but Ruaraidh's voice stopped him,

"They want recompense for the pony… and the prisoner."

Farinas cursed himself for leaving his coin pouch behind; of course, they wanted compensation.

"How do I know she's worth anything?" he snapped.

"She's a sister to the headman. Her father, the last headman, was killed in their attack."

Remembering the druid's words, Farinas breathed a sigh of relief. He moved his cloak aside and took Quistaghyn's pin from his tunic. He threw the pin, and it flashed golden in the air before Conn snatched it. After examining it carefully, he proudly displayed it on his cloak.

"Right, let's get out of here." Farinas was thanking the gods that they could finally leave when a big man stepped forward and seized his horse's reins. The man was young and sturdy, with the brutish look and approach of a bully. Farinas responded automatically, kicking hard with his heavy hobnailed boot. The young man crashed down in the dust where he lay moaning and rubbing his chest.

The atmosphere changed immediately, as the man was helped to his feet. He glared at Farinas, shouting angrily, and looking to Conn for support. The warriors' hands were on the hilts of their swords as they moved in, circling the mounted group.

"He's Tormond, Conn's son. He won't let us go without paying for that insult." Ruaraidh moved closer. "He says he's the one that beat the prisoner. She fought like a wildcat, and he hasn't got any information out of her yet..." Ruaraidh hesitated.

"Go on!" Farinas barked, not sure he wanted to hear, but knowing he had to.

Ruaraidh lowered his voice. "Remember you're a Roman. She's a barbarian prisoner." His warning came just in time, and Farinas remained outwardly calm as Ruaraidh continued. "He said, he... he took his pleasure with her... but he's not finished with her. He wants to keep her... Kill us and blame the Vacomagi."

As Conn considered his options and tempers among Tormond's younger followers rose, Ruaraidh faced them and continued to speak, quietly and calmly. Whatever he was saying seemed to have the desired effect and Farinas felt some of the tension easing as Ruaraidh and Conn continued their discussion. Eventually, Tormond nodded and Ruaraidh translated.

"Tormond says he'll agree to release the prisoner, but only in a trade-off." There followed a heated discussion between Conn and Ruaraidh, with lots of headshaking from Ruaraidh. Farinas had no idea what was being said, but he watched as the warriors gradually relaxed and moved their hands from their weapons.

Ruaraidh, however, was looking worried, as he turned to Farinas. "I'm sorry," he said.

"What for? So long as we can leave, it doesn't matter what you agreed to."

"Tormond's demanding payment for the insult." Ruaraidh paused. "He wants the armband."

Farinas felt as though the breath had left his body…anything but that.

"I told him it was too valuable. The emperor himself had given it to you, but he won't back down."

Farinas hadn't realised the sleeve of his tunic had been pulled up when he threw back his cloak. His hand instinctively went to the armband. He had thought he would never part with Videric's gift, but he had nothing else of value to offer, and the younger Venicone were spoiling for a fight.

Farinas shrugged. He had no choice. He threw the armband to the smirking lout who squeezed it onto his arm. Farinas gripped his sword, wanting nothing more than to cut the arm off and retrieve Videric's band. Instead, he turned his horse and rode out, with Ruaraidh and Keitha following.

Outside the village, Ruaraidh rode up beside him. "We'll ride towards the Roman camp for a few miles. They'll be watching, then we circle back, returning the way we came in, avoiding this village and Hillfoot."

Farinas nodded. He put the thought of Videric's armband, circling the arm of the grinning whoreson, out of his mind. "You did well," he told a relieved Ruaraidh. "I wouldn't have escaped with Keitha…or my life, without you."

A few miles out from Clatchard, they stopped, and Farinas lifted Keitha down from the pony and untied her.

"Water," she murmured, and Ruaraidh hurried over with a waterskin. "Thanks." She drank then they helped her back onto the pony. "I'm fine," she told them. "I would have escaped after I killed the whoreson who used me." She made a face at the word, that didn't begin to describe what had happened to her at the hands of Tormond. Farinas had expected some gratitude, but he just nodded. "You made a good Roman." She offered the compliment, in place of thanks.

Farinas smiled. He liked her spirit.

"We'd best move out, or we could be in danger from the real Romans." Ruaraidh reminded them.

Keitha nodded. "It's probably safe to head back now." She looked impatiently at Ruaraidh and Farinas who were sharing the waterskin. "Now!"

They mounted hurriedly and followed her, as she galloped her pony along the side of the hill, giving Clatchard a wide berth. As it grew dark, they slowed the pace, allowing the animals to pick their way through the undergrowth. When Keitha reined in her pony, they dismounted to rest the animals.

"We're midway between the two villages, so it's not safe to spend the night here," Keitha decided, "but in the dark, we should walk the animals."

"You ride." Farinas dismounted. "I'll lead your beast too." He could see she wanted to refuse, but she was more badly hurt than she wanted to admit, so she nodded and allowed him to help her onto the pony.

"Hillfoot will have watchers out, for fear of another attack," Ruaraidh warned. "We'll just have to hope they're not too alert." Farinas hoped so too, but trouble came a few miles further on. They were almost at the falls, and thought themselves safe, when they heard a cry, and realised the lookouts had been alerted.

"Stop! Who's there?" The question was accompanied by the unmistakable sound of ponies being mounted, and warning shouts to alert the village.

"Ride!" Ruaraidh roared. "Trust the horse!" He and Farinas mounted, and they raced after Keitha, towards the village.

Settling into the saddle, Farinas let the horse speed up, trusting it would find a safe passage. When they still had a way to go, Farinas knew the fresh mountain ponies would have little difficulty catching them. He was considering making a stand to allow the other two to escape when he heard the now-familiar alarm from the Vacomagi village. Shortly after, as his horse eased back on the pace, riders raced past heading towards their pursuers.

Vacomagi lookouts had seen what was happening. They'd raised the alarm and riders had ridden out to engage the enemy. The leading riders were followed soon after by others who flashed past, as Keitha led Farinas and Ruaraidh through the gates.

Once inside the village, Farinas slumped over the horse's head, exhausted but happy. They were safe, and the mission was accomplished. Villagers, wakened by the alarm, gathered around.

Mistress Foirbeis had hurried from the broch to see if any medical help was needed and stood with Cináed. "You were a fool," Cináed was telling Keitha, anger fighting with relief. "You risked other lives—"

"I risked no lives but mine," she glared at her brother. "I would have escaped. I sought no help from anyone."

"What of this alarm? Where will this lead?" He roared, indicating the villagers lining up in readiness.

"We're happy you're safe," Mistress Foirbeis interrupted. "And grateful to Farinas and Ruaraidh." She saw how weak Keitha was. "Escaping might not have been so simple," she told her, before calling men to support Keitha to the broch.

The night air was filled with nervous voices, and cries of children wakened from sleep, but the riders soon returned and reported that the Venicone had retreated behind their palisade. There had been no engagement. Lookouts returned to their posts and others to their homes, hoping there would be no more disturbances that night.

Ruaraidh returned to his foster family, to be greeted as a hero, and Farinas found a quiet corner of the meeting house where he wrapped himself in his cloak and lay down. His only regret, as he lay trying to sleep, was the missing armband. Not even the little carved figure of Uzivelele had meant so much to him, and it could easily be replaced. Videric's armband never could be. His last connection to his friend, it had become even more important to him than he had realised. Thoughts of Keitha and Ruaraidh safely home though, finally brought sleep.

Chapter 40

The smoke in the meeting house was clearing, as fresh air and sunshine filtered in, when Farinas was kicked awake the following morning. "Time to get up, hero." Cináed laughed and settled at the table with mugs of beer, and a bowl of hot porridge for Farinas. He was followed soon after by his advisers and representatives of the families, armed and prepared for further alarms.

Cináed sat with Keitha who looked battered and bruised, but better than she had the night before. Corentyn and the unit leaders joined them as the families' representatives gathered in small groups. Farinas saw Ruaraidh representing his new family. Quistaghyn stood at the front and, when it appeared everyone was present, he raised his staff and pronounced a blessing on the meeting.

Farinas slipped out to clear his head and when he returned, he remained standing by the door, listening to Keitha reporting on her rescue. There were roars of appreciation for Farinas and Ruaraidh, then, as the crowd was settling down, the door burst open, and a huge warrior entered.

He stood on the threshold, legs apart, hands on his hips looking over the gathering of villagers. His red hair was long and thick. It was braided to keep it from becoming entangled in the massive longsword he wore in a scabbard on his back.

Farinas, standing nearest the door, drew his *gladius* and stepped out of the shadows to bar the stranger's passage into the hall. Over the man's shoulder, he saw the massive hilt of the sword. He had moved automatically at the perceived threat, but his training and discipline stopped his sword arm. The stranger threw his head back and roared with laughter. "Ach Cináed, you been buying yourself a mercenary?"

"Eochaid!" Cináed's response and the smiles of the villagers made it obvious the huge warrior was welcome.

Farinas sheathed his sword and moved aside, as Cináed walked through the murmuring assembly to kneel before the warrior. Eochaid raised him and the two men embraced. "I was right sorry to hear of your father's death. A good man, a loyal an' fierce warrior."

"My thanks, Lord." Cináed stood aside to allow Eochaid to walk through the assembly to the front, where he bowed to Quistaghyn.

Cináed sat, as Eochaid called out more informal greetings to others. His last was for Keitha. "Keitha, lass." He embraced her, noted her wince of pain, and drew back to examine her bruised face. "We'll talk later about what happened, and what needs to be done." She smiled and nodded, then he faced the assembly. He removed the sword and scabbard, placed them before him on the table, and addressed them in a voice used to being obeyed.

"We've matters to discuss, and I've ridden long and hard. We'll ask you to gather when we've finished our discussions."

"We still have our dead to send on their way to the Otherworld." Quistaghyn spoke quietly, reminding them of their duties.

Eochaid bowed to the druid. "You're right to remind us, Quistaghyn. Make your preparations and we will join you." The druid nodded and withdrew.

As they were leaving, Ruaraidh made his way over to Farinas. "You took a chance there," he told him. "Not many draw a blade on Eochaid, and live."

"Aye," another man overhearing, nodded. "He's no' carrying yon *claidheamh mór* on his back for the show of it. Calls it *neach-dèanamh banntrach.*"

Ruaraidh was happy to translate. "Widow-maker."

"Two or three o' the youngsters tried to sheath their swords on their backs." Another added. "It wis a fine laugh to see them try tae mount a pony—"

"Or sit doon."

"So, who is he?" Farinas asked.

"Who is he?" They looked at him in amazement.

"He's the Chief o' the Vacomagi."

"I thought Cináed was the chief," Farinas said, and the men shook their heads.

"Naw," one explained. "Cináed's oor headman…the *ceann-cinnidh* o' this village."

"And Eochaid?"

"Well, Eochaid's the chief... *ceannard cinnidh* o' all the Vacomagi villages."

"Aye, you're lucky. He must have liked your style." The men thought this was highly amusing, and Farinas joined in their laughter. Drawing a sword on a stranger did not usually end so well!

As they made their way to the door, Eochaid's voice carried easily over the noise. "The whoreson that barred my lawful way better join us. I like to know the names of my attackers...usually before I slice them down the middle."

Farinas examined the Vacomagi chief as he approached the dais. Eochaid was big and well-muscled under his linen tunic and woollen trousers. He wore a heavy gold torc and silver and gold armbands. His boots were of soft leather and the cloak, thrown over the bench, was heavy and lined with fur. The mighty two-handed sword in its scabbard lay on the table in front of him. It would take a lot of skill and strength to wield it effectively.

Eochaid had pushed his thick red hair from his forehead and looked on Farinas from grey eyes, above a long moustache and beard. He was closer in age to Laeomann than to Cináed, and his hair was flecked with grey, but Farinas had no doubt he could best most younger men.

As Farinas joined them at the table, Cináed was giving his chief a brief history of the newcomer, from fellow slave, to gladiator, to heroic rescuer.

"A man to hold onto, eh Keitha?" Eochaid's comment brought more laughter and an embarrassed look from Keitha.

The tribe's best beer and food were brought, and Corentyn opened the conversation. "How did you get past my watchmen?"

Eochaid laughed and slapped him on the back. "Don't be punishing the lads, now. They were concerned with trouble from the other direction...from the Venicone.   We surprised them...and we're the best," he added with complete conviction. "Choose less obvious lookout points though."

Corentyn stood. "I'll see to it."

"Sit down, man. Eat! Drink! My men are dealing with it," Eochaid assured him, then continued to the main business. "Now, I heard about your wee bit of trouble with the Roman-loving Venicone. Maybe your man here has bought us some time, with his talk o' their friendship with the Roman legions that are coming, but we need to deal with them before they learn it was all falsehoods."

"You'll call others?" Cináed asked.

Eochaid nodded. "Already done! The call has gone out to all the Vacomagi. Otherwise, the Venicone will pick us off, one village at a time —"

Farinas remembered the blacksmith and Oswy's gang. Too much talking seemed to be a common fault in the north. "You need to move fast," he urged. "The Romans are coming. Not as soon as I told the Venicone, but soon the legions will march north and take their bloody revenge."

There was silence as the others considered the coming troubles…just when they thought the Romans had decided to leave them in peace.

Cináed spoke. "First though, we have duties to our dead to attend to."

Work stopped and those not keeping watch, or tending to the sick and injured, gathered at the pyre, huddled into thick cloaks and shawls, against the chill wind sweeping off the hillside.

Farinas joined Ruaraidh, Bearnais and Artair, sharing their sorrow for the lives lost. Quistaghyn led the remembrances and praises for the dead, then the carnyx was sounded and the mourners, led by Eochaid, walked up and touched the pyre, saying last goodbyes to their dead. Eithrig was there, wrapped in furs and standing at a distance from Laeomann's family, Alone, she walked to the pyre.

Finally, Quistaghyn leaned into the pyre and spoke quietly, addressing the dead. Bearnais whispered to Farinas. "He's telling them the way to the Otherworld, so they don't get lost, and have to wander forever in the land between the living and the dead."

Farinas had seen his share of death and taken part in the ceremonies that followed, but he'd missed Videric's funeral rites. He bowed his head, hoping his friend had found his way to his Otherworld, wherever it was. They'd never spoken of death and beyond. That would have been unlucky. His hand moved involuntarily to where he'd worn Videric's gold band and he felt a deep sense of loss, finding it not there. It had become more a part of him than anything else in his life. His only connection to

Videric. Glancing up he caught Keitha watching him, but she quickly turned away.

When Quistaghyn stepped back, torches were thrust into the dry peat and heather, and a sigh rose from the mourners as the pyre was engulfed in flames.

The villagers returned to their homes, many being led away sobbing, as gleaming sparks whirled into the sky, and the acrid, earthy-smelling smoke billowed over the stream and dispersed across the hillside.

Eochaid led Laeomann's family back to their roundhouse, and Farinas gladly accepted Bearnais' invitation to share their meal. The animals the hunters had caught were still being prepared, but there was plenty of vegetable broth, hot and comforting and Farinas was glad of it.

They spoke of the neighbours who had died, and Ruaraidh recounted how they had rescued Keitha, while Bearnais served the meal and Artair kept the beer flowing. "So, gladiator," Artair finally asked, "you intendin' to stay?"

"I'm not sure." He wondered if the connection he felt was only because of Keitha. He shrugged. "Nowhere else to go."

Artair laughed and nudged him. "I stayed for a lass too." Bearnais made a face at that, but she was struggling not to smile.

Farinas could think of nothing to say. Fortunately, Ruaraidh came to his rescue. "I wonder what they're deciding?"

"More fightin'," Artair predicted.

"Aye," Bearnais nodded. "Always fightin'."

When the call to gather at the meeting house came, Farinas and Ruaraidh joined representatives of the other families making their way to hear what decisions had been made.

Eochaid it was who made the announcements. "As far as the Vacomagi are concerned, the matter's done with. They attacked; we took revenge. The real threat lies with Rome."

There was grumbling and one man spoke out "What if the Venicone don't see it that way."

"I've sent out the call, reinforcements will be arriving soon, should they be needed." Tension in the hall eased slightly, now they knew there would be support in the event of another attack, and Eochaid continued. "We're sending the prisoner back to his father." This was greeted with some protests, muted by the presence of Eochaid, their chief, but he raised his hand and added. "We'll fight if we must, but we'll try this first. Anyone disagreeing, can meet me outside later." There was an uneasy silence from the objectors, but Farinas noticed Cináed and Keitha smiling. Clearly, they understood Eochaid's ways and his sense of humour.

Eochaid continued. "Right, now that's settled, here's what we're doing. We're sending the prisoner back...with a demand that his father attends a Gathering with our headmen, at Calasraid. I've sent word to Griogair, chief o' the Venicone to call his headmen to the Gathering...all of them. He was never a lover of Rome. I cannae believe he'd agreed to any treaty with Rome."

"That's true," an old man muttered. "He'd no' join forces wi' Rome." There were murmurs of agreement from those who knew the man or knew of him.

"Suppose they seek support from the Romans at Carpow?" The question worried Farinas. He hadn't considered this when he persuaded Conn that he and Ruaraidh had come as emissaries from the Roman camp.

It was Quistaghyn who answered, displaying knowledge that could only have come from a powerful network of contacts. "They will find no Roman camp at Uisge Dhè. The soldiers have been sent to strengthen defences at the fort at Caladair, in preparation for the coming reinforcements."

"Good to know." Cináed's relief was shared by many, not just Farinas. It was early spring, a time for preparing the ground for planting and sowing, for rebirth, not fighting and killing. Farinas glanced at Keitha, but she showed no displeasure. It seemed no one wanted more fighting.

"Corentyn will go with the prisoner," Cináed added. "He'll let them know about the Gathering and our call for peace, so we can unite against Rome. He'll use his time at Hillfoot to check their defences in case they reject the call. We have information on Clatchard's defences from Keitha."

So it was agreed. Corentyn and the prisoner would leave at dawn the following day. Beitris, from Corentyn's unit, would accompany them. Decisions made, jugs of *uisge beath* were brought, and they drank to their dead, as the harpist played a lament on his *clarsach*.

During the night, lookouts changed, and unit commanders checked the guards and their defences often, while others took turns ensuring the pyre's hot, cleansing flames were fed.

At dawn, Eochaid and his men made a quick breakfast, then left, after promising to make sure a unit of fighters was on its way.

At the same time, the prisoner, Tadhg, rode out, escorted by Corentyn and Beitris. He kept his head down and made no trouble. A short while later, Farinas saw Roibeart, another of Corentyn's unit, ride out in the same direction. When he asked Cináed about it, Farinas smiled and told him Corentyn never left anything to the gods.

The pyre was allowed to die down, and the ashes were scattered on the sacred pool, above the one where Farinas had bathed. There was a tree standing on the bank with its branches covered in offerings to the local spirits. It reminded Farinas of the one above *Eas Dochart*, that Dànaidh had taken them to.

Because of the possible threat from the Venicone, there would be no more trips to the pools. The herdsmen kept the flocks penned in, and the children played close to home. Watchmen were told to look out for the reinforcements promised by Eochaid, riding under the Vacomagi banner. Hunters went out, always keeping to the north.

The previous attack and the tactics used by the Venicone were different to the way the tribes usually fought and the units drilled and exercised daily, with this in mind. Farinas joined the unit commanded by Goraidh. They would be deployed at the rear of the column, to prevent an enemy force breaking through to the village.

An additional unit was formed under the command of Friseal, a young man who had proved himself in the earlier battle, and in the raid on Hillfoot. Their task would be to remain behind, in the event of a repeat of the earlier strategy, of attacking through the village.

The villagers had settled into their new roles, either preparing for spring planting or caring for the beasts, mending tools and weapons, and always, drilling and exercising.

Life had settled into an easy routine that Farinas was enjoying, so when the lookout at the southern end of the glen sounded the alarm, it was even more of a shock than usual.

245

Chapter 41

The alarm continued as everyone moved swiftly to their assigned positions. The vulnerable were assisted into the broch with the animals, and young lookouts were posted on the top floor, with a view of both ends of the glen.

As Farinas watched, one of the lookouts raised his arm and shouted. "Two riders… from the south!"

Soon after, one of the lookouts rode in, leading a pony. Its rider was struggling to remain upright, and Farinas recognised Roibeart who had ridden out after Corentyn and Beitris. Roibeart looked uninjured, but both he and the pony were close to collapsing from exhaustion. Cináed ran and helped Roibeart down.

They spoke briefly then Roibeart was helped into the broch, while Cináed ran to his pony and rode to the head of the column of warriors. His voice carried as they scrambled into their units. "The Venicone have imprisoned Corentyn and Beitris." There was a roar of outrage at this and Cináed held his hand up for silence. "Corentyn ordered Roibeart to follow them, out of sight of the prisoner. While hiding above Hillfoot, Roibeart watched as a force rode in from Clatchard and joined with those from Hillfoot. A joint Venicone war band is approaching. It's not far behind Roibeart."

There were angry mutterings at this further breach of their common rules of warfare. At the very least, the messengers should have been allowed to return in safety.

Cináed stilled them. "Move out fast! Use the time Roibeart has given us!"

There was a loud roar, and Cináed waved the column forward, as stragglers hurried to catch up. They stopped when they reached the farthest-out lookout, posted by Roibeart on his way in. The lookout reported dust clouds in the distance, and glints of sunlight on metal.

When the units were in place facing the route from the south, Cináed rode to the rear of the column. "Don't let the bastards break through, Goraidh!" he shouted, dismounting, and leaving his pony with the youngsters, before making his way to the front of the massed warriors.

As Goraidh's unit got into position, Farinas lined up and waited with his sword drawn, and wondered at his eagerness to engage in a battle for people he hadn't even known, just a short time before. He found his hand resting on his arm where the armband should have been, and he asked the god, Uzivelele, as well as the great god, Mars to protect them. As his mind wandered to the little black carving he'd left at the gladiator school, he sensed a stirring in the column, and a hush falling over the ranks. He checked his weapon and waited as the remaining units lined up, spears in front, swords behind.

Keitha had taken her unit forward, beyond the head of the column, then she had led them up the grassy slope bordering the track. At the tree line, they disappeared into the trees, ready to surprise the advancing Venicone. Quistaghyn was already stationed at the treeline with the carnyx-blower, waiting to sound the signals.

It had all been done with speed and precision, and again Farinas was impressed.

At first, the only sound to be heard was bird song, then the birds fell silent, and they became aware of the sound of marching feet. Those at the front of the column watched as the Venicone war band marched into sight. The ranks faltered, dismayed by the sight of the Vacomagi facing them, ready and waiting. Thanks to Roibeart, and Corentyn's foresight, the Venicone had lost the element of surprise. The eerie stillness and the readiness of the waiting Vacomagi were intimidating and Cináed held the columns in silence until the last enemy warrior had passed below Keitha's unit.

Then from the tree line, the carnyx sounded, and Keitha's unit raced down the slope and charged the rear of the enemy, making retreat impossible. At the same time, Cináed led the others in a frontal attack, and the Venicone found themselves beset on two fronts.

Farinas grasped his sword and followed the spearmen. Thrust into single-handed combat, Farinas and the others had no concept of what was happening outside the small area they occupied, but Keitha's sudden attack from the rear had given the Vacomagi a second, distinct advantage. While some Venicone tried to turn to engage them, others moved forward to fight off the frontal attack.

Farinas soon realised they were fighting a bigger force than before. The Venicone had clearly called on support from other villages, and now significantly outnumbered them. Roibeart's warning had prevented the Vacomagi from being massacred and had given them an initial advantage, but the tide of battle was slowly turning against them. As the Venicone rallied, the fighting became increasingly fierce and brutal. With little in the way of armour, sword slashes cut into skin and bone, and sword points penetrated vital organs.

Screams filled the air and roars of rage and anger blended with the clash of metal echoing from the hillsides. Blood soaked the heather, and men and women, on both sides, fell to be trampled under the feet of those still standing. Farinas, bloodied and exhausted, found it harder and harder to stem the tide of the Venicone, trying to push through. He thought of Ruaraidh and the other young ones waiting just beyond his position, and he fought as determinedly as the others.

As the sun rose in the sky, Cináed fought his way to the tree line, where Quistaghyn stood observing the scene below,

"There's too many," Quistaghyn said. "This is war the Roman way, not a raid for a few beasts or a wee bit of land."

They looked down on the scene. The Vacomagi were no longer attacking; they were on the defensive and falling further and further back. Keitha's unit was all but cut off from the others and it too was being beaten back. "There's been no call for support from the village," Cináed pointed out. "We might need to call up Friseal's unit." He waited, unwilling to withdraw Friseal but aware of the toll the battle was taking on his people.

He had decided to make the order when they heard a cheer go up from the youngsters standing between the battleground and the village, with the ponies and carts. As Cináed and Quistaghyn watched, a unit of warriors under the Vacomagi banner marched through Goraidh's unit and led them in a charge that slowly gathered momentum, as they hacked and slashed the tired Venicone.

"The unit Eochaid promised," Cináed shouted, and Quistaghyn nodded.

"Just in time," he whispered and signalled the carnyx-blower.

As the carnyx sounded out, signalling the arrival of reinforcements, Quistaghyn raised his staff high above his head and, for a heartbeat, all eyes were raised to the sound of the horn. The sight of their druid gave the Vacomagi strength and determination. At the same time, the Venicone, faced with reinforcements, lost much of their resolve.

As Farinas charged forward behind the reinforcements, he saw a big man, wielding a two-handed, broad sword and inflicting serious damage on any who came near. Farinas recognised Conn, the headman he'd dealt with when he'd gone to Clatchard as a 'Representative of Rome'. Taking him out of the battle would seriously affect the enemies' morale. It would also help pay the man back for his treatment of Keitha.

As he battled his way towards him, Farinas saw that Cináed had left Quistaghyn's side and was also fighting his way towards the big warrior, cutting down any who stood in his way. The two clashed, as Farinas forced his way through to assist Cináed. He was stopped by a Venicone who managed to slash his side before Farinas spun on his heel and sliced his attacker's neck. Blood spurted out, signalling a fatal strike and Farinas battled on, ignoring the burning pain in his side.

Cináed and Conn were tired, but they fought hard, oblivious to the other personal struggles going on around them. Eventually, Cináed, with his lighter blade, was able to strike the Venicone under the arm, then he sprang back, avoiding the broad sword, falling from Conn's nerveless grip.

Farinas would have moved in for the kill if Cináed had not slammed his sword aside with his own weapon. A dangerous move in the heat of battle, but Farinas was used to split-second decisions from his time in the arena where fights to the death were uncommon. He stayed his blade from a fatal strike.

Cináed had recognised the man as an important Venicone. "Prisoner!" he roared, over the battle clamour. "Take him alive!"

Farinas's eyes re-focused, and he nodded his understanding. As Conn desperately tried to grasp his sword, Cináed brought the flat of his blade down on the side of the man's head, and he fell in the mud at their feet.

As Cináed and Farinas continued to fight, Keitha rode up, and Farinas realised she had been watching Cináed's battle with Conn and she had brought the pony to take the prisoner from the battleground. Cináed and Farinas threw the unconscious Venicone over the pony's back, in front of Keitha.

"Have him secured and taken back in a cart," Cináed ordered before whirling and slashing a Venicone, trying to seize the pony's bridle.

Keitha, blood-stained and as exhausted as the others, showed no sign of recognising her prisoner, as she wheeled the pony and forced her way through the fighting. The animal was well-trained and found safe passage through the carnage.

Fortunately, fear of injuring their headman kept the Venicone at bay, and Keitha reached the carts with her prisoner. A lad calmed the pony, as Keitha dismounted. Conn, still unconscious and bleeding, was thrown into a cart. "Secure him well," Keitha gasped. "He's strong. Then take him back to Friseal." She left them binding the man with leather strips and returned to the fight where she joined her unit and led them back up the slope.

From her position above the battle, she could see how everything had slowed down. Badly injured and dead lay everywhere.

The Vacomagi reinforcements had come to the battle fresh and were pushing the Venicones towards Keitha's unit. Seeing the battle beginning to go the way of the Vacomagi, Quistaghyn ordered the horn blower to sound the advance.

At the sound of the carnyx, the Vacomagi made a concerted effort to advance on the Venicone who broke ranks and tried to flee the battleground. They had seen one of their leaders taken, and they were finished. Soon, those who could flee, did, leaving their dead and wounded behind. A few Vacomagi followed, caught up in the battle fever, but returned as the carnyx sounded the recall.

There was little in the way of celebration, as they gathered in their units and counted the cost of yet another battle. Farinas again helped carry the injured to the carts and Ruaraidh came over. "You're bleeding," he told him pointing to his blood-soaked tunic. "Get into the cart and I'll take you back with the others."

Farinas looked at the young man in the cart with a sword slash in his arm that was through to the bone and shook his head. "It's nothing," he insisted. "Take these first."

After the wounded and the dead had been taken from the battleground, Cináed and the other survivors, many injured but still able to walk, gathered and looked over the blood-soaked glen. Among them was Roibeart. He had freed himself from the attentions of Mistress Foirbeis at the broch and ridden up to join the battle. The cries of the injured Venicone were almost, but not quite indistinguishable from the screaming of the black crows and ravens wheeling overhead.

"We can't keep killing each other like this." Quistaghyn's words expressed what they all felt.

"Let them come for their dead and injured," Cináed ordered, leading the exhausted survivors from the carnage.

Chapter 42

Back at the village, the young charioteers had taken the ponies from the shafts and led them away to be cared for. The exhausted and bloodied warriors were welcomed back and looked after by their families and neighbours or in the broch. There had been four deaths and some serious injuries. Probably not the final toll but much smaller than it would have been, without Roibeart's warning and the timely arrival of Eochaid's reinforcements.

Farinas took a pitcher of water from a woman and drank deeply as he listened to the wailing and cries from the homes where bodies had been taken. "How long can we keep losing our young?" the woman asked, and Farinas had no answer.

Children and old people came out of the broch to the sight of the carnage left by the battle. The smoky smell from the funeral pyre still hung in the air. Now they would have to build another.

Cináed and Goraidh organised lookouts at vulnerable places. "What are we goin' to do about Corentyn and Beitris," Goraidh asked as they made their way to the meeting house.

"We'll talk about that," Cináed assured him, before making sure Eochaid's unit was being looked after. He asked their leader Seocan, to join them, as well as Farinas, whose sword slash was being bound by Ruaraidh.

The men entered, joining Roibeart Cairistìona and Quistaghyn, as food and ale were brought, and damaged weapons taken away for repair. Even before the unit leaders made their reports, Farinas stood up, and all eyes turned to him.

"The man we captured. His name is Conn, headman of Hillfoot. He and his son took Keitha, questioned, and tortured her, then gave her to us, believing they'd sold her to Rome for more questioning."

Cináed nodded. "We'll question him later. Our first concern must be Corentyn and Beitris." He hesitated and looked closely at the group. "Where's my sister?" he growled. "I know she wasn't hurt."

"Checking her unit?" Torcadall, leader of the spearmen, suggested.

Cináed caught one of the servers by the arm. "Go and tell Keitha she is needed here," he commanded. The server left and Cináed continued. "Our thanks to Seocan. Without you and your unit, the result might not have gone our way and our casualties would certainly have been higher." He waited as the others added their thanks then got back to the main business. "I'll hear the reports of the unit leaders."

The reports were painful to hear, as the dead and injured were named, and there was a moment of silence as they thought of the casualties and remembered the dead. Cináed finally broke the silence. "We need to arrange an exchange, Conn for Corentyn and Beitris."

"Conn is head of Clatchard," Goraidh pointed out. "Hillfoot may not wish to trade for him."

"We should ha' killed the injured, not let them be taken back to fight us again." Roibeart was saying what others were thinking, but Quistaghyn disagreed.

"All-out tribal warfare is never the answer, especially now when we will soon face an even mightier foe. These battles are as nothing to the ones we will have to fight when Rome sends her mighty legions."

The door was thrown open, and the lad who'd gone to fetch Keitha interrupted with his news. "She never came back with her unit."

"I saw her...at the end. She was unhurt." Farinas stood up.

"Sit!" Cináed thundered. "She's surely not gone off on her own again!"

"She may be with the wounded," Quistaghyn suggested, getting up and walking towards the door. "I should go and help Mistress Foirbeis. I'll send her over if she's there."

The boy shook his head. "No one saw her return. She told Curstaidh to bring the unit in."

Quistaghyn left as Cináed roared at the boy. "Bring Curstaidh here!" The boy fled. "Whatever she's got into this time; she can get out of it herself." Cináed's comment was directed at Farinas, who reluctantly nodded his agreement. "We've more important issues to deal with than the fate of one wilful woman, even if she is my sister."

"We returned our hostage to Hillfoot, yet they held our envoys and attacked us," Roibeart said. "And Conn joined them, with others. We can't trust any Venicone."

"An exchange won't work. We'll have to take them back." Goraidh slammed his mug down on the table. "No survivors this time."

"We can call on all the Vacomagi now," Torcadall reminded them.

"Not a good plan. The Venicone will call on other tribes. This war will spread." Cairistìona was not usually so reasonable, and the others listened, realising how serious the situation was.

Cináed let them have their say, and listened as the argument went first one way then the other.

"Eochaid will take the Vacomagi to war," Seocan advised. "But only if there's no other way. He wants the Gathering to take place."

"How long can we go on like this?" Cairistìona asked. Her brother was still in the broch and seemed unlikely to recover from his injuries.

"This is what Rome wants." Goraidh spoke quietly as if he'd just realised what was happening. "What we're facin' is bigger than anything we've seen in generations. Rome tried to destroy the Caledonii before. Her legions massacred many, but we learned to defend ourselves and, with the gods' help, she failed." He waited then added quietly. "Now we're about to do it to ourselves."

That silenced the talk of war, at least for a while, then Roibeart drew the discussion back. "All this talk isn't getting Corentyn and Beitris back!" he roared. "While we talk, they could be dead."

"No," Cináed disagreed, "The exchange will be the first thing discussed at the Gathering. Eochaid will make sure of it, and everyone will abide by the decision."

As they considered this, the door opened and Keitha's second-in-command, Curstaidh entered. Her arm was wrapped in a bloody length of cloth and her face was streaked with dirt and blood.

"Keitha didn't come back with us. She sent me back with the unit. I thought—"

She stopped and the sounds of a pony being ridden hard reached them. As the pony stopped, Keitha's voice carried into the meeting house. "Gladiator!"

"Better see what my sister wants." Cináed shrugged resignedly, and everyone followed Farinas outside. Ruaraidh and a group of villagers had gathered around Keitha who was slumped over the neck of her tired pony. She was covered in dust and gore from the battle, and blood dripped from a gash in her thigh.

When she saw Farinas, she straightened up and managed a tired grin as she threw a blood-soaked bundle at his feet. "My thanks, Gladiator!" As Farinas and the others looked at the bundle, Keitha turned the pony and rode to the stables, dripping blood as she went.

It was Cináed who stepped forward, grasped the cloth, and pulled it off to reveal a bloody arm, neatly cut off just below the shoulder. Above the elbow was a gold armband. Its shine was dulled by grime, but it was unmistakeably Videric's.

Farinas swallowed a lump in his throat. He had been noticing how often his hand moved to the place where he'd worn the armband, and how much he'd missed it. With trembling fingers, he pulled the band off and held it tight.

He was vaguely aware of the others moving away, chattering excitedly about Keitha's latest exploit. Everyone had heard what had happened from Ruaraidh or Keitha. Farinas had not talked of it.

Farinas stood, and a damp rag was thrust into his hand. "You'll want to give it a bit of a clean." Ruaraidh smiled, sharing his emotion.

"You knew what she was doing?"

"When we were looking for our dead and injured, I saw her riding after the Venicone. She took her revenge, and she repaid her debt at the same time. She's too proud to be owing anyone." Ruaraidh smiled. "It's where it belongs." He returned to his duties, as Farinas followed the others back into the meeting house, smiling at the familiar feel of the gold on his arm.

"Make sure my sister gets her wound seen to," Cináed growled at Curstaidh, who nodded and left.

Goraidh was grinning and explaining to Seocan what Keitha had done, and the others were settling down again when the door was pushed open, and a man walked forward to stand in front of the dais.

"Seòras, welcome," Cináed stood and faced the man who was standing awkwardly, but with a determined look.

"My daughter Beitris, and Corentyn, when are we going to get them?"

"We'll exchange our prisoner for them, but he stays here…until the Gathering."

"No!" Seòras slammed his hand on the table. "You know how they treat prisoners...your own sister..."

"Not Beitris," Cináed said. "They won't harm her or Corentyn, now that their chief, Griogair is in talks with our chief, Eochaid. Beitris and Corentyn will be exchanged then...safely." Seòras calmed down and Cináed held his hand out. "Come, join us in the discussion. It's about your lass and Corentyn."

Seòras joined them and Roibeart handed him a mug of ale then turned to Cináed. "We know we can't trust the Venicone...we've just said so. I say we go and get them."

"Not while we have Conn!" Cináed was losing patience, but he understood their concerns. "It will be arranged at the Gathering. It will only be done sooner if they return Beitris and Corentyn… but I will send no one else to be taken or killed."

Corentyn spoke. "These villages have acted alone. It is not our way. We must deal with Griogair the Venicone chief, not the heads of a few villages. What we do now, will determine how we defend ourselves against Rome."

Cináed nodded. "We will talk with Conn now. Roibeart you can tell him of Hillfoot's treachery." He smiled. "Farinas, you can let him know there are no Romans coming to his rescue."

He got up. "We'll meet back here when we've finished with Conn."

Chapter 43

Cináed led the way to the broch, now empty of animals. Quistaghyn and Mistress Foirbeis were treating the injured on the top floor, and Conn was slumped at the foot of the central pole to which he was secured. His wounds had been cleaned and bound. When he saw them coming, he struggled to his feet, shaking his manacles. "This is not how I should be treated."

"Better than you deserve," Cináed answered.

"You're a fool" Conn spat on the floor. "The legions are coming. You'll wish you'd joined with us when that happens."

"Vacomagi do not ally with Rome against their own," Quistaghyn answered him.

"You're finished. When the legions come, the Venicone will be on the side of the winners."

"You speaking for all the Venicone, now?" Cináed asked.

Conn hesitated then answered. "They'll join us." He examined Cináed closely. You'll be Cináed, the village headman?"

"Aye," Cináed nodded in agreement.

"You'll be wonderin' about your sister?"

Farinas wanted to smash the gloating look off his face, but he kept to the shadows.

Cináed remained calm. "My sister?" He shrugged. "She was late back from that last wee fight we had. Taking something back that belonged to our friend here."

Farinas stepped out of the shadows, the armband glinted on his arm and Conn's triumphant look was wiped from his face. "No." He lunged at the Vacomagi, but the chain pulled him back. "Where's my son?" he roared. "Where's Tormond?"

Cináed spoke. "You would sell my sister to be abused, tortured, and killed for information after your son had already mistreated her. What would *you* expect her to do to him?"

Conn's gaze moved from the armband to the man wearing it. All he saw was the Roman official he'd bargained with. He gazed in horror at Cináed, trying to make sense of everything. "You're allied to Rome, through this man?"

"We will never ally with Rome," Cináed growled. "He's Vacomagi."

Farinas wondered at the feeling of pleasure he experienced at this sign of acceptance. He'd not felt he belonged anywhere for a long time, not properly, as a free man. Not since he'd lived in Theveste. He smiled, watching Conn's growing confusion reflected in his expressions.

He'd found out about the death of his son, his grand plan had been overturned, and the Roman official had turned out to be a Vacomagi. One hope was left to him. "Roman soldiers at Carpow will come when they hear of this."

It was Corentyn who answered with an authority that even Conn couldn't deny. "That camp was temporary. It has gone. They have been sent to reinforce the fort at Caladair in preparation for the invasion and the destruction of the Caledonii, *all* the Caledonii. Did you really think they were interested in an alliance with you? The head of a small village."

"You're a fool," Cináed added. "To think they were interested in you."

"We're wastin' time. He's no use to us," Roibeart interrupted. "Your allies from Hillfoot, are holding two of our village. They went there to return a hostage and talk of peace. Your treacherous allies have kept them."

"We thought to trade you for them," Cináed added, "but we doubt they'd want you back. You're not even from Hillfoot."

Roibeart looked at the prisoner. "He's no use to us. Kill the bastard! We'll take our people back."

While they were talking, Conn had been pacing up and down, as far as his chain allowed. He stopped pacing as his situation became clear. The man didn't lack courage. He stood tall and faced them. "Aye well, you've killed my son. You'd best get on with it."

Cináed stepped forward and placed his hand on Roibeart's arm. "We'll decide what happens at the meeting." Turning to the guards, Cináed ordered them to take Conn to the meeting house. Decisions needed to be made quickly before more died.

When the villagers entered the meeting house, anxious to see the prisoner, Conn, bound and guarded, was sitting in the shadows behind Cináed and his advisers. Farinas saw Eithrig enter and stand near the door, keeping to the shadows.

There were roars of anger and muttered threats, but Cináed quickly called the meeting to order. "We have to decide how to get Corentyn and Beitris released."

Conn shook his chains and shouted at the angry crowd. "Release me …I'll return your envoys. No one else needs to die!"

"No!" Roibeart moved towards Conn. "This whoreson can't be trusted. He tortured Keitha and sold her to the man he thought was a Roman official!"

There were more roars from the villagers who surged forward, jostling each other and overturning benches, only to be met by Cináed. "He deserves to die but killing him won't help Corentyn and Beitris."

"Well tell us what will," Seòras roared. "What are they doing to my daughter, while we talk?"

Seeing his death in the faces of the angry villagers, Conn was losing some of his earlier courage, "I will bring your people back to you …I swear."

"You're a liar," Seòras called out. "Just kill him and be done with it."

"I'll ride out now," Roibeart shouted, "with any who want to go wi' me,"

"I'm wi' you!" Seòras growled, and other voices joined in.

"No, you won't, Roibeart." Keitha had entered quietly, and she limped through the angry villagers to face Roibeart. Her voice cut through the confused shouts and silenced them. "I know you feel guilty that you left them there, but you've no need. If you hadn't warned us, many of us…maybe most of us would be dead, as well as Beitris and Corentyn. There would be no one to talk peace and fight Rome."

She struggled up onto the dais and grabbed a beaker of ale, as Roibeart calmed down. Keitha turned to Seòras. "I know well how hard it is to do nothing, Seòras, but if we try to take Beitris and Corentyn by force…believe me…they will be killed. I know these people. I would like nothing more than to see him dead, like his treacherous son, but that wouldn't help."

"So, we do nothing?" Roibeart asked.

"No, we leave it to our chief, Eochaid We know we can trust him." She waited for the murmurs of agreement to die down. "Conn may yet be of some use."

There was more talk, but Keitha had been convincing, and the meeting ended with the decision, once more, to take no further action, unless provoked.

"Roibeart, see that the old storehouse is made secure and guarded. He can be kept there," Cináed ordered.

"It's too small." Eithrig's words were greeted with gasps from the hall, not so much because of what she said, but because she had spoken at all. Few had noticed her standing by the door. She had been watching Conn and even she seemed surprised by her outburst, but she was defiant as she faced Cináed.

"It's good enough for a treacherous whoreson who ill-treats women, attacks without warning, and deals with Rome." Cináed looked at his stepmother, as surprised as the others by her interruption, and added. "Since his imprisonment concerns you, you can see to his needs, while he's our prisoner."

Roibeart led the prisoner out, followed by Eithrig, and the villagers returned to their duties, wondering what lay in store for Corentyn and Beitris.

Chapter 44

For the next few days, life seemed almost normal, although the flames and smoke from the new funeral pyre were a constant reminder of recent battles and losses. Defences were strengthened, more pens were built, and additional watches set. It was also important to prepare for possible shortages, so more land was prepared for planting, and hunters went out regularly, always to the north, away from Venicone land.

Farinas hadn't seen Keitha since the meeting to decide what to do with Conn, but Cináed kept him informed about her injury, which was healing well. He had thanked Quistaghyn for the brooch which had saved Keitha's life, possibly his and Ruaraidh's too. The druid's smile indicated that he was already well-informed of the events.

A few days after the meeting, Farinas was on his way to the forge to lend a hand to Marcas when he passed close to the small turf structure where Conn was being held. A guard stood outside, and Farinas heard a woman's laughter from inside. As he approached, he saw Eithrig coming out carrying an empty bowl and jug. Her smile lit up her face and Farinas thought how much happier she looked. He wondered at her interest in the prisoner, but the widow was not his concern.

Coming over a rise, he saw Keitha training a group of youngsters with wooden swords. He remembered his time training with Videric and Cináed, on their way to the port at Gesoriacum and wondered where Teo was and what he was doing. He'd trained them well and made the journey interesting, despite the chains. Farinas hoped he was well and successful.

"Pay attention Cailean," Keitha was shouting. "You've stood by the carts and watched the fighting. You've brought the dead back. Do you want to be brought in a cart, to your funeral pyre!" The lad shook his head and attacked his partner with plenty of energy, unfortunately he lacked any skill.

Seeing Farinas approaching, Keitha left the youngsters and walked over to him.

"Wound healing well?"

Keitha nodded. "It was a clean cut, no poison."

"Thank you…for this." He touched the armband.

"Aye well, thanks for my rescue."

"You would have got away without our help."

"Maybe." They grinned at each other. Farinas had never found himself with nothing to say to a young woman, but he was finding it hard to get his tongue working.

"How's Ruaraidh's training going?"

"He's good. He learned well at the gladiator school," Keitha said. "He's better than others his age."

Farinas had seen youngsters not much older than Ruaraidh in the battle lines. This was not good news. "That means he'll be joining the warriors soon?"

"Probably, but we'll give him time to get settled and learn our ways first." She smiled. "Maybe Eochaid and Griogair will arrange a peace. Give us time to prepare for the Romans."

Farinas turned and watched the youngsters. They were trying, but there was a way to go before they could be sent into battle. Cailean especially was finding it very difficult, and he was older than the others. His opponent, a younger girl, was slightly more skilful but she was depending on brute force to beat her opponent, and he was becoming more and more frustrated. After her sword point touched his chest for the second time, the girl's mocking laughter rang out and she beat him across the side of his head with the flat of her sword.

"Teàrlag! I've told you before. Touch only!" Keitha shouted, but the girl just laughed.

"He's going to get killed the first time he fights. He's useless!"

The boy made no reply, but he clearly agreed with the girl's opinion. He threw his sword down and walked away. Farinas picked up the sword. "Hey!" The boy turned and Farinas threw it to him. Cailean caught it expertly in his left hand. "He uses his left hand."

Farinas turned to Keitha, but she was standing, hands on hips, watching him. "We didn't need a famous gladiator to tell us that," she told him. "We know."

"Told you!" Teàrlag smirked. "He's useless." She walked away, and as she passed Cailean she hissed. "I'll send my wee sister to beat you next time, *amadan*."

"I'll need to give him someone else to practise with. Teàrlag's no help, but she isn't good enough to practise with any of the others."

"Why doesn't he use his left hand?" Farinas asked, watching as Cailean transferred the sword to his right hand and made some clumsy moves with it.

"He has to fight like everyone else," she answered. "It isn't good to be *làmh chlì*."

Farinas saw the boy listening and he stated the obvious. "Well, it's not good for him, to try to be right-handed." Before Keitha could answer, he continued. "There was a left-handed gladiator at Trimontium, Nahresi. No one wanted to fight him. He'd learned to fight against right-handed gladiators, and he'd got good at it. We hadn't fought against any left-handed gladiators except him. We were bad at it." He smiled at the lad. "Aye, Nahresi definitely had an advantage."

Cailean moved the sword to his left hand and practised the exercises he'd been taught. He was hesitant at first but soon increased his speed, eventually, laughing out loud as he felt comfortable with the sword. "He could be good," Farinas noted.

Keitha watched. "Maybe." She paused. "I wouldn't put him in a shield wall, though." Cailean joined in their laughter.

"I helped Videric train new recruits for the gladiator school. I could maybe help here?" Farinas suggested.

Torcadall was training youngsters with spears, and he'd stopped to watch. "You managed a spear well enough. You could maybe help with that too."

They were discussing training methods when an alarm sounded. "*Daingead*! Not the Venicone again!" Torcadall roared. "To your places!" and they raced down to prepare for another raid.

Soon, a lookout came riding through the stream. "Riders! Three! From the south!"

"You're sure there's only three?" Cináed asked.

"If there's more, they're a good distance behind. Lorcan's keeping watch. He'll let us know if any follow."

Cináed nodded. "Go back and stay alert. This could be a trap." He called out to a young girl who was helping line up the ponies and carts. "Cara, ride to the lookouts in the north. Warn them this may be a trap. Tell them to watch for any riders coming their way. Ride back as soon as there's anything to report."

Cara mounted a pony and raced through the glen, as everyone waited for the riders from the south, from Venicone land.

As usual, there was no panic, just an air of readiness, and expectancy, as the riders appeared and then there were cheers, as Corentyn and Beitris were recognised, riding in with a stranger. Seòras called out his daughter's name and ran to help her from her pony.

As Corentyn came closer, he called out. "We come alone. There's no alarm!" and Cináed signalled the unit commanders to stand the men down. As the units broke up and everyone moved away, there were many backward glances at the stranger who had dismounted to stand beside Corentyn.

"You're well?" Cináed asked, and Corentyn nodded. "We could do with some food and ale, though. This is Griogair, chief of the Venicone."

Cináed was not the only one to regard the Venicone chief with suspicion, but he trusted Corentyn. "You're welcome, my lord."

"We have much to discuss," Griogair answered, "but, as our friend said, some food and ale would be welcome after our journey."

Cináed led the way, calling to Keitha as they passed, to summon his unit heads to the meeting. "Farinas, you come too," he added. "Cailean, go and tell Cara and the lookouts in the north that there is no alarm…for now. Tell them to stay alert though."

As they walked to the meeting house where the servers were already seeing to the food and ale, Farinas smiled to see that the best the village could offer, was being laid out for the Venicone chief. The Venicone had already seen how well-prepared and battle-ready they were. Now they would believe they had an ample supply of provisions, despite the hard winter. It sent a warning to any thinking to attack the village in the future.

As they passed Conn's prison cell, Eithrig came out, and they could hear Conn demanding to be released, but his tribal chief gave no indication of having heard him.

Inside the meeting house, Farinas and Cináed sat with Corentyn and Griogair as the others entered. Cináed seemed surprised to see Eithrig coming to join them on the dais but made no comment. It seemed it was her right to attend such meetings, even if she rarely chose to do so. Roibeart came in and made straight for Corentyn. "How are you? Did thae whoresons treat you right? How's Beitris?"

Griogair gave no sign of having heard the insult, and Corentyn laughed. "We're fine! Beitris is with Seòras. We missed good food and ale... and the company. The Venicone are miserable bastards, and their food's tasteless." Farinas noticed a reaction from Griogair at the comments, but he was keeping himself in check.

Others entered and greeted Corentyn before starting on the food and ale. There was the best mead too, and roast deer. It was the only meat they had, but Griogair did not need to know that. Corentyn was told of the events following his capture, allowing the Venicone time to eat and drink his fill, before Cináed questioned him.

"It seems we have you to thank for the release of our envoys, imprisoned in clear breach of our customs."

The Venicone chief pushed the bench back and stood. He was tall and broad-shouldered with long thick hair arranged in two braids. His moustaches curled down on either side of his mouth and his gold torque glinted in the firelight. His clothes were richly dyed wool, and his sword and dagger were sheathed in bronze scabbards. He stood proud and tall before the company which continued to increase, as more representatives entered the hall,

"I am Griogair, chief of all the Venicone. Your chief, Eochaid sent word of my people's attempts to win favour with Rome." He paused this voice became a growl. "I'll no' deal with Rome, and I'll take down any o' mine that do."

Silence followed his words, then Quistaghyn spoke. "You can answer for all the Venicone?"

"Aye. I can. I'm the chief." His hands curled into fists, and his face turned red, as he struggled to control his anger. Whether it was at the question, or at his renegades, wasn't clear, but he made a menacing figure. "They answer to me."

"Not what the funeral pyres have told us." Farinas thought he might have been unwise, as Griogair's hand moved towards his sword, and Cináed thought perhaps he should have removed his visitor's weapons.

"You'll be the gladiator," Griogair growled, and Farinas nodded as his hand moved to his own sword. "I've heard you make a good Roman... and a better Vacomagi."

Farinas nodded and smiled, and as the tension eased, Griogair relaxed and sat down. He drained his mug and sighed. "Aye, you're right. I've been too concerned with the legions and their comings and goings on our land. There's war ahead. Two headmen, and a few men from other villages, defied me." He drank from his refilled beaker and wiped his mouth. "They'll no' dae that again."

No one questioned this statement.

"And Conn?" It was Keitha who spoke.

Griogair turned slowly and examined her. "You'll be the lass he and his son captured and misused."

She nodded, and he spoke directly to her. "I hear you dealt with the son, as was your right. Conn is also yours to deal with. I've already replaced him. Clatchard and Hillfoot have new headmen of my choosin'."

No one had expected this, and his words were considered in silence. Keitha nodded but said nothing. Conn's fate would be decided by them all.

Cináed refilled Griogair's mug. "Two of your villages have allied with Rome. Some of them may still wish to join with Rome. How would you feel, fighting against your kinsmen?"

Griogair's answer was absolute. "They're no' kinsmen o' mine when they join with Rome."

"I need to talk with my advisers," Cináed told him. For now, you're our guest. You can talk to Conn, but he remains our captive."

"I'll take him to the prisoner." Keitha walked to the door, and Griogair followed her outside. Cináed and his advisers relaxed but there was much to consider. Eithrig was hardly noticed, sitting quietly among them.

"Can he be trusted, Corentyn? You know him best," Quistaghyn asked. "Decisions we make today will be important, not just for us, but for all the Vacomagi, and the Venicone."

Corentyn's brow furrowed as he considered his words. "He didn't know about the headmen sending envoys to the Romans, or about the attacks on us. I'm sure of that. As soon as Eochaid told him what had happened, he rode in and demanded our release. He questioned everyone, and put his own men in, as he said." Corentyn considered as the others listened. "Griogair doesn't trust Rome. He'll not ally with them."

Quistaghyn interrupted. "His druidess, Aneira, has told him about the killing of the Roman Governor. She has warned him there will be no treaties. Rome already lands ships close to Venicone land, on the *Uisge Tatha* and will probably build a fort there to protect the harbour once the legions begin marching north. That port's on Venicone land."

Farinas remembered the Roman camp at Carpow. "There was a camp very close to Clatchard, until a few days ago. Griogair must know his people are in danger."

Roibeart nodded. "And the Romans have used that harbour in the past. Griogair needs allies…not more enemies."

Keitha returned and Cináed waited for her to speak. "I thought Griogair would kill Conn when he started whining about his treatment. Griogair asked him about his treatment of me, then laid him out with one solid blow. He threw a bucket of water over him and told him to stop complaining, and hope we didn't kill or enslave him, as was our right."

"Where is he now?" Cináed asked and Keitha smiled. "He wanted to see the smithy. I left him and Marcas discussing the best weapons for the coming war with Rome." She looked around, noticing suspicious frowns. "Don't worry. He's not spying. I trust him."

"What do you want to do about Conn?" Cináed asked her, and Eithrig looked up, clearly concerned.

"I've dealt with his son. The matter's done with. We need men, so I'll trust Griogair to control him...or kill him."

"Griogair would be behaving differently, if the Venicone had beaten us, and taken our village," Roibeart suggested, and there were a few nods of agreement.

"Maybe, but they didn't, so we have the power," Torcadall pointed out.

"To use for good or ill," Quistaghyn noted.

"So, it seems like we have an ally in the Venicone chief," Cináed suggested, to nods of agreement from everyone.

"Better than having him and his Venicone as enemies," Keitha said, quietening the few remaining objections.

"And we will have peace…until the legions return," Corentyn added, as they fell silent, remembering tales of what Rome had done in the past and realising what it would be capable of in the future.

"Right!" Cináed said. "We need to make good use of the time to —" The door slammed open and Griogair walked in but remained standing on the threshold.

"I'll be leaving now, to prepare for the Gathering at the spring equinox," he announced. "I'll see some of you there?"

Cináed nodded. "Aye. I'll be there.

"Am I to take Conn, or leave him to your justice?"

"Take him! He's no use to us here. You might get him to fight Rome with you," Cináed answered.

Quistaghyn added. "So long as he has no power to influence others or make treaties with our enemies."

Griogair nodded in agreement.

"And there will be no further raids?"

"None…I swear it."

Keitha got up. "I will come with you. No one leaves us without food for their journey." Griogair made a very pleasing bow, and left, smiling.

"A good man to have as an ally, I think." Corentyn expressed the feelings of the others, as the door closed behind them.

"We still have to scatter the ashes from the pyre in the sacred pool," Quistaghyn reminded them.

"Let's hope it'll be the last for a while," Torcadall said.

"Explain to your families and neighbours what has been decided," Cináed told them. "So that they understand why the prisoner is being allowed to leave."

They were walking down to the pyre when Keitha passed with Griogair and Conn. Farinas, who had begun watching Eithrig, noticed her standing by the gate, as the two Venicone rode through. There had been something unsettling in the look that passed between the young widow and Conn.

"At least we can show respect to our dead, without fear of an attack," Cináed was saying to Corentyn, as they followed Quistaghyn and the others taking ashes to the sacred pool to be scattered on the water.

"I'm still setting extra lookouts, and they know to be on their guard," Corentyn told him. "Best not trust the Venicone, just yet."

"I'll leave it to you," Cináed agreed, "but I think Griogair's a man that's true to his word."

They scattered the ashes and once again, life returned to normal with everyone hoping for peace, at least long enough to grow another harvest, and bring a few new lives into the world, both human and animal.

Chapter 45

Along with the regular work, preparations for the Gathering were taking place. A few men and women were busy sewing and embroidering garments, lining cloaks with fur, mending, and polishing boots and fashioning gold and silver jewellery, scabbards, and horses' bridles. There would have been more to do, but Cináed had let it be known he would only be taking Farinas with him. Cheese, honey, and salted boar meat were prepared to add to the provisions for the Gathering. Everything that could be done to impress their neighbours, Vacomagi and Venicone, was being done.

Quistaghyn left the village, suitably robed and wearing gemstones on his fingers and braided into his hair, on a pony equally impressive, to meet with his fellow Vacomagi and Venicone druids. They would exchange information and celebrate the spring equinox in an oak grove on sacred land between the two tribes. These festivals would normally be held separately but, by coming together, the druids hoped to strengthen the peace between the two tribes. Later, they would attend the Gathering together. The druids feared Rome as much as the tribes did. Rome recognised the power of the druids and had tried to wipe them out on many occasions and in many countries.

Cináed discussed his decision with his advisers. "I'll take Farinas," he told the group. "The others need to meet him and get to know him as a friend and ally. We also need our defences intact in the event of a raid, and I'll feel better knowing the village is secure while I'm away. Farinas is familiar with what happened here and at Conn's village. He also understands Rome's intentions."

"Shouldn't you have protection?" Keitha asked.

"Our protection will be the law of the Caledonii…and both chiefs will ensure everyone's safety." He paused, then added, "Fewer delegates mean less talking, fewer disputes. We need to agree on peace between tribes, and on tactics to use against Rome, and we need to do it quickly. Keitha will take my place while we're away." He looked at Corentyn and added. "If she tries to bugger off on her own…truss her like a fat *capall coille* and put her in Conn's old cell. Keep her there 'till we get back."

Corentyn grinned. "Aye, my lord. I'll do that." Keitha glared but made no response.

"The Venicone could be using this to draw you away, to mount another raid on the village," Roibeart said.

"That's why I'm leaving you here. Stay alert and send word at the first sign of a threat."

"Might be they want to kill or capture you at the Gathering," Farinas suggested, but this was met by an outcry from everyone.

"That won't happen," Cináed explained. "We'll be on Damnonii land. The chiefs, including the chief of the Damnonii, will be there to ensure peace.

"The villages should be safe too. Our only danger comes from renegades like Conn." Cairistìona pointed out. "No matter what Griogair has promised, men like Conn are only to be trusted when they're dead. Don't worry," she added. "We'll be prepared. We still have Seocan and his unit. They'll stay until you return."

"Send a messenger if there's any trouble," Cináed repeated. "We'll let the chiefs know, and it will be dealt with, under their authority and we'll return as soon as we hear anything."

Later, as Farinas was training the youngsters with Keitha, Cináed came over to watch.

"Do we walk or ride to the Gathering?" Farinas asked.

"There's a good cart track to take us most of the way, so we ride," Cináed told him. "If we leave at sunrise, we should arrive before dark."

"Stay with Cináed and avoid marshes," Keitha advised.

"And naked warriors running through them displaying their tattoos." Farinas and Cináed laughed, remembering Videric's words, while Keitha looked puzzled.

"You might even find yourself a woman from the Damnonii," Cináed suggested.

"There's plenty of fine women here!" Keitha snapped.

"That's true, but he hasn't shown much interest in any of them," Cináed pointed out. "Although Cairistìona seemed interested for a while, and Ceitidh was definitely interested. I just thought—"

"There hasn't been much time for women," Farinas struggled to find words to rescue him from his embarrassment.

"Well, we'll see when we're there." Cináed was watching his sister, enjoying her annoyance. "It's good to bring in new blood."

Keitha glared at him, then turned back to the youngsters. "Keep your swords up; use them to defend as well as to attack!" Her shout echoed off the hills, and the youngsters immediately straightened their backs and attacked with more energy.

"She likes you," Cináed said, leaving Farinas wondering.

Cináed and Farinas left for the Gathering soon after Quistaghyn. Their horses were waiting beside the light cart that would carry their contribution to the food, and some wineskins of their best wine, including some imported wine, extra clothes, and blankets. Since the headmen were trying to impress each other, the meals would be made from the best each village could provide.

Cailean was driving the cart as a reward for his progress in training. He wore a sheathed sword proudly on his right hip, and he was anxious to attend such an event, even though he would also have to help with the cooking and serving. He wore a fine new tunic and warm woollen trousers, and his cloak had been trimmed in fur.

Cináed and Farinas were also dressed to make an impression. The spring sun shone on gold torques and armbands, rings and sheaths decorated with coloured gemstones. Their cloaks were richly dyed wool, with fur-trimmed hoods. They were pinned in place with large bronze and enamel brooches, as decorative and pleasing as any Roman *fibulae* Farinas had seen. Their heavy waterproof cloaks were rolled up and fastened to their saddles with packs of food and full waterskins. Leather boots, bridles and reins were gleaming, and the silverware shone. Everything was designed to show the village's wealth, with the swords and sidearms also proclaiming their readiness to fight.

Farinas in his finery, felt as he had done going into the arena, part of a spectacle. At least he hoped there would be no killing at this event. He had let his hair grow and it curled round his face which he continued to shave. Cináed's long hair and moustaches were washed and arranged with lime water. He had chosen to ride a horse with a saddle, as he had often done on his travels, before being captured and sold as a slave.

"I can't have you looming over me when we ride in," he said. "They'll think you're the village headman. Especially now you're looking like a civilised Vacomagi."

"Never thought I'd hear Caledonii described as 'civilised'," Farinas said.

"We have to intimidate the others with our wealth," Cináed said. "They'll be doing the same."

"You've impressed me," Farinas admitted. "I've yet to see the naked, tattooed barbarians Videric told us about."

"I told you it was lies," Cináed said. "Except for the fighting bit. We're bonny fighters."

"Your curls are bonny." A young lass overheard and came from the crowd of well-wishers to attach a bunch of purple and white heather to Farinas's horse's bridle. "*Fortan dhut,*" she said, and Farinas looked to Ruaraidh who'd come to see them off, to translate.

"I think she's offering more than some heather and good luck," he laughed.

"Maybe you should be taking this more seriously," Keitha growled, pushing the girl aside.

"Told you she liked you," Cinácd said as they moved out into a morning that was bright and clear. As usual, however, distant clouds threatened rain at some time during the journey.

Farinas thought he recognised the countryside they passed through, as they headed down the glen, either from journeys to Hillfoot and Clatchard or from his journey to the village with Ruaraidh. This time though it was daylight, and the atmosphere was more relaxed. Beyond the Three Sisters, Farinas looked out for Dànaidh or his hound, but the land lay quiet, apart from the sound of the river, which became a roar as they passed the falls. The sun was shining on the clear water and the hills glowed with purple heather and yellow gorse and Farinas was beginning to see why Cináed loved this country so much.

Past the falls, the going was easier as they followed the track south. Early in the afternoon, thunder rumbled in the distance and rain poured down on them, and so it remained until they rode into Calasraid, the small Damnonii village that had been chosen for the Gathering. There were ruins that were clearly Roman scattered about, but Cináed said people had been living there long before the Romans came; back before Rome even existed, in the time of the Old Ones.

The village's meeting house had been made available for the delegates to bed down, and for meetings to take place. The young servers were housed in hastily improvised shelters. Cailean took charge of the cart and horses.

"Keep an eye on the cart," Cináed called to Cailean. "Come and get me or Farinas if there's any trouble." Cailean nodded and left, as Cináed led Farinas into the meeting house. The wind slammed the doors behind them, and heads turned to examine the visitors.

"Cináed! Farinas!" Eochaid came forward to greet them. The big man looked just as impressive in his finery as Farinas remembered, but without his longsword sheathed on his back, less war-like. Smiling he led them to a dais where the main delegates were sitting. Farinas recognised Griogair of the Venicone, and they exchanged warm greetings, then Eochaid took them to meet a striking-looking woman dressed in the Roman style. She wore a long softly gathered tunic under a woollen *palla*. Her dark hair was piled on top of her head and her blue eyes examined the newcomers intently. Her jewellery was as elegant and rich as any the visitors wore. As Eochaid introduced them, her full red lips parted in a smile of welcome, and Farinas gave his most charming smile in return.

"Antia is the Damnonii chief, and our host," Eochaid said, then named Cináed and Farinas.

"You are welcome," Antia said, "and I hope the Gathering will be successful. Cináed, my condolences on the loss of your father, Laomann. By all accounts, he was a good and strong headman to your village." She smiled. "I am sure you will have much to discuss with the chiefs, and later with the heads of the villages."

Cináed bowed, a more elegant gesture than any Farinas had seen him make before, and Antia signalled to a young woman standing by the side of the room. "This is Caesennia," she said. "She will look after you while you are here." She and Eochaid returned to the dais, joining Griogair who was sitting with

Quistaghyn and his fellow druids, in a show of spiritual solidarity and friendship.

Caesennia led Cináed and Farinas to a bench at a long table in the hall. Places were made for them, and platters of food and jugs of ale were placed before them. Conversations were resumed, as they ate and drank. Cináed greeted those Vacomagi he had met before, and Farinas examined his companions. He sensed unease among them and some tension, particularly among the Venicone.

"I'm Niall." The man on Farinas's left glared at him, as though ready to start a fight, but Farinas was beginning to realise that was just their way. Maybe a lack of sunshine led to a dour disposition. "This is my adviser, Donnchadh." He indicated a dark-haired man, tall and well-muscled who bared his teeth in what Farinas took to be a smile.

"You're the gladiator, then?" Donnchadh asked and there was silence as others listened to the exchange.

"I'm Farinas. I used to be a gladiator," Farinas agreed, wary of where this questioning was going.

The man, big and bearded as many men in the north seemed to be, nodded. "Griogair put me in as headman in place o' Conn, at Clatchard. I've no wish to ally with Rome." There was a growl of agreement from the others at the table. Cináed introduced himself, and there was a visible lessening of tension, as he made no reference to the recent battles with the Venicone.

Niall explained what was happening. "We're waiting for one of the Venicone headmen to get here, but the chiefs have already begun their talks. There's been one or two wee disputes so far, but nothing serious."

"Aye," Donnchadh nodded. "Just some land issues between villages or a dispute from way back, in their grandfathers' or great-grandfathers' time. We've more important things to think about now. The local Damnonii are closest to the Romanised areas. They've been warning us of what's coming. The Romans aren't happy."

A server put down a jug of ale and told them what they'd heard. "The Romans used to live on our land without much bother between us, but we think things are going to be different soon. Soldiers are moving north, and there's talk of them rebuilding the wall."

The door banging open halted the conversation and a man and a woman came in, seemingly blown in by the wind and rain. They slammed the door shut and were welcomed by Griogair who took them to meet Eochaid and the druids.

"That's Faolan," Niall explained. "Griogair made him head of Hillfoot when he took over and Siùbhan is his adviser They've had a lot of work to do. Some of their houses burned down recently."

No one continued this conversation, and Farinas guessed this had been discussed previously, and the matter was now considered closed. He noticed Cináed watching Niall and Donnchadh to see if they wanted to take the issue further, but no more was said. Faolan and Siùbhan joined them, and the meal passed without incident.

The talk among the village heads and their advisers had been about the need to come together to prepare for Rome's retaliation; something the tribes were not good at. They tended to be fiercely independent, owing allegiance only to their chief.

The chiefs, village heads and druids left to continue the serious discussions, in a house set aside for them.

Farinas joined various groups, listening to gossip, and learning what he could about the people he was now so closely involved with. He was questioned about his birthplace, and about his time as a gladiator, mainly by the young women, although some of the men were interested in the weapons and armour used in the arena.

There seemed to be little enmity between the Vacomagi and the Venicone, but Farinas couldn't think there was any real friendship...or trust. He was becoming aware of too many tribal disputes and issues from the past that had been simmering for generations.

The atmosphere lightened when hunters who had gone out earlier, returned with a boar which was taken to be prepared for roasting. They were cheered into the hall, as everyone looked forward to enjoying fresh meat.

When the main discussion broke up, the group returned to the hall. "How are your talks going?" Farinas asked Cináed.

"Well enough, I think. Petty differences keep being raised but Eochaid and Griogair seem to be in agreement. They're keeping things peaceful with Antia's help. We'll put our decisions to the whole group as soon as we can…Then we can go home."

As night fell, food was served, and entertainment was provided by Damnonii musicians and bards, but it had been a busy day and soon everyone settled down to sleep.

Farinas rolled himself in his cloak and lay down at the back of the meeting house. As he lay listening to the rain, again drumming on the thatched roof, he felt a hand opening his cloak. He relaxed as a soft, warm body slid in beside him. He briefly thought of Keitha but his body, deprived for so long, took over and he rolled into the soft embrace of Caesennia.

Chapter 46

When Farinas woke, Caesennia was dressing to attend to her duties. Throughout the hall, others were quietly doing the same, picking their way between the sleeping bodies of men, women, and hounds. Farinas rolled over to go back to sleep and saw Cináed clasped in the arms of Faolan's adviser, Siùbhan.

When Farinas next woke, servers were bringing in oatmeal and ale, as everyone got ready for the day. The doors were opened to clear the air and the sun sparkled on raindrops and puddles. Farinas and Cináed were enjoying their porridge when raised voices disturbed pleasant thoughts of their bedmates.

"There's no point facin' the legions across a battlefield. We need to pick them off when we can, while they're marchin' or bedded down…"

"Aye, you Venicones are no' very good at pitched battles," a voice called out. "Took a beatin' when you tried it against the Vacomagi."

"At least we don't set fire tae folks, whilst they're sleepin'."

Voices were being raised across the hall, and the peaceful atmosphere was beginning to take on a more familiar warlike aspect.

Cináed looked as though he was about to add his voice to the discussion, to calm things down before blood was spilt and fighting broke out, when a clear voice carried across the room. The Lady Antia had entered and was making her way to the dais.

"Enough!" The demand, coming from the young woman who had said little until now, shocked the tribesmen into silence. Antia was dressed in a light cloak of soft wool the colour of the heather. It hung open over a long linen robe, fastened at the waist with a gem-encrusted belt. Her dark hair was piled on top of her head, allowing her gold earrings to sway gently and catch the light. These were matched by a long gold chain and an amethyst pendant.

"You sound like bairns squabbling over foolishness, while the grown-ups decide important matters."

"Burning down houses isn't foolishness!" The comment was met with a few shouts that quickly died away, as Antia looked at the man who had called out.

"No, it is not, but we have dealt with that matter, and" she paused looking round, "the unprovoked attack that led to it."

There was silence and she waited a few heartbeats before adding. "We have to come to an agreement to live in peace, at least until we've driven out the Romans…again."

There were some cheers and laughter and it seemed as though she had won them over until a huge Venicone stood up. "Nobody calls me a bairn!"

"Sit down, Iagan!" Griogair commanded. He had joined Antia, leaving Eochaid and the druids quietly watching the proceedings. Iagan hesitated, unwilling to back down. "Sit down, or I'll let Caitrìona know how you kept warm last night."

Roars of laughter greeted this threat, and even Iagan allowed a small smile to cross his face, before sitting down and raising his cup of ale to his lips.

"We fight. That's what we do, an' we're good at it." Eochaid had come forward to stand with Griogair, and roars of approval greeted his assertion. "But, like the Lady Antia said, we're no' about killing each other now. We're saving the fighting for the Romans." Eochaid paused then raised his fist.

"*Fuil Ròmanach!*" The cry echoed throughout the room. Venicone and Vacomagi united for the moment, in the cry for the blood of Romans. "We leave here united," Eochaid said. "If anyone has a dispute, bring it to us."

"For now, drink your beer, and give us peace," Griogair grumbled. "We've serious talking to do."

There was laughter, and talk of hunting, as the servers cleared the tables, and the main delegates left to continue their discussions.

Cailean came to clear the tables, and Farinas waved him over. He hadn't been to the practice grounds much, but he was interested in the lad. "How's the training going?"

Cailean smiled. "Good. The others don't know how to fight me, so I usually get the better of them."

"And Teàrlag?"

Cailean's smile disappeared. "After I beat her in practice, she stopped coming to training." He looked worried. "The Lady Eithrig said she needed a personal servant and demanded Teàrlag. I think Teàrlag had been visiting her and persuaded her to take her as her servant. She picks on people she doesn't like…causes trouble for us…then the Lady Eithrig protects her."

"Maybe I could—"

"No…thank you…but it's fine." Cailean smiled again. "We're working on it. The older ones are protecting the younger ones from her and Eithrig. It's best we sort it ourselves."

Farinas nodded. "Aye but if things get worse—"

Cailean nodded. "I know. I'll tell you." He smiled and waved to a young man calling to him. "I'd best get the tables cleared for later."

Farinas put on his cloak and went out into the sunshine, pleased he'd spoken to Cailean and deciding to get more involved in the training when they got back.

The air smelled clean and sharp, and water from the snow-capped bens tumbled over rocks to form sparkling streams and cascading waterfalls on the way to the river in the valley.

"You think you could get used to our mountains?" It was Caesennia, on her way to collect water from the stream. Her brown hair was blowing wildly, and a woollen shawl was fastened around her shoulders, against the sharp wind. Farinas ran his fingers down her throat and in between her breasts. She shivered but it had little to do with the cold wind off the hills. Farinas took the buckets from her.

"Yes," he answered, surprised that he felt this way. "I think I could."

They walked together to the stream. "My name isn't really Caesennia," she told him. "My mistress likes all things Roman, so she changed my name. My real name is Floireans."

"I like that," Farinas said. "It's very…flowery…"

The girl laughed as he filled the buckets with water and walked back. "Flowery?"

Farinas shrugged. "*Flores* is the Roman word for flowers."

"I don't think my mistress knows the pure Roman tongue. We live near the Antonine Wall, and we've got used to Roman ways…some more than others."

A thought struck Farinas, listening to the girl talk about her mistress. "Will your people side with Rome, against the other tribes?"

"Never! Antia likes Roman clothes and jewellery…and their food. She lives in a villa with colourful mosaics, glass windows and a bathhouse, but she'll fight for Caledonia. Anyway, our tribe wouldn't follow her if she was for Rome. We'd choose another chief."

"Is it that easy?" Farinas asked.

"Of course, succession usually goes through the mother, but leaders stay in power by our consent."

Farinas left her washing pots in the yard and walked over to the smithy where the smith was mending a plough. Farinas watched quietly, enjoying the use of fire to shape and mend. Eventually, the smith looked up, examined his work, then nodding with satisfaction, he placed it down by the door and lifted an ale skin. He drank then passed it to Farinas. "You'll be enjoying the heat," he said with a smile.

"Aye," Farinas agreed. Handing the ale skin back. "I'm not used to this cold."

"Cold! This isn't cold, man. Nature's warming the soil slowly, ready for sowing, and I expect we'll have a fine crop of bairns in a few months, with the goings on in the night."

Farinas laughed. "I expect so." It was something he'd never given much thought to.

"More for Rome to kill." The smith had become serious.

"You have children?"

The smith nodded. "They're still young enough to think war's about excitement and danger, and others dying…no' them." He looked up. "You know what I mean?"

Farinas nodded. "I know what you mean," he said.

The smith went back to work, and Farinas joined a group of archers competing at a makeshift target, in an open space away from the houses.

"The chiefs don't trust us," one of the spectators told him, when he mentioned that all the competitors seemed to be Vacomagi. "They ordered us to compete in tribal groups, to avoid fights."

"That sounds reasonable," Farinas said, then laughed and moved aside as two spectators, both Vacomagi, began punching and kicking each other over a decision.

The man shrugged, "Fighting's what we do, but at least they probably won't kill each other; they're brothers."

Farinas left him helping to separate the fighting brothers.

As everyone gathered in the hall for the evening meal, the smell of roasting meat filled the air, ahead of the servers. The chiefs and druids were already seated at the table on the dais.

"They seem quite pleased with themselves," Farinas said, as Cináed sat down beside him. "I hope that means your talks were successful."

"Aye, they went well today, so the chiefs will likely make an announcement soon." Cináed drained his mug of ale and refilled it. "I don't like being away, especially with Conn out there."

"He has no power now," Farinas told him, hoping he was right. "And the defences are strong," he added.

"Aye, you're right." Cináed agreed. "Still, it'll be good to get back."

The meal was almost finished, and everyone was relaxing with drinks, when the chiefs, Eochaid and Griogair stepped to the front of the dais. The announcement was quick. The details had already been agreed. The Venicone and Vacomagi would live together in peace. Should a dispute arise, it would be taken to the chiefs and their decision would be final. There would be no truces with Rome. They would not band together to fight Rome in pitched battles, but they would support each other against any invasion.

The news was greeted with silence. There were issues between the two tribes that went back to the time of their ancestors. They knew enough of their history with Rome though, to make the proposal one they could grudgingly accept. It helped that Griogair had already replaced the two renegade headmen.

The druids stepped forward and it was the first time any there had seen so many in one place. They pronounced a blessing on the venture, their words setting the seal on the rulings and silencing any objections.

Before trouble could start up again, Antia's servers refilled the cups with *uisge beath* and served more food, unfamiliar but delicious sweetmeats like the fried cheeses rolled in honey.

"To us!" Eochaid roared and Griogair joined him, as cups were raised throughout the hall, then the new battle cry echoed once more, *"Fuil Ròmanach!"* uniting them against one enemy.

The decision made and accepted, everyone settled down to drinking, singing, and talking; mostly boasting and wild threats about what they would do to the Romans. A few feuds were settled, perhaps to be resurrected when the alcohol wore off, and the chiefs agreed to another Gathering when the harvests were safely in. With the drink flowing, friendships blossomed, oaths were sworn between one-time enemies, and songs and laughter filled the hall.

Cináed disappeared from the meal as soon as the announcements were made. Farinas realised why when he could see no sign of Siùbhan.

"Your headman's walking in the moonlight with Siùbhan." Caesennia sat down beside Farinas and helped herself to an oatcake sweetened with honey. "She's here as Faollan's adviser, a Venicone, obviously."

Farinas nodded. He wasn't interested in tribal politics, but he supposed any connections between the tribes would be useful...and difficult. He concentrated on eating, drinking sparingly, and later, bedding Caesennia.

The night passed without incident and the morning dawned crisp and clear. Sunshine set a soft glow over the purple heather on the hills and sparkled in the clear water flowing down to the stream. Most of the delegates were unable to appreciate any of this. They were nursing sore heads and upset stomachs after a night of drinking and over-eating. Friendships were forgotten as they struggled to get ready for their return journeys.

Farinas had been careful with his drinking since leaving Trimontium and he had enjoyed the company of Caesennia with a clear head. They had parted on good terms. He realised he missed Keitha, and he was sure Caesennia had other, more refined bedmates at the villa.

Cináed was also clear-headed, and the two mounted their horses early and rode out with Quistaghyn. Cailean followed in the cart. Having made the required impression earlier, most of their finery was packed away in the cart, and they prepared to enjoy the ride home.

Quistaghyn and Cináed discussed serious matters arising from the discussions held at the Gathering, and Farinas enjoyed the sunshine. Once, when they stopped, he could see below them the Falls of Dochart and he looked again for Dànaidh, but it was quiet by the river. A few miles further along the pathway, however, they saw two figures ahead of them. As they approached, Farinas recognised Dànaidh with Faileas loping alongside him.

Hearing the sound of the horses, the old man dropped the stick he'd been leaning on and grabbed the hound, trying to drag it into the bushes. As he struggled with Faileas, they could hear his distressed cries. He was clearly terrified but unwilling to leave the animal. Faileas however, was standing his ground, with hackles raised, and teeth bared.

"Wait!" Farinas called out, but the sound of his voice only caused the old man to struggle more, and his cries became terrified wails. "It's Dànaidh, the old man who helped me and Ruaraidh," he explained, dismounting and handing the reins to Cináed.

"I'd watch out for that hound," Cináed warned, but Farinas was already close to them.

Dànaidh was struggling with Faileas, still trying to protect him.

"Dànaidh!" Farias quickly realised the old man was in a world of fear, unable to either hear him or understand that they posed no threat. He tried speaking to the hound. "Faileas, Faileas," he whispered. *"Bonus canis es."*

The dog wasn't listening either. Its master's terror had carried to the hound and was dictating its behaviour. It was standing with its hackles raised and snarling, as Dànaidh's wailing increased. Farinas was wishing Ruaraidh was there to talk to the old man, when he became aware of someone standing behind him.

"Suidh!" At the command, the dog sat, whimpering softly, and Dànaid looked up to see Quistaghyn gazing down at the now submissive hound. The sight of the druid in his robe and holding his staff was too much for the old man and he collapsed, trembling on the ground.

"*Thig!*" At Quistaghyn's command, the dog walked forward and stood by his side.

"*Sios!*" The hound lay down with a sigh, as though happy to give over the responsibility for the old man to the druid.

Fuirich!" At the final command, the hound relaxed completely. "What's the old man's name," Quistaghyn asked.

"Dànaid," Farinas told him. "His name's Dànaid."

Quistaghyn walked over to the old man. "Dànaid." The old man looked up and Quistaghyn spoke. At first, there was no response, but as he changed the language slightly, the old man quietened and replied. Finally, Quistaghyn held his hand out and helped Dànaid to his feet. As they walked past Faileas, Quistaghyn clicked his fingers, and the hound rose and quietly followed them to the cart.

Farinas helped Dànaidh into the cart beside Cailean. He put a blanket over him and patted him on the shoulder. "It's Farinas," he whispered, "Farinas."

The old man looked at him for the first time, and his lips trembled. "Farinas?" He seemed to be thinking, and then he smiled. "Farinas and Ruaraidh?"

"Aye," Farinas nodded. "Farinas and Ruaraidh."

Quistaghyn spoke, and the old man relaxed. On another click of the druid's fingers, Faileas jumped into the cart and crawled under the blanket beside Dànaidh.

Cailean standing beside them, holding the reins, moved back from the hound, keeping a wary eye on its fangs. Faileas seemed to sense the lad's fear and every so often he bared his teeth in a warning snarl. Now though, it seemed like a token gesture.

Quistaghyn spoke, but Dànaidh was back in his own world, calm but still fearful. "We'd best just leave them for now," Quistaghyn said. "Where should we take them?" he asked Farinas.

"I think we'd best take them with us," he finally decided. "They were running away from someone, and I don't think he had kin back where he lived, none that cared for him anyway," he added, remembering Dànaidh's isolated hut.

"Maybe we shouldn't waste time here," Cináed called, as they considered what to do. "We don't know what they were running from. We'll question him when we get back."

"What happens if the hound doesn't like us taking them away?" Cailean asked, watching Faileas lying at his feet.

"You'll be fine, lad." Cináed was surprisingly reassuring, considering how he'd avoided going anywhere near the animal. "Just don't annoy it," he added but Cailean didn't look reassured, as he edged farther away from Faileas, and moved the cart out after the others.

"We need to find out what frightened the old man," Cináed said, as they rode on towards the Three Sisters.

"When we came by here, the band that chased us carried a dead sheep," Farinas reminded them. "We wondered if it could have been one of the sheep Dànaidh was tending."

"We'll find out, once they've been looked after," Quistaghyn said. "I'll get Ruaraidh to help. The old man seemed to remember him."

Chapter 47

As soon as they arrived back at the village, Cináed and Quistaghyn joined the unit leaders to report on the Gathering. Farinas waited with the cart, as Cailean jumped down, quickly followed by the hound. Dànaidh however, shivering and fearful, pressed against the front of the cart as people crowded around, although a low rumbling growl from Faileas soon had the onlookers moving back.

"Faileas!" Ruaraidh's shout set the hound's tail wagging, and he allowed Ruaraidh to climb into the cart and crouch down beside Dànaidh. He spoke softly and soon the old man climbed down and stood leaning on Ruaraidh.

"Where can we take him?" Farinas asked. "He's too frightened to speak, but we need to know what happened to make him so afraid."

"He'll come wi' me." Farinas turned to see Mistress Foirbeis standing watching them. "I'll look after him, and you can talk to him when he's sorted."

"What about the hound?"

Mistress Foirbeis looked at Faileas, and they seemed to reach an agreement, woman and hound. She nodded. "Aye, him too." She clicked her fingers, and Faileas walked over and stood by her side. "What's the poor man's name?"

"It's Dànaidh." Ruaraidh and Farinas watched as Mistress Foirbeis held her hand out to Dànaidh.

"Come wi' me, Dànaidh. We'll soon have you feelin' better." She wrinkled her nose. "Aye…an' smellin' better."

The old man looked at her, his lips trembled, but he seemed to trust the hound's instincts and, with Ruaraidh helping, he walked towards her. Mistress Foirbeis took his arm and the odd trio walked away, ignoring everyone, although Faileas gave a warning growl, if anyone came too close.

"I'd best go and tell Cináed I've sorted that out," Farinas said, smiling as he walked away.

"Aye, like you sorted out the Romans back home." Ruaraidh laughed. "I'll go and see if I can help Mistress Foirbeis with Dànaidh. He looks like he needs a friend."

Inside the meeting house, Cináed was reporting on the Gathering. He stopped as Farinas came in. "How's the old man?"

"He's fine. Mistress Foirbeis took him and the hound away. She said she'll sort him, then he can answer questions."

He sat down as servers came in with food and beer. The food was oatmeal and cheese, Farinas noted, so still not much luck with the hunting. There was no sign of Lady Eithrig. Farinas had seen little of her since Conn left but that was not unusual. The young widow rarely ventured outside, now she had the young lass, Teàrlag as her servant.

"That's grand there's a truce." Torcadall pushed his bowl of oatmeal away. "We can get the hunters out."

"Something's happening on Venicone land. It may be nothing but stay in the north until we find out," Cináed warned, thinking of the frightened old man and his dog.

Heard you enjoyed the Gathering." Cairistìona was smiling at Farinas and there was some laughter.

"Aye," Goraidh nodded. "I've won a bonny wee knife from Comhnall. He was that sure you'd no interest in the lassies, after living wi' all those good-lookin' gladiators for so long."

Farinas hadn't realised that his preferences in bedpartners had been widely discussed. "If I'd known bets were being laid, I'd have obliged sooner," he said, as the laughter grew.

"I'd have been happy to oblige," Cairistìona answered. She grinned at Keitha who was scowling at her, then added. "Still am, any time."

"If we've nothing important to discuss. I'll check that the youngsters are carrying on with their training. There's still the matter of the Romans to prepare for." Keitha walked out, leaving the others grinning.

The meeting was almost over when Mistress Foirbeis came in. Her solemn expression was enough to bring a hush to the room, and she took a seat in silence. Farinas noticed Eithrig slipping in behind her and sitting close to the door.

"How is he?" Cináed asked.

"He'll be fine, just fine, once he's over his fear and he gets some good food inside himself. He's no' overkeen on people. They haven't treated him well. He's lucky he's got the hound." She hesitated but no one spoke, realising she had more to say.

"He looks after the sheep belonging to people living close by the Falls o' Dochart. A while ago…he's not so good with days and such… a band of hunters came by and tried to steal the sheep. The sheep ran to the hills, but a Roman soldier killed one with a spear and they carried it off. His own people tied up his hound and beat the poor man for losing the sheep. He's been out on the hills, every day since, in all weathers, with his hound, trying to find them. He was frightened to go back without the sheep. The poor man's cold, hungry, and frightened."

"That's the ones that chased me and Ruaraidh when we came here; four Caledonii, and two that looked like auxiliaries. They had a dead sheep," Farinas said.

"We need to find them and deal with them," Goraidh banged his mug down on the table. "They're too close; it'll be our beasts they're stealing next."

"It's more serious than that," Cináed said. "Villagers will be looking to blame neighbouring villages if their beasts go missing. The peace we have will not stand in the face of such accusations."

Mistress Foirbeis waited for the murmurs of agreement to die down then continued. "There's more. While he was out on the hill, a few days ago, maybe. He's not sure. He saw smoke coming from the houses...lots of it, and flames. He crept down, keeping hidden and saw the same men, with another five, setting fire to the houses and driving the people out. There were no soldiers that time. He's sure of that. He saw people burned alive, trapped in their houses. They set fire to his home too, and now he thinks they're after him."

"If they were auxiliaries, they'll have been from the camp, so they'll have moved out now," Corentyn said. "The others must be from local tribes."

"Anything else?" Keitha had followed Mistress Foirbeis in.

"Dànaidh's still frightened. I've left him talking to Ruaraidh, but I doubt he'll get any more from him."

"He didn't seem to be part of the community," Farinas said. "There was a man treated like that in Theveste, but he was a leper. No one wanted to catch the sickness from him."

"The poor soul doesn't have a sickness, but his mind isn't that quick, and his speech isn't too clear. They were maybe a bit fearful of him, for his differences," Mistress Foirbeis agreed.

"Ignorant folk," Quistaghyn shook his head. "Fearing what they don't understand."

"How is this helping us find and hunt down these men?" Keitha asked.

"We should go and find them," Cairistìona said, and for once she and Keitha were of the same mind, but Cináed disagreed.

"No, we need to talk to Faolan, the new headman of Hillfoot. The band seems to be operating mostly on his land. We do not make raid on his land unannounced...even against lawless bands. We show Faolan due respect."

"You'll be going?" Farinas asked Cináed, smiling at the thought of Cináed and Siùbhan, Faolan's adviser. "To discuss this with Faolan... and his adviser?"

"I will, and Corentyn. We'll decide what to do, but only with Faolan's agreement. You can come too," he added, looking at Farinas. "It's as well our people get to see you, or they might take you for a Roman."

"Aye, especially if they smell that perfumed oil you use," Keitha added. She was smiling, until Cairistìona leaned towards Farinas and sniffed appreciatively.

"I like how he smells." Her smirk was directed at Keitha who glowered at her.

"Right," Cináed broke the uneasy silence. "We leave tomorrow. "Keitha, make sure security's kept up. I expect they'll move onto our land sometime soon. Be ready."

He turned to Seocan, "I told Eochaid at the Gathering, how well you and your unit fought against the Venicone. We are grateful but we should be able to handle any trouble ourselves now. You'll be wanting to get home."

Seocan nodded. "The men are getting fat on the good food and beer you've provided but there's work to be done at home. We'll be leaving at dawn, and I'll report to Eochaid about these raiders."

"In the meantime, going to Faolan about the raiders is the best way to deal with them," Quistaghyn added. "It shows him respect and will help to keep up the agreements made at the Gathering."

It was Keitha who expressed everyone's concern. "You best keep a look out for them. They're hiding out somewhere in the south, probably quite close to Hillfoot and Clatchard. Maybe display less gold and jewels tomorrow?"

Chapter 48

They followed the advice, and when they rode out the next morning there were no jewels or gem-encrusted scabbards in sight. As Farinas had come to expect, the sky was overcast, and a fine mist covered the hills and soaked into their cloaks.

"This weather might keep these brigands by their hearths," Corentyn suggested.

"Best place to be, most of the time, in this land," Farinas muttered but he felt more cheerful when the sun came out, and they stopped at the pool below the waterfall, as they had done before their attack on Hillfoot, to eat and rest the horses.

"I hope the people are friendly," Corentyn said, spreading his cloak out to dry. "After what we did to them."

"One certainly was." Farinas grinned at Cináed, and Corentyn laughed.

"Aye, we heard about your bedmates...both of them."

"Cailean needs a good talking to," Cináed warned, "spreading talk like that," but he was smiling, and they continued in good spirits until Corentyn began dropping back, then catching up again. "What is it?" Cináed finally asked.

Corentyn shrugged. "Could be nothing. Just a feeling...as if we're being watched."

Farinas remembered Keitha warning them to be on the lookout for danger, and he became more conscious of rustlings and creaking in the undergrowth beside the track.

They were still a distance from Hillfoot when the horsemen appeared; a small band of mounted Caledonii, riding towards them from the direction of Hillfoot. Corentyn was a little way behind, and his warning shout alerted them to a similar band approaching from the rear.

Farinas automatically touched his armband, before sliding his sword from its sheath, as Cináed wheeled his horse, so he and Farinas were covering each other. There was no way they could break through. The attackers had them penned in. Farinas had never fought on horseback, but the pony was well-trained, and he was able to concentrate on fighting, as the ponies struggled to avoid the attackers, but they were outnumbered.

Cináed roared as he brought one down, blood spurting from his neck, and Farinas stabbed another in his chest, as he brought a battle axe down on him. The sword strike caused the man to drop the axe, which hit Farinas's arm, almost causing him to lose his grip on his sword. Ignoring the pain, he swung his sword and sliced the neck of another man, as he heard Corentyn cry out.

Cináed turned his horse and pushed through to Corentyn, who was lying over his pony's neck with blood running from his shoulder. He was still grasping his sword but, as Cináed reached him, he slid from the pony into the mud. Farinas could see nothing of what was happening behind him, but he heard Cináed cry out Corentyn's name, and he knew they were finished.

He swung his sword at a black-bearded, grinning tribesman and roared as his sword slashed a clean cut across his throat. They could never win against these odds, but he was determined to take as many with him as he could. He knew Cináed was still fighting. He could hear him bellowing curses and insults, but Corentyn was silent. As Farinas hacked and slashed, he wondered if he would soon be feasting with Videric and the gods, or if he would be reunited with his gentle mother.

Farinas's arm was throbbing, and his sword felt too heavy to lift but he fought on, encouraged by Cináed's voice, although it was weakening. Suddenly, through the curses and groans, he heard the clear note of a horn from the direction of the village. He had no idea what the horn meant. Were more men coming from Hillfoot to join in the attack?

Suddenly the attackers drew back, their shared looks indicating alarm, then they broke away, urging their ponies back towards the fall, yelling insults and threats as they retreated.

Farinas saw Cináed dismounting to kneel in the mud beside Corentyn and he rode back and pulled up his pony in front of them. Rubbing his injured arm, he remained with drawn sword, ready for whatever the horn heralded.

Cináed was helping Corentyn onto his pony when a band of Venicone rode into sight. They stopped when they saw the bruised and battered men, and the leader rode forward. Farinas sheathed his sword and Cináed called out as he mounted his pony. "You left that a bit late,"

"We thought you could handle them," Faolan answered with a laugh. "We came as soon as our lookout got back with the information. "How's your man?" he asked, looking at Corentyn.

"He'll be fine with a bit of attention to his injury, a slash across his shoulder. It's not too deep. He must have got a blow to his head too." Cináed looked back in the direction the attackers had gone. "You not going after them?"

"I'm not risking more men. There could be others back at their camp. We'll deal with them later," he promised. "Let's get back and get you seen to." Faolan turned his pony and led the way along the track.

Cináed and Farinas rode on either side of Corentyn, making sure he stayed on the pony. Farinas recognised the oak tree and, a little farther on, the place where their archers had waited above the village. As they rode down the hill, he was pleased to see no sign of the fires they'd set. The villagers were going about their business and paying little attention to the riders.

Outside the rebuilt meeting house, they dismounted, and men came to take Corentyn to be looked after. "He'll be well taken care of," Faolan told Cináed, knowing he wanted to go with his friend, partly through concern for his injuries and partly because he didn't yet, fully trust the Venicone. "You two need any treatment?"

"Not me," Cináed said, although he had dried blood on his tunic, from a cut in his neck, and his eyes were bruised and puffy. "You?" He looked at Farinas.

Farinas rubbed some dried blood from his face, flexed his fingers and rubbed his arm. "I'm fine."

"You could do with some food and drink, though." Faolan led them inside, where Siùbhan was sitting at a table, set with platters of food and jugs of beer.

They ate and drank, then Cináed told them what he knew of the robber band. It wasn't much, only what they'd seen, and what Dànaidh had been able to tell them.

"We know of them," Faolan admitted. "We also know that Conn joined them, along with a few others dissatisfied with Griogair's decisions. Conn managed to escape when Griogair was at the Gathering and we believe Conn is now the band's leader, using them for his own ends."

"Conn wasn't part of the attack on us," Corentyn pointed out, and Faolan shook his head.

"He's keeping back just now. Sending men out, while staying safe and drawing others into his band."

"Some of ours left the villages while we were at the Gathering," Siùbhan said. "They didn't like Griogair making Faolan headman, in place of Tàmhas."

"Tàmhas and his son, Tadhg, remained here. They're loyal." Faolan's tone made it clear there would be no argument about the men's loyalty. "They'll fight with us."

"And the auxiliaries?" Farinas asked.

"Like you said, probably two from the temporary camp who'd joined them for the hunting. We've no reports of Romans in the area since the camp moved," Siùbhan explained.

"We were glad of your help," Cináed said. "We were having a bit of trouble back there."

"Since learning about Conn and his band we've set extra lookouts. They were alert for any sign of trouble —"

They were interrupted by the door opening and Corentyn came in, followed by Niall, the headman from Clatchard and his adviser, Donnchadh. They threw off their cloaks and nodded a greeting.

"We met this wounded Vacomagi outside," Niall explained. "Says he's a friend."

"Aye, Niall," Cináed smiled. "Corentyn's with us."

Corentyn slumped down onto a seat at the table. His face was pale and badly bruised, but it was his shoulder that was causing the most pain. A pad of herbs and moss was held in place by linen bands and his right arm was strapped tight across his body by a cloth sling. He grimaced as he helped himself to food and ale.

"You got here, then." Niall and Donnchadh filled mugs with beer and grabbed pieces of meat from the platter on the table.

"Thanks to Faolan here." Cináed nodded. "We had some trouble on the way."

"Aye, we heard," Niall said. "We came as soon as we knew what was happening. Our lookouts keep us well-informed of strangers on our land." The last was said almost as a warning, and the Vacomagi took it as such.

"Conn and his bastarding whoresons have been robbing and burning villages close by," Faolan added, quickly defusing the situation.

"This attack seemed more planned, though," Siùbhan said. "They had set up an ambush, so they knew you were coming."

"I've been wondering about that," Corentyn admitted.

There was silence, then Farinas said what Cináed and Corentyn didn't want to consider. "Someone told Conn we were coming here."

"Aye, you have that right," Donnchadh said, and Faolan nodded.

Cináed stood so abruptly, he toppled his stool. "No! My people are loyal!" He looked to Corentyn and Farinas for confirmation but saw only a thoughtful look passing between them.

"Sit down, Cináed," Siùbhan said, refilling his mug and handing it to him. Cináed took the mug, righted the stool, and sat down, but he was troubled.

Farinas decided he should say something about his suspicions; should have voiced them earlier perhaps. "I did wonder at Eithrig's interest in Conn…when he was our prisoner…and she's been acting a bit strange."

"Eithrig's always been a bit strange." Cináed growled, unwilling to believe where their thoughts were going.

"She hardly speaks to anyone." Corentyn voiced his suspicions as the others listened. "She shows no interest in the babe, or village affairs. She never leaves the village, not even to wash clothes in the stream … a woman does that for her, and now she has Teàrlag to run errands… I'm sure she feels no loyalty to us."

"It would maybe have been Teàrlag took the message…she would know how to avoid the lookouts... but Eithrig would have sent her," Farinas added, sure his suspicions were correct. "She must have been in contact with Conn since he left Griogair's village," he added.

Cináed was still finding such disloyalty to the tribe hard to believe. "Eithrig, my father's widow…and her maid?" Farinas looked at Corentyn who nodded.

"Makes sense." Niall nodded in agreement. "They were waiting for you. Someone told them you were coming here. Can you think of anyone else who would betray you?"

They waited while Cináed considered the possibilities then Corentyn spoke. "There is no one else. It must be them and they will be dealt with. Oath-breakers they are. Traitors to the tribe."

Cináed nodded in agreement. "In the meantime, though, we have Conn and his renegade band to deal with. We thought to work with you on that matter." Cináed's suggestion surprised the Venicone, and Farinas already knew enough of tribal politics to appreciate how unusual this offer was.

"And why would you want to do that?" Niall asked.

"Not because of a few renegade tribesmen." Cináed was determined to convince the others of the threat from Rome. "We know Conn was in talks with the Romans when they were camped near Clatchard...He'll do it again when the legions return, and he'll take with him a sizeable band if he's not stopped. The Romans may be a lot of things, but they're not fools. They'll use his men and their knowledge of the tribes against us."

"And he's drawing men to him all the time," Donnchadh nodded.

"They might take him seriously if he takes a sizeable fighting force with him," Faolan said. "The traitorous whoreson that he is!"

"The emperor is determined on a final push north to wipe out the Caledonii. The killing of his man is just the excuse he needs. You're all renegades to him," Farinas told them.

"So!" Corentyn, always the practical one, raised his head.

His hair was caked in dried blood, his eyes were bloodshot and unfocused, but his voice was firm. "We deal with Conn first. Wipe him and his renegades out. Then we can think of strategies against Rome."

"Strategies that don't include pitched battles," Siùbhan said, and the others agreed.

"To the heroes of Mons Graupius," Faolan said, raising his mug of ale. "Our biggest mistake in living memory."

"Didn't know you were that old," Siùbhan smiled, and the mood lifted as they drank.

It was Corentyn who brought the discussion back to important matters. "Where is Conn getting his men from?"

Niall answered. "When Griogair was at the Gathering, Conn and a few others came back here and joined the robber band. Some of Clatchard and some Hillfoot men joined him."

"Those that joined him won't be missed," Faolan added. "Useless bastards they are, but quick to fight and good at it. They'll make a lot of trouble for our people, especially those living outside the main villages."

"Aye," Cináed nodded. "Folks like Dànaidh." He quickly added a few details about the old man and the burned houses.

"None of ours left," Corentyn stated.

"You sure?" Niall asked. "None of your workshy wastrels, that might not be missed."

Corentyn shook his head. "None. I'd know if any had gone." The others nodded, accepting his word, but Niall added a warning,

"None yet," he said.

"Aye, you're right." Cináed sighed. "Eithrig's already got at least one working with her and Conn. Others may not have joined because the band's mostly Venicone. That doesn't mean they don't want to. Eithrig may have been working on them."

"Or Teàrlag," Farinas said. "She may have been talking to the younger ones, although she's not well-liked."

"I'll tighten security when we get back," Corentyn promised, and none doubted his word.

They drank in gloomy silence then Siùbhan drew them back to the main business. "What do we do about Conn?" she asked.

"Have your men found his lair? Corentyn asked.

Faolan nodded. "We think it's south, just past the Three Sisters, by the Falls of Dochart."

"That's where Dànaidh saw them set fire to the houses," Farinas said.

"That's where they'll be." Donnchadh nodded. "They'll have patched up the houses, and now they're gathering others to them."

"We need to take them by surprise." Corentyn was used to advising Cináed, but Farinas could see Faolan and Niall were not so happy, being advised by an outsider, especially with such obvious advice. He smiled as Siùbhan stepped in to ease the tension.

"You think so? Really?" She smiled, and Corentyn laughed.

"Sorry, sorry, I'm so used to giving advice, even when it's not needed."

"Aye, we've got used to it," Cináed said.

"To a dawn raid!" Farinas snatched up his mug, and the others raised theirs and drank.

"That's agreed then," Faolan said. "A dawn raid, the sooner the better."

"Tomorrow!" Niall's shout surprised everyone. "Well, we can't risk the word getting out to Conn," he explained. "I can get men here in time to leave for a dawn attack." He looked at Cináed. "You?"

Cináed didn't take long thinking about it. "Aye. I can get men here."

Corentyn, obviously still suffering from his injuries, but determined to be involved spoke up. "I'll ride back and send men out under Torcadall. I'm in no fit state to fight tomorrow," he grudgingly admitted.

Cináed nodded. "Tell Keitha she's in charge, but to listen to your advice."

"If we bring twenty men each, that should do it," Faolan said, and the others nodded.

"Just swords or battle axes," Niall suggested. "Less likely to hit one of our own in close fighting." He paused then added. "Have them bring shields. Conn's men won't have shields...our men will be able to recognise each other by them."

Corentyn got up, holding his injured arm. "I'll go now." He stumbled and all the colour drained from his face.

Cináed caught him and sat him down, smiling. "You stay here. Stubbornness won't keep you on a horse. Farinas will go!"

"Right!" Farinas smiled. "Torcadall, me and eighteen men... Swords and shields... maybe battle axes."

"I'll see to our unit," Siùbhan said, getting up.

"Use Tàmhas and Tadhg," Faolan advised. "They can prove themselves in the front line."

Donnchadh got up with them, to go to Clatchard to select men for their unit.

As the three reached the door, Faolan called after them. "We'll come up with a plan while you're gone. When you get back," he promised, "we'll celebrate our newly formed *co-chòrdadh*! Venicone and Vacomagi fighting together instead of fighting each other. That'll surprise the gods!"

Chapter 49

Farinas rode as fast as he dared while keeping a lookout for any of Conn's men, but he had a clear ride back to the village. The sentries had reported seeing him coming through the glen, and Keitha and the unit commanders were waiting inside the gates, as he dismounted and led them to the hall. Villagers crowded round, anxious to know about Cináed and Corentyn. "They're both well," he shouted. "We need to plan."

Inside the hall, Quistaghyn joined them, and Farinas explained what had happened, and what they needed to do. When he finished there was silence, then Cairistìona explained. "Eithrig isn't here. She must have gone to join Conn sometime last night. Teàrlag's gone too, but they left the bairn."

"Eithrig was never much of a mother to him," Keitha said. "Our brother is better with us."

Farinas tried to hide his impatience, as he got to the purpose of the meeting. "Torcadall, you've to take men to Hillfoot. We're moving on Conn's band at dawn tomorrow, from Hillfoot. Niall's bringing men from Clatchard. Twenty fighters from each village."

"We're fighting with the Venicone?" Goraidh wasn't the only one nervous about fighting alongside their old enemy.

"It was Faolan saved us from Conn's ambush. He could have left us to Conn's band, but he saved our lives. He and Niall know the real danger is from Rome. We need to be united."

Farinas waited to see if there were any objections, but the news of the ambush had decided them. They trusted Cináed and Corentyn. They'd go with whatever plan they were working on.

"Keitha, you'll take Cináed's place here —"

"No! I'm going!"

"Conn may try to take the village while we're away, and your defences will be weakened by twenty fighters...as well as Cináed and Corentyn," Farinas pointed out. "You're needed here," he insisted.

Quistaghyn added. "Conn now has Eithrig and Teàrlag giving him all the information he needs about our defences. Teàrlag got past the lookouts," he reminded them. "Corentyn will want to find out how she managed that. She can also let Conn know who might be interested in joining them. Our best hope is to destroy his band completely, while keeping a strong force here."

Although not said, everyone also accepted the need for a successor, ready to take over, should Cináed be killed. Keitha wasn't happy with the decision, but she nodded.

"Right!" Torcadall was convinced and eager to get on with preparations. "Cairistìona, Goraidh and Farinas – you'll be going."

They nodded and Cairistìona slammed her hand on the table. "Bastard traitors! I hope we meet them tomorrow!"

"I'll start getting our defences tightened and send out more lookouts." Keitha was on her feet ready to leave. "Torcadall, you need to let me know who's going with you."

"Wait! Farinas stopped them. "We take swords or battle axes only, no spears or arrows. It will be close fighting. We're to bring shields, so we can be recognised by the Venicone. We don't think Conn's whoresons will be carrying shields. They're more used to robbing unarmed villagers and travellers. Those that attacked us had none."

"We'll leave before dark," Torcadall told them. "I'll bring the men in here and explain."

"I'll get Cináed's shield and one for Farinas," Keitha said. "I'll send food in."

Torcadall and Keitha left, and Farinas was explaining more about what had happened at Hillfoot, when Torcadall returned with those he'd chosen to take part in the attack.

"Keitha's letting everyone know what's happening," he said, before telling his unit what was planned, with input and explanation from Farinas. When the food arrived, they ate in uneasy silence. They would be going in as part of a larger force made up largely of Venicone warriors. No one could remember anything like that happening before and no one was happy about it.

When the horn blew, the war party gathered their weapons and formed ranks at the gates. Farinas was surprised to see Ruaraidh and Cailean standing in two carts, waiting to drive them out. The shields were in the carts and Keitha picked out one and held it up.

It was a rectangular black shield, with gold and amber-coloured Celtic markings in the shape of an animal's head. The bronze boss shone in the light of the dying sun.

"Your shield, Farinas," she called, as the others cheered. "We weren't sure about the lion's head, Leo Africanus, but we did our best."

Farinas called out his thanks and assured them the Celtic lion was perfect. When Keitha moved to place it back in the cart, he insisted on taking it from her. "I'll carry it," he told her, surprised by how emotional he felt, knowing the Celtic lion symbolised his acceptance by the tribe. "I need to get used to the feel of a shield again."

He shifted his sword to his right side, and with his left hand, he found the handle behind the boss and slipped his hand in. It fitted perfectly into the indentation. The shield felt lighter than he'd expected but strong, and he'd no doubt it was well-made.

The war band marched out to the cheers of the villagers, although the carts trundling ahead reminded them some would be brought back, injured, or dead.

Farinas marched at the rear, unwilling to be seen struggling with the shield, but glad of the time to get used to it. Better to struggle now than in a battle. Wearing the sword on his right side would not be an issue once he'd drawn it.

He knew Videric would have smiled at the lion. He would have chosen a plainer design. 'You don't want to make yourself a target', Farinas could imagine him saying, disregarding the fact that his black skin already made him easily recognised, in this land of pale skin.

They passed the falls without stopping, and soon lookouts from Hillfoot came to lead them into the village. The houses were quiet, but small fires burned in the grassy areas where men had arranged cloaks and blankets to keep them warm until ready to move out. In the small village, so many extra people crowded the empty spaces.

Torcadall made his way to the hall, and his men took blankets from the carts and found spaces to build a few fires they could lie close to. Farinas was sure the groups were decided, not just by tribe, but by village. When he collected a blanket, he gave his shield to Ruaraidh who admired it and told him he'd helped in its design.

"Aye, I thought so," Farinas smiled. "I'm grateful. I'm sure you were the only one with any idea of what a lion looked like." He looked at the design as Ruaraidh carefully placed it with the others. "It's sure to give me courage in battle."

"Just so long as it doesn't make you reckless," Ruaraidh warned.

"Why you and Cailean?" Farinas asked.

"We're the oldest in training. Me, because I came late to the village, and Cailean because he couldn't be trusted when he had to fight right-handed. We'll be going into battle soon." Ruaraidh and Cailean looked delighted at the prospect, Farinas not so much. He left the lads tending to the ponies and made his way to a fire where he settled down under his cloak and a blanket.

He tried not to think of everything that could go wrong.

Chapter 50

The sound of a horn had them scrambling up, kicking out the embers of any fires still burning, and gathering their wits. The three headmen, Cináed, Faolan, and Niall were standing by the gates. Although not going with them, Corentyn stood with Cináed's unit, as the men gathered in front of the leaders.

Faolan stepped forward and spoke for them. "Right, we're going to finish Conn and his whoresons for good. Our scouts have reported them camped in the ruins of the houses they burned down, just beyond the Falls of Dochart. They number upwards of forty, armed. We outnumber them but don't take chances. Niall will lead his men in an attack from the east, Cináed will lead his men in from the west, and my men will go in from the north. Between us, we'll finish them. We go in fast and quiet. Get ready."

Farinas, like the others, checked his sword and dagger and made sure his boots were laced tight. They left their cloaks in the carts and collected their shields, ready in the event of a pre-emptive strike by Conn. Cináed waited at the carts, talking to his men, and answering their questions; mostly about whether the Venicone could be trusted.

The horn sounded soon after, and the units lined up ready to march out. This time it was Cináed who addressed them.

"This is the first time we've agreed to fight together, Venicone and Vacomagi against a common enemy. Conn will not expect it. He'll think we're too busy fighting each other to deal with him, but we'll show him." The men cheered at this. It sounded weak, but Farinas thought he could feel the stirrings of unity from the tribesmen. Cináed continued. "This can be a practice for when we come up against Rome's legions. We'll show them too!"

The war cry from the Gathering was taken up and echoed from the hills. *"Fuil Ròmanach!"*

In the silence that followed, a voice called out, "Prisoners?" The three headmen shook their heads and Faolan answered. "No prisoners. Conn was a prisoner, and we see the trouble he's causing. They've chosen to live outside our laws. Kill, as quick and as clean as you can, but kill them all." He paused and waited for any objections. "We need to concentrate our efforts on the Romans, not on a few renegade traitors bringing fear and destruction to our villages."

There were no arguments and Niall stepped forward. "You're carrying shields, all of you. Look at them, take note of them and use them to recognise your friends when battle fever takes over. Look at the faces above the shields, these are the faces of our allies, and whatever some of you may think, allies are good."

There was some laughter, and they did examine their neighbours' shields and faces. Farinas thought the three headmen had done as well as they could. The men were ready, and as united as it was possible to be, in the short time they'd been together. On the order, the units marched out.

Corentyn left to ride north, leading Cináed's horse. Lookouts from Hillfoot and from his own village would ensure his safety on the way.

Farinas walked with a feeling of pride and a sense of belonging. He remembered first feeling something like it while waiting with his uncles to attack the Romans. Then it was more an appreciation of how the others felt. Here he felt it himself and touched his armband, hoping Videric was with him in some way.

They moved forward in silence, scrambling through the undergrowth and wondering what the others were doing. Some still believed they were walking into a trap laid by the Venicone.

Between the Three Sisters and the Falls of Dochart, Cináed led the unit across the river then up to a stand of trees where they could see the houses that Conn had taken over for his robber band. The houses were in darkness, and they could see no activity. Nor could they see the other units.

"No sounds," Cináed warned. "We go in on the sound of the horn. Watch out for the others. Hillfoot will be coming in from our left. Clatchard will be coming towards us."

"And Conn's ruffians on our right," a voice growled, "and us, caught in a neat wee trap." There was a tense silence as the others heard their worst fears put into words.

"I trust them." Cináed spoke with authority, stilling any further objections. "We're here. Do you want to go home, Anndra? Turn tail and run?"

"Naw, I don't run away from a fight. I was just thinkin'—"

"Well don't! Do what you're good at...fighting! Leave the thinking to others." Cináed turned away, as the others grinned at Anndra.

It was quiet in the dawn light, and nerves were stretched to breaking point when they heard a rustling behind them coming from the direction of the river. Heads turned, hands grasped weapons, eyes peered into the gloom, but discipline prevailed and not a sound was heard from them. The man who stepped out was holding his hands away from his body and he had a curved horn slung over his shoulder on a leather strap.

"Asgall...from Hillfoot," he whispered. "Hillfoot and Clatchard are in position. I'm to sound the horn when you're ready."

Cináed waited as his men drew their swords and lined up, clutching their shields in suddenly sweaty hands. "Ready?" he whispered, and the men nodded.

"Aye," Anndra spoke. "We're ready. Let's get on with it."

Cináed nodded at Asgall, and he blew a loud clear note followed by two shorter notes. As Cináed led the charge through the undergrowth into the quiet village, they saw Hillfoot men charging down the hillside.

A few men and women staggered from the houses. Some grasped swords, but others, still befuddled by drink or sleep, simply stood watching death and destruction sweeping down on them as the attackers' own momentum carried them forward, but the horn sounded, stopping the rush into the houses. The men gathered and waited, knowing they would be at a disadvantage inside the houses. They heard alarmed cries and angry roars from the houses, and then the band surged out, disunited, and panicked but screaming in defiance.

Farinas noted there seemed to be more men than they'd expected but they lacked any discipline. He hefted the shield and grasped his sword, then they were on them. They had no strategy to foil an attack, only ferocity and desperation. Farinas was glad of the shield, as he fought off attacks from all sides. From their position, Cináed's men were unaware of how the other units were faring. They could hear the shouting and the clash of weapons, but their concentration was centred on their own area and their own survival.

Some of the band were fleeing towards the river, and Cináed's unit was all that stood between them and safety. These men had no stomach for a fight against armed men, but Cináed's orders made it clear, none were to escape. Farinas and the others found themselves constantly chasing men towards the river and cutting them down, while trying not to be trapped too far from the rest of the unit. The robbers who were willing to stand and fight, managed to inflict some damage, and Farinas found himself forcing his way through to stand with Torcadall, as two of Conn's men turned on him.

These men were more skilled with the sword, than the others and Torcadall was already bleeding from a wound in his side. Farinas cut down one attacker, as Torcadall brought down the second man, but he was losing too much blood and he collapsed.

Farinas stood over his fallen comrade, protecting him. He stabbed an attacker in the chest as he charged forward and fought others off. Sooner than Farinas expected, the sounds of battle died down to be replaced by the moans and cries of the injured. The sun had risen, and the ground glistened dark with blood.

Cináed's unit had forced those trying to flee, back into the main group being attacked by Hillfoot and Clatchard. As the field of battle became more concentrated in the space in front of the houses, the number of men fighting decreased. Some had thrown down their swords, but the instructions given before were upheld, and others quickly realised there would be no mercy.

Farinas was reminded of bouts in the arena where he felt like an executioner, and so it became as Conn's followers were cut down and overcome by the weight of numbers, and the determination of the attackers. During a lull in the fighting, Farinas bent to see how Torcadall was faring. The wound in his side was bleeding and he was still unconscious. Farinas knew he would bleed out if the wound wasn't seen to. After a quick look round, he stuck his sword in his belt and began to drag Torcadall closer to the waiting carts.

A sound caused him to turn, as a wild-eyed robber, panicked and desperate, bore down on him brandishing a war-axe. Farinas twisted away from the axe and as the man tried to check his advance and turn, Farinas slid the short dagger from his belt and plunged it into his back. With no time to remove the dagger, he drew his sword, raised his shield, and took up his position again over Torcadall as another of Conn's men attacked, aiming a blow at his sword arm. He slammed the shield up under the man's chin and was finishing him with a sword thrust, when he felt Torcadall moving.

Farinas looked down to see Ruaraidh and Cailean dragging him the last few paces into the undergrowth where they lifted him and carried him back to the carts. Farinas wiped the sweat from his eyes and retrieved his dagger before forcing his way back into the main fighting. By now, the three units had become one and they circled the remainder of Conn's band. Farinas saw Conn, bloodied but still standing, being attacked from all sides. He eventually disappeared, brought down along with the rest of his men.

As the sun lit up the scene, men moved back from the final killing ground and collapsed on the grass, wiping sweat and gore from their faces, and checking minor injuries. Others were tending to the injured and helping them into the carts that had been brought over. Farinas went to check on Torcadall who was struggling to get down from the cart. His side was wrapped tightly, and the bleeding seemed to have stopped.

"It's fine," Farinas told him. "They're done, and you'll start bleeding again if you don't stay still."

"I'm not getting driven back in a cart," Torcadall complained. "They're needed for the badly injured." He got down and they watched as two men were loaded into the cart.

"That's the only badly hurt we've got," Ruaraidh said. "You might as well get in. We're going back now." He handed Torcadall a bundle of linen strips and a waterskin. "You can look after them 'till we get them to Mistress Roibeart."

Clatchard and Hillfoot don't have many injured either," Cailean added. "They're loading their carts now."

Farinas bundled Torcadall into the cart. "You'd only start bleeding on the way back and hold us up," he told him.

The other cart was loaded up with the men's shields and the two carts headed back onto the track. Farinas returned to the men standing with Cináed. "Anyone seen Torcadall?" he was asking.

"Aye, he took a sword to his side, but he's fine," Farinas told him. "He's gone back in the cart with two others."

"That'll be Ealar and Filib." Cairistìona named the injured. "I saw them being taken away. Did anyone see Eithrig and Teàrlag?" she asked.

"Probably killed by men from one of the other units," Corentyn said. "If they were here."

"I'll go and see what's to be done." Cináed walked through the bodies and met up with Faolan and Niall. After a brief discussion, they returned to their units.

"Bodies to be thrown in the houses then we set fire to them," Cináed ordered. "Goraidh, take three men. Check first that there's no one in there, children or old folk, and no livestock. Watch there's no one that could be a danger," he warned.

Farinas went with the others, and they dragged the bodies into the houses. Eithrig's body was found beside Conn's. Teàrlag's was at the edge of the field, where Hillfoot had fought. A bloodied sword lay beside her body. It looked as though she had been cut down trying to escape.

They found no one inside, and once everyone was accounted for, the village was set alight, and flames were soon shooting into the sky. The three units were briefly united as they watched the final destruction of Conn's band. Only Farinas noticed Cináed and Siùbhan sharing a brief moment together before the units formed up and marched out.

The mood on the march back was subdued. Giving no quarter was not their way, but they were realising their ways would have to change if they were to survive the new onslaught planned by Rome. At least they had shown the tribes could cooperate when necessary.

Chapter 51

Their spirits lifted as they marched back to the village. With Conn and his band eliminated, they could concentrate on their families and their daily lives, even though the threat of Rome hung over them.

The sun was shining and for the first time, Farinas was able to appreciate its warmth. Maybe Caledonia wasn't so bad, he thought. They found the wounded recovering well in the broch, and then returned to their homes to tend to various cuts and bruises.

Cináed walked with Farinas to the meeting hall where food and drink waited. They sat with Quistaghyn and the unit commanders, and Cináed gave a brief report on the battle.

"Vacomagi and Venicone worked well together because each worked under the command of its own leader," Corentyn noted. "Useful to know for the future."

"Eithrig and Teàrlag were killed with Conn," Goraidh said. "The traitors have been dealt with."

"Ruaraidh and Cailean did well," Farinas said, grateful to the lads for their help. "They took Torcadall off the battleground."

"Aye," Keitha nodded. "I thought they were ready. They'll go in with us next time."

"With peace between the tribes, we can hope that won't be soon," Quistaghyn said.

"I'll drink to that!" Cairistìona raised her cup, and the others joined her. Quistaghyn had supervised the painful and bloody removal of her brother's left arm a few days before, but he would live, and she was grateful for that.

The sun was sinking behind the hills when Farinas left the hall. He scratched the stubble on his face and felt his clothes sticking to his body. There was dried blood from a few minor cuts, and mud and gore covered much of his body. He collected what he needed and walked down the glen to the pool. Gazing at the clear water and listening to the birds singing, it was hard to believe he'd been fighting for his life earlier that day.

He still hadn't got used to the cold water, but he welcomed its freshness. He shaved his face quickly using perfumed oil, smiling as he remembered Keitha's words, then pulled his clothes off and plunged into the water. The shock, as always, drew his breath from him, and he washed as quickly as possible, before swimming the short distance between the grassy banks.

His fingers were touching the opposite bank for the third time when he heard a splash and felt ripples of water against his skin. Turning quickly, he saw a pale body shimmering under the water while long strands of glossy red hair floated on the surface. Farinas's breath caught in his throat as Keitha rose from the water, glorious in her nakedness. A green stone hung on a gold chain around her neck, and the same stones hung on gold wires from her ears.

Like a nymph in the gladiator school's bathhouse mural, there was nothing brutish or savage about the creature standing in front of him, squeezing water from her hair, and smiling wickedly at him.

Keitha was examining Farinas just as he examined her, and they came together as an iron nail drawn to a lodestone. They held and kissed, then Keitha broke free and hurried out of the water.

"It's so cold. Come and heat me up." Her laughter rang out across the pool and Farinas imagined he could hear the water spirits sharing her delight.

He waded out and grabbed his cloak before joining Keitha on the grass. They pulled the cloak over themselves and clung together. Farinas felt his body relaxing as he rubbed her skin and felt warmth flowing back into their bodies.

"What took you so long," she whispered as their lips met, and the hurt and loneliness, the fear of the future and the Romans, disappeared.

When they dressed, Keitha, in a long blue woollen robe and woven shawl, looked nothing like the warrior Farinas had become used to, but there was a wicked-looking dagger hanging from her belt, and he smiled. She would always be a warrior he supposed, but with the Romans coming, she would need to be.

As they walked together into the peaceful village and were greeted by its people, Farinas thought that at last he had found something and someone worth fighting for.

Author's Note –
The Romans did return.

Ulpius Marcellus was sent by the emperor Commodus, to suppress a serious revolt in 180, after northern tribes breached Hadrian's Wall and killed Marcellus's predecessor, and his guards, during an inspection of the wall.

The Roman writer, historian and senator, Dio Cassius called the uprising, the most serious war of the emperor Commodus' reign, and reported that the Romans took almost four years of punitive raids, to quell the revolt.

Languages used

My apologies, if any are needed, for my use of foreign words and expressions. I do realise they come from complex languages, and an online translation service is not the best way to discover authentic, grammatically correct words and phrases, but I hope they are not too far off the mark and that they cause no offence.